IN THE SHADOWS OF THE STATE

ALPA SHAH

In the Shadows of the State

INDIGENOUS POLITICS, ENVIRONMENTALISM, AND INSURGENCY IN JHARKHAND, INDIA

Duke University Press Durham and London 2010

Designed by C. H. Westmoreland
Typeset in Carter and Cone Galliard with
Quadraat Sans display type by Keystone Typesetting, Inc.
Library of Congress Cataloging-in-Publication Data and republication
acknowledgments appear on the last printed pages of this book.

WITH A DROP OF *HADIA*,

TO BA AND BAPUJI,

my grandmother and my late grandfather,

otherwise known as Motiben and Somchandbhai

Punamchand Raja Kheta Lakha Rajpar Nayani Shah

Contents

List of Illustrations

Acknowledgments

This book has its origins in my contemplating the pursuit of doctoral research. The fieldwork for it began in January 1999 when I landed in Ranchi City, Jharkhand, India, as a research assistant on a project evaluating a development project funded by the U.K. government. Three months later, at the end of this assignment, I was convinced that I wanted to pursue independent academic research in Jharkhand. I moved to the market town of Bero, where I stayed until June 1999. Having enrolled in the Ph.D. program at the London School of Economics and Political Science in September 1999, I returned to Jharkhand in November 2000 for a longer period of field research that lasted until June 2002. This time I was based in the village I call Tapu, but I also rented rooms in Bero and Ranchi as I wanted to situate Tapu in the broader context of what was happening in the state and national arena. I returned for further periods of fieldwork: January through February 2004, and January through March 2007 and 2008.

The book is thus the result of nearly a decade of my life, and I have acquired many debts along the way—too many to do justice to here. I first thank the Economic and Social Research Council for the funding I have received through doctoral and into postdoctoral research, without which this book would not have been possible. I am also extremely grateful to the Wenner-Gren Foundation and their awarding me the Richard Carley Hunt Fellowship, which made completing this book a pleasure. I am also grateful for the various smaller fellowships and awards I received along the way, all of which have made a difference and allowed me to keep working on this project: the LSE Malinowski Award and Metcalfe Scholarship, the Newnham College

Cambridge Jean Mitchell and Piddy Funds, and the Royal Geographical Society Violet Cressey-Marks Fisher Scholarship.

In the late 1990s, Linda McDowell, Bill Adams, and Stuart Corbridge greatly influenced my interest in anthropology, and it was Stuart who first introduced me to Jharkhand in 1999. In Jharkhand, various people helped me as research assistants, and I would like to acknowledge in particular the efforts of Indumati and Pratibha Dwivedi. Thanks are also due to Ram Dayal Munda and Shri Prakash, and especially to Sanjay Kumar and his family, and the late Vikram Pramar and Hannah Pramar for their hospitality and many long hours of discussion. Kathinka Sinha-Kherkoff and Vinod Sinha were a constant source of intellectual, emotional, and moral support, nursing me through malaria and a broken leg. To them I am deeply grateful. For reasons of confidentiality, I cannot specifically name those to whom I owe my greatest debts in Jharkhand: the family I acquired in Tapu, and my friends there and in the Bero area more generally. The kindness and generosity I received there was immeasurable, and I owe to these friends not just the material of this book, but also the lessons they taught me about life in general.

As the book has taken shape, a number of friends and colleagues have provided crucial support, advice, and critical engagement. I would like to thank André Béteille, Maurice Bloch, David Gellner, Chris Gregory, Thomas Blom Hansen, Deborah James, Lucia Michelutti, David Mosse, Will Norman, Ben Rogaly, Orlanda Ruthven, Orin Starn, Nick Thomas, Harry West, and Virginia Xaxa. Conversations about my doctoral thesis with the late Olivia Harris, John Harriss, and Jonathan Spencer helped me think through the kind of monograph I'd like to write. Of the Brighton Syndicate, Lars Buur, Steffen Jensen, and Dennis Rodgers read several chapters, as did Edward Simpson. Harriet Bury, Tobias Kelly, Yasmin Khan, and Emma Mawdsley read the entire manuscript (in some cases, several times). Their critical commentary, careful editing, and moral support were crucial. My doctoral supervisors, Chris Fuller and Jonathan Parry, have supported me beyond the call of duty. Their deep interest in my research has seen me through the dark times. They remain my most profound critics, and their own research and passion for intellectual endeavor is a source of inspiration.

My greatest debts are to my family. I thank my *faibas*, Surbhi and Nutan; my *fuas*, Sirish and Pankaj; my sisters, Mala, Seema, and Deepa; and in particular my mother, Kundan, and father, Madhusudan, who have stood by my side no matter how far I have strayed.

Paintings by Kundan, Seema, and Deepa have been reproduced in this book, and I am very grateful to my father-in-law, John, who kindly helped to get the artwork and map ready for publication. I could not have completed this book without the kindness, love, and support of my husband, Rob, who painstakingly read several drafts, was a great source of both criticism and encouragement, and has made all things possible.

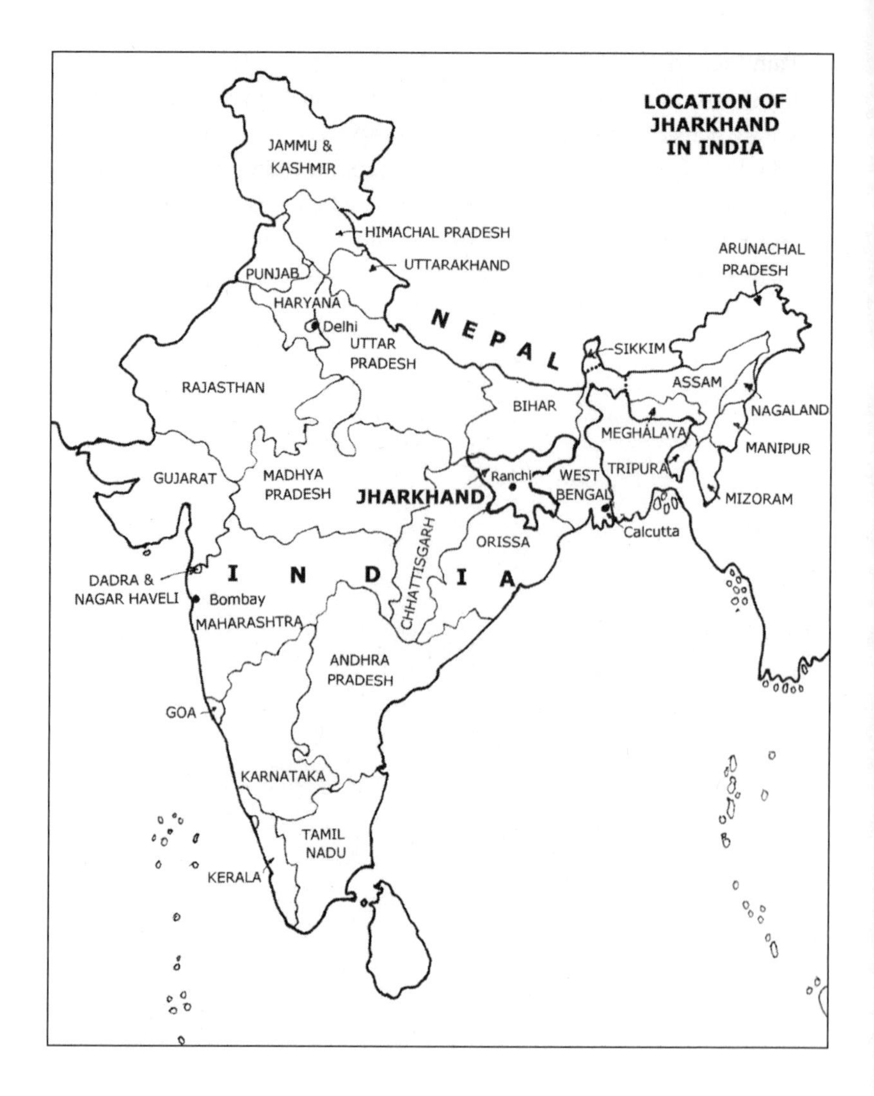

Map showing the location of Jharkhand in India.
Map prepared by John Higham.

Prologue

6:00 A.M., 4 DECEMBER 2000

Knock, knock, knock. The flimsy wooden door of my mud house was rattling.

"Not again," I thought, waking up from deep sleep, rubbing my eyes.

"Alpa, Alpa! Get up! Get up! This is the Jungle Raj, the Forest Kingdom! In Tapu village you can't sleep till midday,"[1] teased Safid Khan.

I lay in bed, registering that I was waking up in this little-known part of India, in the newly formed State of Jharkhand, listening to the rhythmic pounding of rice in the house next door.

"Come on, Alpa! Get ready! It's market day!"

"Okay, okay, I'm coming!" I replied, clumsily climbing out of my blankets and spilling the hay that Somra Munda—my neighbor, who later became my adopted brother—had put under my thin mattress to keep me warm.[2]

Safid Khan is dead now, but I often smile to myself when I remember the glint in his eyes; his large, smiling face; and the spindly legs that supported his hunched back. I didn't particularly like being woken up that early every day, but I was fond of the old man. His teasing and joking helped to break many boundaries for me in the early days.

It was less than two weeks since I had arrived to live in Tapu, but I was already aware that the village was deeply divided. On the one hand, there were the poorer tenant descendants of the old landlord system, who made up about 80 percent of Tapu's 102 house-

The house I lived in, Tapu village, Jharkhand. *Painting by Seema Shah.*

Tapu. *Photo by author.*

holds. Most of them were *adivasis* (indigenous people or Scheduled Tribes), and the majority of these adivasis were of the Munda tribe, but there were also a handful of Muslim households and some *dalits*, members of the Scheduled Castes. And on the other hand, there were the remaining 20 percent of the village, who were *sadans*, middle and higher castes, who in Tapu were mostly descendants of the historically dominant Yadav caste landlords. Despite my conscious decision to live in a house in a Munda courtyard, most of the adivasis seemed extremely shy and kept away from me. It was the landlord descendants who wanted to wine and dine me.

I opened the door into the courtyard. Characteristically, Safid Khan had already left. It was a cold morning, crisp and clear. I wrapped my shawl tightly around me, closed my eyes, and took a deep breath. I could hear the swish of dry leaves against the mud floor. Somra Munda's wife, Ambli, was sweeping the courtyard. The steady rhythm of her broom was pierced by the jingle of bells. Brass on brass, I thought, but also the occasional hollow ring of wood on wood. Old Onga Munda was shuffling his water buffalo and oxen out of his house and into the courtyard, to take them to graze in the forests. Mangra Munda, his nephew, came out to call his children into the house to eat some rice.

Seeing me, Mangra said, "Come on, you come with me to the market today." I tried to hide my delight as I replied, "Definitely."

Mangra had barely spoken two words to me since I arrived, and I was thrilled at this invitation to walk with him to the market town of Bero. Market days were like ritual occasions. From the time I had lived in Bero in 1999, I knew the crowds it attracted from the surrounding villages, its exciting buzz, and the smell of dust and dry spices it left in the air. Adivasis went to Bero to buy the week's supplies, sell their wares, and meet friends and relatives from other villages. On their way back home, many stopped in the forest for a drink of rice beer or *mahua*—wine made from the flower of the same name—brewed and sold by male and female villagers who poured it from their clay and aluminum pots into cups sewn together from *sal* leaves or into small steel bowls.

A few hours later, Mangra came to get me, saying: "Let's go, I need to come back quickly." He had made an effort to dress in his market best. His skin was glowing against his clean white shirt, and he had put on his one good lungi. His hair was slickly oiled, parted, and neatly combed. As he turned, I caught a waft of the mustard oil moisturizing his body. In one hand, he carried an empty cloth bag.

The market in Bero. *Photo by author.*

Drinking rice beer on the way back from the market. *Photo by author.*

"Is there nothing to take to the market today?" I asked.

"The tomatoes and eggplants are not ripe yet. I'm just going to buy the weekly supply of kerosene, soap, salt, sugar, and spices."

"Where's *bhavji*?" I was conscious that by calling his wife my sister-in-law, I was stating that he was my brother.

"She's gone to chip stones and look after the goats," he replied. Mangra had four young children, and although—like everyone else in the village—he had some land, the family was finding it difficult to make ends meet. Whenever they could, both husband and wife spent their days digging and chipping stones for the sadans, who supplied local contractors with gravel from Tapu.

We made our way onto the mud track that snakes from Tapu to the next village, climbs into the sal forest, and then descends into the Chotanagpur Plateau. Here, the track joins the paved road that leads into Bero and eventually, thirty-five kilometers or so later, is engulfed by Ranchi, the growing capital of Jharkhand.

We walked in silence. It was an hour's walk to Bero, and there was no one else from Tapu who looked likely to join us. Mangra was shy, and I wondered how best to break the ice. I noticed that, although he was dressed in his best clothes, he had come barefoot.

"Why have you left your slippers?" I asked.

"I've lost so many in the market. I leave them somewhere and then forget them." He smiled wryly. "The problem is I'm not used to slippers. So now I've just given up wearing them to Bero."

I laughed and nervously joked back, "Well, now that Jharkhand State is formed, Tapu will develop. Electricity will light up the village, and water will spurt out of taps. Tapu's mud houses will become brick mansions. Everyone will want their children educated. You won't have to walk as far as Bero to see a doctor. And shops will open in the village. You will be inundated by people trying to sell you slippers! There'll be no problem if you leave them in Bero."

I felt rather stupid for having made such a silly remark. But Mangra grew serious and asked, "I heard that there might be some change in *sarkar* [the state]—has Jharkhand sarkar formed?'

Before I could reply, he reflected on his own question. "In any case, what does it matter? What will it bring? As far as I'm concerned, it will probably only bring our *soshan* [exploitation] closer."

I was stunned by Mangra's comment. Less than a month earlier, on the stroke of midnight, 15 November 2000, India's twenty-eighth state, Jharkhand, had been created. Mangra and I were standing less than fifty kilometers from its capital, Ranchi. On the day of its creation, at 12:05 a.m., Governor Prabhat Kumar had taken his oath of office and had later paid tribute to all the adivasi martyrs of the Jharkhand movement for independence from Bihar. The Jharkhand movement was often described as one of the oldest autonomy movements in India, having made its first demands for a separate state within India to the Simon Commission in 1928. After the independence of India, these demands were reiterated to the 1952 States Reorganisation Commission. The struggle for autonomy initially revolved around the idea that the culturally autonomous indigenous people, or adivasis, were exploited and oppressed by the high-caste Hindu governments that had ruled them from Patna, the capital of Bihar. Therefore, activists argued that adivasis such as Mangra had the right to a separate state.

On 15 November 2000, I had arrived in India to pursue fieldwork in rural Jharkhand. Reading the front pages of national newspapers such as *The Pioneer* and *The Economic Times* at a friend's house in Delhi, I had realized that a mixture of celebration and anxiety would welcome me a few days later in Ranchi. The first government called itself a National Democratic Alliance, and it was led by Chief Minister Babulal Marandi of the Bharatya Janata Party, the Hindu nationalist party, rather than by Shibhu Soren, leader of the Jharkhand Mukti Morcha (Jharkhand Liberation Front, or JMM) that had spearheaded the long fight for autonomy.

Nevertheless, when I arrived in Jharkhand, I found its separation from Bihar was a cause for great celebration by many people in Ranchi. Activists from different parties were euphoric and made merry for days. While separation from Bihar took place at the behest of the Hindu nationalist government, undoubtedly the long history of the struggle for autonomy led by Jharkhand's activists was crucial. Moreover, the separation of Jharkhand from Bihar intensified the activists' campaigning and advocacy to protect the region's adivasis. The streets of Ranchi were jammed with demonstrations for the protection of adivasi "jungle, *jamin*, and *jal*" (forest, land, and water). Indigenous rights activists promoted Sarna as an adivasi religion of nature worship, and one of the many annual festivals, Sarhul, was celebrated with great pomp and ritual in Ranchi as *the* adivasi festival of the year (equivalent to the Muslim Id, the Christian Christmas, and the Hindu Diwali). The newspapers were full of articles against the migration of adivasis out of the area, and for an antimigration bill to be passed. And workshops were held to point out the shortcomings of current forms of local governance, and to argue that legal recognition be given to indigenous forms of self-governance.

The formation of Jharkhand State was a success not just for India's adivasi activists, but also for indigenous rights activists around the world. The long struggle for independence had been fought in the name of the many adivasis living in rural Jharkhand. Therefore, I expected them to share this excitement. But I did not realize then that many of the poorest adivasis I would meet in rural Jharkhand, people like Mangra, did not really know, and moreover did not care, much about these major political changes.

We walked down what is considered to be a national highway. The pavement under Mangra's feet must feel hot, I thought. Suddenly the town of Bero burst upon us. Brick buildings and construction had exploded everywhere around the central hub of state administration which catered for the surrounding 114 villages—and included the local police, forest, and the block development offices. The latter was the most localized office of the Ministry of Rural Development in India, and through it thousands of rupees are distributed each year to develop the area's marginalized communities of adivasis in the forest fringes. Bero was also the destination of a growing number of sadans, whose migration to the town had made its population rise from a mere 3,500 in 1991 to at least double that figure in 2007. The sadans were leaving their mud houses in the forest; opening small businesses, mainly shops; and seeking the benefits of running water, easier access to the development resources coming into the area in the name of the poor, better schools for their children, and at least sporadic electricity.

Mangra dropped his head and started to walk faster, as if trying to stay ahead of me. He seemed to be having second thoughts about being seen with me in the market. I knew what he was about to say.

"You wait at Odhar's shop," he said. "I'll go to the market and come back to get you."

I didn't really want to wait at the shop of the Tapu sadan. But I didn't want to push the boundaries with Mangra, either. A bit disappointed, I agreed.

Neel Odhar was sitting behind a rotting wooden counter in the shop. Against the peeling blue paint, his crisp blue-and-white checked shirt, beige trousers, and gray Nike running shoes made him stand out. On one side in front of him, his brother's scooter was parked; on the other side was a line of bicycles. I recognised Gego Munda from

Tapu repairing the bicycles. Behind Neel were stacks of dusty red chairs, piled almost to the ceiling. His brother rented the chairs for weddings and other functions. Neel pulled a chair out, wiped it with a rag, and called me in.

Chatting to Gego, Mangra loitered around the front of the shop for a few minutes. Neel looked disapprovingly at him. "Couldn't you even have got a bicycle to carry her on?"

"I really enjoyed our walk," I piped up, a bit embarrassed and trying to defend Mangra.

When Mangra left, I told Neel how surprised I was that he did not even know that Jharkhand had been formed. Neel responded, "Ah, this *jangli log*!" I grimaced in distaste at his derogatory use of the term "forest people," by which he meant they were savage, wild, dirty, backward, and uncouth. He continued, "What would they know about such matters? All they think about is one day at a time. They eat, drink, and are merry. Why should the formation of Jharkhand matter to them? It matters to us, us *parha-likha* [educated] people. Jharkhand's formation is going to bring more money to the rural areas for us, more state contracts, more development, and more benefits. It's great for us."

I was struck by the contrasting perspectives on Jharkhand's independence held by Neel Odhar, Mangra Munda, and the indigenous rights activists who represent people like Mangra internationally. Why did some Tapu adivasis, Mundas in this case, not care about the formation of Jharkhand State? How did Munda views about the formation of Jharkhand coexist and interrelate with other imaginings of Jharkhand—for instance, those held by rural elites (usually higher caste, though sometimes adivasi) and by indigenous rights activists living in the larger urban centers of Jharkhand? This book is my journey to understanding how, *in the shadows of the state*, these contrasting perspectives coexist in Jharkhand; what implications they may hold for transnational debates on indigenous people, rights, and development; and, relatedly, what the unintended consequences of global indigenous rights activism may be for poor, rural indigenous people in Jharkhand, India.

1. *The Dark Side of Indigeneity*

The last two decades of the twentieth century witnessed increasing transnational concern about the lack of a universal system of protection for indigenous rights and development. This concern gained prominence with the formation of the United Nations Working Group on Indigenous Populations (UNWGIP) in 1982. United Nations established a Permanent Forum on Indigenous Issues in 2000 and appointed a Special Rapporteur on the situation of human rights and fundamental freedoms of indigenous people the following year.[1]

More generally, the first United Nations International Decade of the World's Indigenous People (1995–2004) promoted global interest in the protection of indigenous rights and a second such decade began in 2005. While indigenous peoples are highly heterogeneous in their views and agendas,[2] advocates for most groups make certain familiar arguments. These include the ideas that indigenous people around the world have been marginalized for centuries, various settler populations have stolen and colonized their lands, their numbers are in decline, their cultures are threatened, and they live in states that give more weight to the values and interests of the nonindigenous than to those of the indigenous.

The global spotlight on indigenous issues goes hand in hand with an increasing interest in global warming, environmentalism, and people-centered nongovernmental organizations (NGOs). Indigenous communities around the world have collaborated with NGOs such as the Minority Rights Group International, the International Work Group for Indigenous Affairs, the Environmental Defense Fund, the Forest People's Movement, Survival International, Human Rights Watch, Cultural Survival, and the Rainforest Action Network. Some anthropologists who seek to defend indigenous rights to land and resources have also championed the cause of these peoples.[3] A number of scholars argue that these indigenous actors are resisting their historical subjugation not through the "hidden transcripts" of "weapons of the weak," but through flamboyant "open transcripts" of overt representations and public acts of opposing the nation-states in which they live.[4] Thus they are part of the genre of (new) social movements that lies between mass revolution and small-scale resistance,[5] and that offers marginalized people a political voice besides that offered by mainstream development or Marxism and socialism.[6] The idea is that poor, colonized, exploited, indigenous populations must be protected; their cultures must be preserved; and their rights must be enshrined in U.N. human-rights legislation. As I will show, these are controversial arguments made in the name of the protection of indigenous rights. Globally, they have produced renewed and heated debate among scholars.

India, a country which some say has the second largest indigenous population in the world,[7] is home to over eighty-four million people classified as members of Scheduled Tribes—that is 8.2 percent of India's total population. The official position of the Indian government, however, is that there are no indigenous people in the country. The government's claim is based on the country's complex migration patterns which means that unlike in other nations such as Australia or Canada, it is impossible to identify the original settlers of a particular region. However, beginning in 1985, Indian activists have participated in the UNWGIP meetings. These activists sought to claim indigenous status for India's adivasi populations, peoples previously known as tribals, and who are recognized officially in government censuses as members of Scheduled Tribes. In 1987 the Indian delegates to UNWGIP represented a newly founded Indian Council of Indigenous and Tribal Peoples, affiliated with the World Council of Indigenous Peoples. The leading members of the Indian group were from what is now the State of Jharkhand.

The Jharkhandi activists claimed that India's Scheduled Tribe populations qualified for the new transnational term "indigenous peoples" because they were culturally different from mainstream Indian society, and especially because they had been internally colonized and dominated by a system of values and institutions maintained by the ruling groups of the country. They argued for the need to secure "the collective right of self-determination" in order to restore "land and forest rights" to India's indigenous people[8]—something that they felt would be possible through negotiation via internationally approved rights and safeguards.

This argument has historical roots. Activists in Jharkhand had been struggling for the autonomy of the region from Bihar State, within the Indian federal union, since the late 1920s. The initial struggles argued for a separate state on the basis that the region housed culturally autonomous indigenous people, classified as Scheduled Tribes by the government, and more popularly known as adivasis.[9] Later, realizing that the demographic reality meant that a significant Jharkhandi population did not count as members of a Scheduled Tribe, at least according to the census, the independence promoters became more inclusive. Their new rhetoric was that Jharkhand was an internal colony of Bihar—that Bihar was reaping the benefits of Jharkhand's mineral, forest, and land resources. This enabled the movement to broaden its social base while maintaining that the area's identity emerged from the exploitation of its population and its distinct cultural heritage,[10] and therefore the region should be restored to its original "sons of the soil."[11] The linking of the cultural politics of Jharkhand with transnational concerns some sixty years later was thus the latest phase of an old movement. Nevertheless, Jharkhand's separation from Bihar on 15 November 2000 was in many ways a triumph for Jharkhand's transnational activists.

The implications of such transnational indigenous rights activism for targeted people in specific localities, however, are far from clear and have received very little in-depth scrutiny. In this book, I explore the lives and experiences of some of the poorest adivasis in rural Jharkhand to analyze common claims made at a global level on behalf of indigenous populations. For instance, I will examine the promotion of special forms of indigenous governance (chapter 2), the way development takes shape in the name of the poorest people (chapter 3), what I will call the eco-incarceration of indigenous people through arguments about their love for and worship of nature (chapter 4) as well as their attachment to their land (chapter 5), and claims that they harbor revolutionary potential (chapter 6).

I show that the opinions, desires, and concerns of the poorest rural adivasis often contradicted and subverted those of the well-meaning urban-based middle-class activists, as well as those of local rural elites aspiring to rise up the class hierarchy. I move between the small village of Tapu, surrounding villages, the local administrative town of Bero, and Jharkhand's capital city from January 1999 to March 2007. I follow the everyday lives of some of the poorest villagers as they chase away protected wild elephants, try to cut down the forests they allegedly live in harmony with, migrate to work in distant brick kilns to experience amorous relationships, maintain a healthy skepticism about the revival of the indigenous governance system, and escape Maoist guerrillas who claim to represent them. I juxtapose these experiences to the accounts of the village elites, as well as to the rhetorical arguments of the Ranchi-based indigenous rights activists fighting on behalf of the villagers. My central proposition is that the activists' arguments actually further marginalize the people they claim to speak for.

In writing this book, my hope is to open up grounded scholarly examination into the unintended effects of well-meaning measures for indigenous protection and development. I want to move the debate beyond both the arguments that consider the concept of indigenous people anthropologically and historically problematic, and those that consider indigeneity a useful political tool. I focus on one specific locality, a region in Jharkhand, to illuminate the broader point that there may be a dark side of indigeneity that it is well worth highlighting, especially to those who urge us to shelve our critical scholarship in case we weaken the advocacy of promoters of indigenous rights and development.

The dark side of indigeneity suggests that local use of global discourses of indigeneity can reinforce a class system that further marginalizes the poorest people. This class dimension to the indigenous rights movement is likely to get erased in the cultural-based identity politics it produces. Moreover, the transnational movement for indigeneity may obscure those spaces of hope, of a good life, that may lie beyond the shadows of the state. These are the spaces inhabited by people like those of the Jungle Raj in Tapu, the spaces from which a radical politics could emerge to better serve the poor.

Before I explore the history of debates and concerns that leads to the arguments of this book, I would like to make a brief comment about my style of writing. I hope this book will engage not only a varied academic audience but also journalists, human rights and political activists, environmentalists, development workers, policymakers, and the general reader. In this endeavor, I have tried to make my theoretical analysis emerge from the stories of Jharkhand without burdening the body of my text with the conventionally voluminous academic references to comparative, theoretical, and regional literature. For the specialist, I have developed my engagement with the latter through extensive endnotes. Where particular authors are absolutely central to the arguments being developed, I have tried to make them appear and disappear from the text like my Jharkhandi friends and informants. I hope that these decisions will mean that the book is detailed enough for the specialist while being accessible enough for the generalist. The writing of academics is a political act, and I believe we should make every effort to make our texts as accessible as possible to a wide audience.

TRIBES OF MIND?

The transnational concerns over indigenous people, rights, and development have reignited a controversy over indigeneity.[12] On the one hand, there are those who argue for the special categorization and protection of indigenous peoples. On the other hand, there are those who question whether indigeneity is a product of the mind, whether those classified as indigenous are in fact an "invention of the primitive," to borrow Adam Kuper's phrase,[13] and whether policies should actually be aimed at assimilating these people into the mainstream of society. To understand how the Tapu situation speaks to these transnational concerns, it is important to historically trace the key issues in the Indian context. As in many other countries, in India debates central to indigeneity have a much longer history than the recent transnational concerns.

The contested issue of tribal status goes back at least as far as India's colonial period, when British anthropologists and administrators viewed the country's aboriginals as primitive tribes. The need to order Indian society was at the heart of nineteenth-century anthropology in India.[14] At first sight a confusing kaleidoscope, India presented the administrator and the anthropologist with the challenge of meaningfully ordering a hierarchical society in which caste was understood to embody racial and cultural difference. Race and racial ideology were the norms of a broader political order at the time and affected the categorization and classification of India's primitive tribes.[15] For one of India's most influential administrators, H. H. Risley, who directed the 1901 Census, caste status was inscribed on the permanent physical exteriors of Indian bodies. In particular, Risley saw what he called the nasal index as a guide to the status of the nose's owner. Those with the finest noses (and lightest complexions, closest to those of Europeans) were descendants of the Aryan invader upper castes such as Brahmans, Rajputs, and Sikhs, and those with snub noses (and dark complexions approaching those of black Africans) were the aboriginal primitive tribes, the forest and hill dwellers, occupying the oldest and lowest strata in India.[16]

This racial anthropology was conveniently appropriated by some Indian elites seeking to both justify local hierarchy and assert parity with upper-class Europeans.[17] Some scholars argue that Indians played a greater role in colonial constructions of the tribe.[18] Nevertheless, one conclusion is that members of the Indian elite and colonial administrators and anthropologists together created the representations that have a powerful effect on society and politics in India today—stereotypes of the forest folk as living in a timeless harmony with nature, disturbed only in recent times by the market and the state. Twentieth-century isolation of remote jungle tribes is, then, not just some survival of an earlier period but a product of the mind of both colonial rulers and Indian elites.

THE PRODUCTION OF ADIVASIS

While the nineteenth century in India was, in many ways, a period that marked the invention of the primitive, a number of policies and events also served to unite a wide variety of communities living in India's forests and hills. One set of policies were those that extended state control over land and forests, via revenue collection. This state expansion was enabled and accompanied by a new influx of exploitative state officials from outside the region, moneylenders, and landlords, forming the trinity of "sarkar, *sahukar*, and zamindar." Where they could not hide or flee from this officialdom, some affected people, like those in western India, mobilized through a religiously inspired purifying struggle espousing upper-caste norms.[19] In other areas, most notably in the Chotanagpur region of eastern India that is now Jharkhand, there were a series of more violent rebellions.[20] Despite these multiple reactions, increased state control in many forested and hilly tracts created a shared experience of domination and subordination, and thus united a wide range of people.

A unifying event, especially for inhabitants of the Chotanagpur Plateau, was the reaction of the colonial administration to the nineteenth-century resistance movements. The government made some effort to provide a range of protectionary measures for adivasis based on a codification of their customary rights to land. For instance, following the 1830s Kol rebellion, the Wilkinson Rule provided for self-rule in present-day Singhbhum. There, tribal village councils were given authority to function independently. After the 1855–56 Insurrection, the Santhal Parganas Regulation Act included provisions for the nontransferability of land in Santhal Parganas. Similarly, the 1857 Sepoy Mutiny and the 1859–65 Sardar Movement led to the protectionary measures of the 1869 Chotanagpur Land Tenures Act. This act recognized *bhuinhari* tenures (special common ownership rights over lands of the original settlers in Oraon areas) and set up a system to demarcate such lands in a survey. This was followed by the 1908 Chotanagpur Tenancy Act, which prohibited transfers of land to nontribals, and ensured community ownership and management of the rights of forest communities over *khuntkatti* areas (where descendants of original settlers held common ownership over certain lands in Munda areas). The Birsa Rebellion of the 1890s also preceded this act. Thus, along with adivasi rebellion, and colonial imagery of isolated tribes, more humanitarian colonial measures also encouraged the institutionalization of tribal autonomy.[21]

Christian missionaries in the nineteenth and early twentieth centuries were a third important factor in creating adivasi autonomy—although today's Indian indigenous activists, in their quest to institutionalize an adivasi religion, often underplay this history. For some scholars, it is in fact Christian missionaries who produced the term "adivasi."[22] After the first missionaries arrived in Ranchi in 1845, the German Gossner Evangelical Lutheran Church, Anglicans, Roman Catholics, and, in particular, Jesuit missionaries played an important role in generating a greater social consciousness and organizing the tribals against exploitative economic relations along ethnic lines.[23] An important part of this project was the introduction of Western education, and with it a new system of values, to the population. Thus while Jesuits such as Father Hoffman[24] were busy helping to draft special laws for the Chotanagpur Tenancy Act in order to protect the area's tribals, a new class of adivasi elites was also developing. Educated, urban based, and usually Christian, these new elites contributed to the emergence of the Jharkhand Movement. They met the Simon Commission in 1928 to put forward what was probably the first demand for a separate adivasi state, leading to the promotion of adivasi as a category to describe a range of people living under similar circumstances.

The educated Christian tribal youth that formed the emerging adivasi middle-class elites in Chotanagpur organized themselves into a range of societies. Their aim was to demand from the colonial government better educational facilities, economic avenues, and job opportunities for tribals, and more generally the removal of backwardness from the region — this implied efforts to socially, economically, and politically advance the area. In 1910, Anglican missionaries formed the Dacca Students Union (later renamed the Chotanagpur Improvement Society), and in the 1920s, the Catholics formed the Chotanagpur Catholic Sabha, representatives of which won two seats in the first Indian provincial assembly elections in 1937.[25] In 1938, all these Christian Sabhas and non-Christian tribal groups merged to form the Chotanagpur Adivasi Mahasabha (which in the 1950s formed a political wing, the Jharkhand Party). This was a significant move which aimed to unite adivasis by fighting rulers from outside the region, or the *diku* raj, in order to improve the socioeconomic and political conditions of adivasis. It also further promulgated the struggle of adivasis in Chotanagpur to a wider Indian audience.[26]

TO PROTECT OR ASSIMILATE?

When India gained independence from British rule in 1947, the question of how to incorporate the Scheduled Tribes and Scheduled Castes into independent India was a crucial concern for the makers of the new nation. One of the earliest detailed critiques of the concept of the tribe in India developed against this historical backdrop. In 1943, four years before independence, the sociologist G. S. Ghurye, a nationalist and a promoter of assimilation policies, wrote a book with the aim of showing that India's "so-called aboriginals" could be best described as "backward" Hindus.[27] Ghurye gave evidence to show that the distinction between animism and Hinduism was very blurred, that the so-called aboriginals had always embraced Hinduism, had had intimate connections with Hindus for a long time, and often saw themselves as Hindus. As a puritan and a reformer, Ghurye concluded that the proper description of these people must refer to their place in or near Hindu society, and not their supposed autochthonism.[28] This was an argument in line with Gandhian activists and other nationalists who, at the time, were committed to incorporating tribals into the mainstream of Indian society, and who felt that the colonial policy of divide and rule, nowhere better evidenced than in the Chotanagpur region, had played a significant role in isolating India's tribes.

In stark contrast to Ghurye, others sought to protect India's tribes from aggressive and insensitive outsiders. The most prominent voice in this line of thinking was Verrier Elwin, a man some accuse of romanticizing tribal society and having an antimodern agenda.[29] A self-proclaimed anthropologist, who initially came to India from Britain as a missionary but resigned from the church after living for some years with the Gonds in central India (and marrying an adivasi woman), Elwin took the view that anthropology must lead to administrative reform and improve the living conditions of the people. Unlike the work of his most vehement critic, Ghurye, who charged Elwin with wanting to put the Baiga tribe in a zoo, Elwin's writings were based on living with and loving India's tribal populations.[30] Elwin's actions to protect tribals, not in a zoo as Ghurye had charged, but at helping them deal with the onslaught of modernity at their own pace—had a significant effect on the tribal protection policies of Jawaharlal Nehru, India's first prime minister.[31]

The Constituent Assembly debates which began in 1946 mirrored the debate over assimilation and protection, with those who believed that modernization policies had to be based on assimilation passionately arguing with those who demanded protection for India's tribals. The result, which replicated some of the provisions of the Colonial Government Acts, was that the new Indian constitution provided special protection for what it called India's Backward Classes, the Scheduled Castes and Scheduled Tribes (then about 15 and 7.5 percent of the population, respectively). The government reserved for these Backward Classes a fixed quota of vacancies and promotions in government employment, reserved seats in Parliament and the state assemblies, reserved places and scholarships in state-run educational institutions, and preferential loans in order to start businesses. In 1979, the Mandal Commission reviewed the quota system and recommended that it be extended to other lower castes as well, to a broader collection of Socially and Economically Backward Classes.[32] These recommendations were controversially put into place in 1990 under V. P. Singh's populist government, leading to 49.5 percent of all jobs in central government services and public undertakings being reserved for Scheduled Castes, Scheduled Tribes, and Other Backward Classes.

While offering them similar privileges, the attitudes toward the Scheduled Castes and Scheduled Tribes held by the makers of India's constitution were nonetheless quite different. The Scheduled Castes' economic deprivation was linked to their low ritual status, and an erasure of difference was the eventual goal for them. The Scheduled Tribes, however, were exoticized and seen as requiring longer-term protection and development. Thus, besides affirmative action policies, tribal areas (called Scheduled Areas) further benefited from being treated as separate administrative categories in order to protect the rights of Scheduled Tribes over their land, forests, and water. The constitution's Fifth Schedule and Sixth Schedule carried over the principles of the Scheduled Districts Act of 1874, which excluded Scheduled Areas from the operation of ordinary laws in British India.

Since its formation, however, like many of the special tenancy acts in adivasi areas, the Fifth Schedule has been under constant threat of amendment in order to allow transfers of tribal lands to nontribals and corporate bodies. Much of India's mineral resources are located in protected Scheduled Areas — in Jharkhand, Orissa, and Chhattisgarh — and in recent years the alliances of neoliberal state policies and multinational corporate interests have sought to harvest these riches to fulfil the dream of "India Shining" (the development slogan of the Bharatya Janata Party (BJP) government of 2000–2004). The latest threat to the Scheduled Areas has been the formation of special economic zones (SEZs) which give special legal rights to private companies, allowing them to buy up land. These threats to scheduled land rights have given rise to alliances between a wide range of NGOs and activists and those adivasis whose lands are targeted for acquisition. In 2007, for example, there were violent protests against the establishment of an SEZ in Nandigram, West Bengal, and protestors blocked parts of Orissa's main north-south highway after the 2006 massacre of their companions by the police at another proposed SEZ site in Kalinganagar.

The debate between protection and assimilation has thus marked the development of discussions about indigeneity in India in which complex political agendas, often but not always intended to secure an adivasi constituency, have been central. Some groups — for example, the neo-Marxists and indigenous rights activists — have sought to reassert a separate tribal identity and/or reclaim rights to resources around a shared subaltern experience of dispossession and resistance. Others have tried to assimilate adivasis in a broader project of nationalism, most notably the extreme right-wing Hindu militants for whom adivasis are merely backward people who should be brought into the fold of mainstream Hindu society. From this perspective, legitimate indigenous Indians are Hindus (and not, of course, Christians or Muslims).

The 1980s saw the steady rise of Hindu nationalism in India through a family of organizations known as the Sangh Parivar,[33] which seeks to replace India's version of constitutional secularism with the ideology of Hindutva—that is, the Hindu domination of Bharat India and the subordination of Muslims, Christians, and other minorities.[34] Its political party, the BJP, first came to power as the head of India's national coalition government in 1997. The years that followed have seen a series of horrific communal riots. However, the issue of the relationship between adivasis and the Hindu right was brought to the center of public attention in India after the bloody violence in Gujarat, western India, in 2002, when about two thousand Muslims were killed, several thousand displaced after their homes were destroyed, and many women raped and mutilated by the Sangh Parivar. Whereas support for the Hindu right was previously thought to emanate from middle-class Indians, in the Gujarat violence, adivasis actively participated in attacks against Muslims.[35] From the late 1990s in eastern India, the threat that Hindu nationalists would gain the support of adivasis led Jharkhandi indigenous rights activists to revive an older campaign to stress the cultural autonomy of adivasis from the Hindu mainstream.

In the 1950s, the political wing of the Chotanagpur Adivasi Mahasabha, the Jharkhand Party, had demanded a separate state of Jharkhand within the Indian federal union, further developing the autonomy movement. The Jharkhand Party had become the chief opposition to the Congress Party in the state of Bihar after taking the majority of seats from south Bihar in the 1952 state assembly elections. Initially, the struggle had been based on the idea that the culturally autonomous adivasis of the region had the right to a separate state. However, as Susana Devalle has shown, a "myth of the tribe," which had its roots in colonial categorization, was being produced in Jharkhand when in fact there was internal differentiation and class divisions among those called tribal.[36] The ideology of tribal economy and society that presented the tribals of Chotanagpur as an undifferentiated mass of simple cultivators exploited by nontribals needed, as Stuart Corbridge argues,[37] to be critically deconstructed. As early as the 1891 census, only one-third of the population of Chotanagpur belonged to a Scheduled Tribe.[38] Moreover, economic transformation, especially industrialization, later attracted the immigration of Bihari upper castes, which further changed the ethnic composition of Jharkhand.

Given that this demographic reality of the region meant that a significant population did not count as tribal, at least according to the census (the 2001 census shows 26.3 percent of Jharkhand to be members of a Scheduled Tribe), the independence promoters necessarily became more inclusive. Sadans, nontribals with a long history of living in Jharkhand, were also incorporated under the broad umbrella of indigenous Jharkhandis. To become practical, Jharkhandi regionalism needed a program of opposition based on a more abstract and general sense of injustice than that of solely ethnic politics.[39] As a result, scholars and activists of Jharkhand came to represent the area as colonized by dikus, nontribal and exploitative outsiders. These foreigners were accused of establishing economic, political, and cultural hegemony over the region, especially by ruling from Patna (Bihar's capital). Further, they were blamed for degrading the natural environment. The stress was thus now on Jharkhand as a colony of Bihar: while the development machinery of Bihar performed disproportionately poorly in Jharkhand, Bihar was reaping the benefits of Jharkhand's mineral, land, and especially forest resources. The demand for a Jharkhandi state evolved into a regional movement enjoying the support of a range of people but with the common understanding that the area's identity derived from an exploitation of its population and its distinct cultural heritage.[40] This view formed one basis of the struggle for Jharkhand's independence from Bihar within the Indian federal union: that the region should be restored to those who rightfully owned it and could best manage it, to its true "sons of the soil."

Following the separation of Chhattisgarh from Madhya Pradesh and Uttaranchal (now Uttarakhand) from Uttar Pradesh, Jharkhand finally became independent from Bihar in November 2000. Scholars have argued that separation was granted on the basis of political bargains struck between India's political elite, on the basis of expediency and opportunism, rather than because of the long history of struggles from within the state or genuine concerns for the democratic and developmental potential of smaller states.[41] Indeed, the separation was led by a state government dominated by Hindu nationalists—the BJP, considered by many as the party of the outsiders—rather than by the JMM, which had led the fight for independence since 1972.

Granting Jharkhand independence from Bihar had been on the BJP agenda since 1988, but the party's view was that the new state should be called Vananchal[42] and its citizens *vanavasi* (rather than adivasi). Although both mean "land of the forests," unlike Jharkhand, Vananchal has Sanskritic and Aryan connotations.[43] Jharkhandi indigenous rights activists claimed that such a renaming would enable the BJP to divorce the region from the JMM and bring it into the Hindu fold. Although the new state was ultimately called Jharkhand, indigenous rights activists mobilized to prove the historical basis for Jharkhand rather than Vananchal.[44] They led a renewed and reinvigorated campaign focusing on a separate identity of indigenous communities, mobilized around protection of their "jungle, jamin, and jal." This campaign, whose effect is analyzed in chapter 4, renewed the representations of adivasis as being forest dwellers and having lived in harmony with the forests for generations.[45]

In the rural areas of Jharkhand, however, there are other competing forces that may seduce new generations of educated adivasi youth. Rather than the threat of Hindu nationalism that is the case in western India, today's adivasi youth is being increasingly targeted by the extreme left in the form of the spreading Naxalite insurgency, inspired by Marx, Mao, and Lenin. Seeing adivasis as a potential revolutionary force, as harborers of "elementary aspects of peasant insurgency"[46] whose class consciousness no doubt needs to be developed, the Naxalites view adivasi areas as the ideal base for a radical politics to create a Maoist belt from Nepal to Andhra Pradesh. The conventional assumption, explored in chapter 6, is that given the Naxalites' anti-elite, antistate approach, their main support comes from the poorest rural adivasis.

SCHOLARLY ROLE IN THE DEBATE

The debate over whether indigenous populations should be assimilated with other populations or protected from them remains a highly charged one, the ripples of which are felt far beyond the Chotanagpur Plateau—indigenous people in many parts of the world have become an active force in contemporary politics.[47] They are also felt beyond the desire to secure an indigenous constituency, as academics continue to debate what role scholarly endeavors should have in these political discussions. As Michael Brown puts it, the global movement for indigenous rights today presents anthropology with difficult dilemmas.[48]

An important body of scholarly work continues to warn against the dangers of constructing an autonomous indigenous community. A range of monumental studies shows that the communities described as tribes cannot be defined independently of the state systems with which they are associated.[49] Claims to tribal isolation and ancient heritage might be externally defined and enforced as a result of European quests and colonization.[50] We need to be aware of embracing indigenous claims to total heritage through measures of legal separatism that place native cultures off-limits to outsiders. Such measures may possibly result in undemocratic reverse discrimination.[51] The idea of an essential indigenous culture is seen to be problematic because culture is not a static entity, but a constantly changing process. Thus, the very concept of indigeneity relies on obsolete Victorian anthropological notions, and on a romantic and false ethnographic vision.[52]

In India, following Ghurye's account, the sociologist André Béteille, one of India's most respected public intellectuals, has argued against the idea of indigenous people. In an essay on "Tribe and Peasantry," he states that the country's tribal populations are like peasants anywhere in India.[53] In this essay, Béteille takes each of the four criteria that are usually used to differentiate tribes from castes—size, isolation, religion, and means of livelihood—and argues that in each, there is no distinction between tribe and peasantry in India. In his later work,[54] Béteille controversially shows the problems of positive discrimination or affirmative action policies in India,[55] and in 1998, he returns to the indigenous people debate in an essay for *Current Anthropology*. Here he shows how the words "native" and "tribe" have been replaced by the term "indigenous," as allegedly more politically correct and with roughly the opposite moral signification.[56] He reiterates some of his earlier arguments about the complex interaction between tribals and nontribals, pointing out that in India (as opposed to Australia and the New World) no given population can claim indigeneity because there are no other populations that can reasonably be described as settlers or aliens. In some ways, his argument mirrors that of Crispin Bates, who proposes that the term "adivasi" is a colonial invention and argues that we need to admit that in one sense all Indians are adivasis.[57]

But there is also a more serious warning about the potential dangers of the idea of the indigenous in Béteille's writings. Béteille asks: "Is there now such an essentialist view of indigenous people in which they carry their identity with them wherever they go and whatever they do? Has the crude anthropological association of race and culture acquired a more refined form in the concept of indigenous people?"[58] In a line of thought reiterated by other Indian scholars,[59] he cautions that the growing popularity of the idea of the indigenous provides ideological ammunition to those who would reorder the world according to the claims of blood and soil.[60]

Adam Kuper more forcefully articulates Béteille's concerns about the undemocratic, even fascist arguments underpinning this recent appropriation of indigeneity.[61] Kuper argues that in the recent "return of the native," culture has become a euphemism for race.[62] It may lead to ethnic conflict, and it has meant defending positions—for example, that descendants of the original inhabitants of a country should have privileged rights to its resources—which are similar to ones made by extreme right-wing parties in Europe.

Such attacks on the concept of indigeneity, central to indigenous people's movements and to the work of many human-rights organizations, have prompted heated reactions from those scholars and activists who feel morally obliged to protect the world's indigenous populations. They take issue with juxtaposing indigenous movements to Nazi or apartheid ideology. They say this polemic ignores the context of extreme discrimination faced by indigenous peoples, and their many experiences of dispossession by more powerful groups.[63] They argue that what is essentially a peaceful movement should not be made to look aggressive. Moreover, they point out that the concept of indigeneity is not a Victorian notion but has been appropriated by diverse people across the world to draw attention to their marginalization and dispossession, and the resilience of their social, economic, and religious practices.[64] Thus we may need a relational approach to indigeneity—one that takes seriously how the people concerned experience the term.

A third way or middle ground proposed by some is that although anthropologically or historically the concept of indigeneity might be problematic, politically and legally it may be a very useful tool for oppressed people who need special rights. Used that way, it may mark a move toward equality rather than away from it.[65] The political use of an essentialized notion of indigenous culture is then merely a reflection of the strategic invocation of a reductionist, rights-based language of the law rather than any preexisting entity called "culture."[66] Rather than exposing the gaps in the concept of indigeneity, perhaps we should explore how particular groups position themselves as indigenous. This would encourage us to follow what James Clifford has called "the predicament of culture," and to explore the ways in which culture is translated and transplanted from multiple positionings.[67] This would involve also the production of ethnographic accounts of indigenous activists, or "culture makers,"[68] and an exploration of their involvement in what Tania Li, drawing on Stuart Hall, has called the cultural and political work of articulation.[69] Indigenous groups might be merely following the logic of what Dipesh Chakrabarty calls a "politics unlimited"—that is, "the idea that the poor or the oppressed, in pursuit of their rights, have to adopt every means at hand in order to fight the system that puts them down."[70] Like ethnicity, then, indigeneity is a political concept. And who are we to deny the ethnic identity or the indigenous identity of others, however unscientific such a claim may seem to us?

In India, this approach is called for by several scholars who argue that not only has the term "indigenous people" come to have a real and lived relevance for people in the country, but it has also become an important tool of articulation for empowerment.[71] These scholars argue that while the precise meanings and characteristics of the terms can be debated, "adivasis" and "indigeneity" in India are social facts.[72] Moreover, being indigenous is a new way of placing oneself in the world and therefore of pursuing a new type of politics, a cultural politics. Although indigenous people might not always be the most marginalized, in this new form of politics, for those fighting for marginalized and dispossessed adivasis, the term "indigenous" becomes useful precisely because it is difficult to pin down, because it has become a powerful rhetorical device. And, perhaps, we need to move beyond the sterile debate of whether or not the concept of indigenous people is relevant.[73] One way forward is for us to investigate how this new kind of cultural politics emerges, what its processes and shifts are: we should treat it as an object of ethnographic and historiographic study.[74] We cannot say that the concept of indigeneity is fabricated because it is already being used by people around the world, and it means certain things to them in the present. In taking the most extreme version of this line of argument, some scholars and activists even argue that to bring critical attention to indigeneity in India is to undermine the struggle of such marginalized groups.[75]

In this vein, anthropologists like Anna Tsing[76] argue for an ethnographic openness to the romanticism and commitment of activists who put themselves on the line. Others argue more explicitly for what Nancy Scheper-Hughes has called a "militant anthropology," whereby anthropologists become not just friends or patrons but comrades.[77] Charles Hale, for instance, in analyzing his own involvement as an activist anthropologist in the land-rights struggle of an indigenous community in Nicaragua, urges anthropology to move away from mere cultural critique and engage fully in activist research as a method.[78] By this he means a political alignment with those who are involved in organized struggle, from the initial design and conception of the research to collecting the data and analyzing and using the results.

These are admirable calls for anthropology, but questions about this position remain. Are the organized battles equally valuable for all those on whose behalf they are allegedly fought? Indigenous communities are undoubtedly stratified by gender and class differences, and alignment with the struggles of middle-class activist leaders that activist research will necessitate might not allow us to hear the voices of the rest. More important, what if those activist intellectuals fighting for indigenous populations are unknowingly complicit in the task of further marginalizing those they claim to speak for?

There are lessons to be learned from Gayatri Chakrabarty Spivak's engagement with subaltern studies.[79] A genre which sought to read against the grain of mainstream historical accounts, subaltern studies —emerging from historians writing about South Asia[80]—tried to locate the voice of the economically dispossessed, the "subaltern" of Antonio Gramsci's work. In asking "Can the subaltern speak?" Spivak warns that postcolonial intellectuals reclaiming the collective voice of the marginalized, even if they also claim to be "subaltern," may unknowingly be complicit in the task of imperialism because the subaltern is not homogeneous.[81] In the case of those speaking for indigenous populations, the danger is that the political project of this identity politics, this "culture-making," flattens a vast diversity of agendas and interests that are in fact affected by the complex interrelations of, for example, gender, class, and caste, which undercut people's identity.

In the Latin American case, debates regarding whether the subaltern can speak came to a head with the controversy around the testimony of Rigoberta Menchú, winner of the 1992 Nobel Peace Prize. With the publication of her autobiography,[82] Menchú was championed by many as the voice of the voiceless, a voice of the poor, oppressed Guatemalan Indians who supported a guerrilla war because of the extreme violence they had suffered at the hands of the Ladinos who ruled the country. In 1999, David Stoll published a book which drew attention to the fiction in some of Menchú's testimony. In line with his questioning of indigenous support for the rebels during the 1970s and 1980s in Guatemala, whom he claims were caught between two armies,[83] Stoll accused Menchú of fabricating and distorting her story in order to serve the needs of the revolutionary movement.[84] Menchú, Stoll claims, played the card of the authentic oppressed indigenous person who supported the war, because it would appeal to Western expectations about indigenous people and the romantic possibilities of this disenfranchised poor as revolutionaries. Stoll's point is not simply that Menchú was untruthful, but that many of us wish to privilege a voice that supports our own aspirations even at the cost of misunderstanding the situation. We see here a reflection of Spivak's warning that the subaltern is not homogeneous. Menchú's story, like the story of all poor Guatemalans, potentially flattens the diverse stories of different poor Mayan populations who might not all have sided with the guerrillas (even if their stories were more complex than just being caught "between two armies"). One result is that these diverse and complex stories have been discounted in conventional representations of the war. Stoll's exposé, while gaining him widespread fame, has made him highly unpopular as he was accused of taking an antileft and antisolidarity position.[85]

Perhaps more immediate dangers to the poorest from the unintended consequences of well-meaning indigenous rights struggles have been documented in the work of those who have explored its class dynamics. Take, for example, the case of the San—more popularly known as Bushmen—of southern Africa. Renee Sylvain argues that the emphasis of cultural representations of San connection with the land has ignored the material implications of political economy and class exploitation faced by some of them.[86] The San of the Omahake region—who were a landless underclass of farm laborers and did not conform to the indigenous stereotype in the same way as the Ju/'hoansi of Nyae Nyae—were either left out or forced to conform to popular stereotypes, which in turn reproduced the class inequalities sustained by the stereotypes.

Class inequalities produced by indigenous rights movements, and the way in which they are embedded in the broader political economy, are also important in the case of Alaska, where corporate capitalism has produced surprising allies. Kirk Dombrowski shows how—in order to bypass federal environmental restrictions on timber clearing on state-controlled lands—corporations involved in timber clearing and pulp production encouraged, with the complicity of some state legislators, the recognition and expansion of native claims to land in Alaska. These initiatives exacerbated and consolidated social divisions among and within native groups, as some gained shareholder status and others did not.[87]

In India, Amita Baviskar's research also warns of the need to pay attention to the class dynamics of indigenous rights struggles. The activists through whom Baviskar was introduced to the Narmada River region used the hill tribes as the face of a struggle against the building of the Narmada Dam. The imagery of the threat of displacement affecting the poor dispossessed "sons of the soil," the ecologically noble primitives, had an emotional impact everywhere. But, as we find out in the postscript to the second edition of Baviskar's book *In the Belly of the River*,[88] when the dam was built, the main supporters of the antidam movement—the wealthy, middle-caste landowners and a group of educated adivasis who had the resources to look after their own relocation—were cared for. However, there was nobody to support the poor hill tribes. When the fight against the dam was lost, the activists moved on to other issues, leaving the poor hill tribes to their own devices, with little knowledge about their relocation entitlements.

So where does this leave scholarly endeavor? We may agree with Béteille that an essentialist notion of indigenous peoples is philosophically, anthropologically, and/or historically problematic. However, do we agree that this may have implications for the political strategies of those who are seeking to regain rights to the lands of their ancestors, or who want to link their causes with those of other people on different continents in similar positions? Should we, then, as Michael Brown asks, hold our tongues when advocates of indigenous rights construct essentialist ideologies?[89] As scholars, should we aim to understand the complexities of local situations, or should we join the enterprise of a politics unlimited? Our scholarly enterprise requires a degree of objectivity and detachment. However, sometimes our activist positions beg us to put our academic rigor back onto the shelf, lest we weaken our advocacy. Surely, as Ajay Skaria writes, however laudable our politics, we also need to pay attention to the weapons and images we fight with, and the profound disrespect and violence that may be involved in our strategies.[90] But should we subordinate our scholarly priorities to those of our activist inclinations? Should we be prepared to hide certain observations and censor our reports, in order to support a particular kind of political program?

This book shows the need for anthropologists to give priority to a commitment to the labor of critical ethnography rather than to a predetermined political program. This involves the need for a sympathetic understanding of the tricky politics involved in concepts such as indigenous rights, without losing critical distance. In analyzing the relationship between anthropology and human rights activities, Iris Jean-Klein and Annelise Riles argue for the need for such a commitment to ethnographic engagement, disciplined description, and analytical care as a professional commitment to humanitarian ethics.[91] Such an engagement does indeed demand taking a risk. In this case, the risk is that we will produce an analysis that is profoundly unsettling for indigenous rights work and activities, that contradicts and subverts the empirical and moral premises of the arguments of activists.[92] Yet, it is such risk-taking ethnography and analysis which sets anthropologists apart from other engaged actors, and which may in the end enable anthropologists to more honestly and productively engage our political and moral commitment to our informants and subjects. This is the political and moral perspective that this book seeks to promote, as it explores indigenous politics in Jharkhand. Before the themes that form the core of the book's arguments are laid out, it is important to turn to a general background of the social relations central to the ethnography presented.

THE SOCIAL CONTEXT IN JHARKHAND

The village of Tapu, the base from which I explore the wider region, has around 102 households and a population of about 550 people. Less than fifty kilometers from Ranchi, it is situated in the undulating landscape of forest typical of this part of the Chotanagpur Plateau. As explained in the prologue, the village is divided, both socially and historically. Sadans from the Yadav caste, who are descendants of the old landlords, form the elite, together with a few adivasi descendants of revenue-collecting families. The remaining adivasis, including members of the Oraon, Badaik, and Maheli tribes; dalits, including members of the Lohar caste; and other lower castes and Pathan Muslim families make up the majority of the village's population, Roughly 40 percent of the villagers are Mundas (adivasis). In this book I concentrate on Munda perspectives, which in general terms, and vis-à-vis the rural elites, are representative of the other adivasi and dalit families in Tapu.

The antagonism, mutual disparagement, and contrasting values of the rural elites and the Mundas are partly explained by the socioeconomic history of the region. In the eighteenth century, the higher-caste landlords of the area displaced lower castes and tribes from other areas and brought them as servants to villages they controlled. In return for their servitude, the landlords gave them small amounts of land to cultivate. In 1932, while the average size of a landlord landholding in Tapu was 43 acres, that of a Munda was about 20.5 acres. By 1992, however, the land reform changes, discussed in detail in chapter 3, meant that the disparity in landownership had somewhat lessened. The landlord descendants then had an average landholding of 6.7 acres, and the Mundas 4.4 acres. As a result of these land ownership changes, coupled with the end of Munda servitude to the landlord descendants, the latter have sought alternative routes to maintain their local dominance. As chapter 3 explains, while landlord families once derived their local dominance from their control of the land, today they maintain their dominance through control of state resources, whether directly (from government jobs) or indirectly (for example, through winning development contracts). Although only two have actually moved to the nearby administrative town of Bero, in the eight years I have known the village, the sons of the landlord descendants increasingly sought to move away from their village roots and looked to education to provide their passport out.

In 2001, literacy rates in Tapu were negligible for the Mundas but were also low among the sadans. Of those no longer in school, 15 percent of Tapu's residents had completed grade school, 8 percent had passed matriculation exams (the equivalent of having finished high school), 4 percent had passed intermediate exams (the equivalent of qualifying for college), and 2 percent had obtained bachelor's degrees.[93] The sadans also had very different aspirations from the Mundas, whom they look down on and whom they often call by the derogatory term "jangli." In contrast to those above them in the class hierarchy, the poorer majority were in fact often proud to be of the Jungle Raj and to hold the values that they felt this involved. They generally sought to keep the government away, living off tilling their land and manual labor. The main source of their livelihood was arable[94] and livestock agriculture, fruits and leaves from the trees, and manual labor in the village stone-chipping industry and government schemes in Tapu or the surrounding area.

By 2007, however, a handful of Munda men had passed the matriculation exams. The seed of desires and aspirations different from those of their parents could be seen germinating among them. To their parents' distress, the young men did not want to farm; like their educated adivasi counterparts in other villages, they wanted to network and hang around the State Development Offices in Bero to join the rural elites. Although in chapter 3 I discuss the political activities of some of these educated adivasi elites in other villages, and in the conclusion I will come back to the handful of these men in Tapu, I do not concentrate on them in this book: they are only just emerging as a class, and they do not represent the majority of the poorest adivasis in this region. It will, however, be interesting to see how they eventually begin to affect the themes and arguments set out in this book.

The indigenous rights activists, whose rhetorical positions and actions I compare with the experiences of the poor rural adivasis, are urban based and highly educated middle classes—some even have Ph.D.s from foreign universities. This book is not about them, and thus I do not engage in a detailed sociology of the activists. However, it is important to know that some are adivasis who come from Christian convert backgrounds. Many others go only by their first name, to hide their upper-caste identity and the fact that they are recent immigrants to the area.[95] The ancestors of some were the elites (sometimes adivasi) of villages like Tapu. Often inspired by Marxist ideology and depressed by the social inequalities around them, they feel driven to express revulsion toward the promises of a relatively comfortable life and work for the most oppressed among the indigenous poor. Inspired by selective colonial accounts of tribal culture,[96] and the image of Jharkhand as a place of forests and forest-worshipping people who are rooted in their land and have their own forms of governance, as presented in the anthropology and history books, their aim is to preserve what they think remains of these images and to recreate a glorious Jharkhand indigenous past, though certainly not a jangli one. While there are a variety of activists, and conflicts between them emerge, differences often get ironed out through a politics of inclusion and exclusion determined by the need to represent one rhetorical idea of Jharkhand's history and identity.

Among these varying perspectives, the question I am most concerned with is whether we will ever hear the multiple voices of the masses in the rural areas, whose concerns and opinions may very well be opposed to the ideas of both the activists and the rural elites. The odds are stacked against the masses, of course. It is the middle-class activists who travel to Geneva for meetings of the UNWGIP and to the United Kingdom and elsewhere to attend academic conferences, as representatives of India's indigenous people. These activists are recognized as advocates of Jharkhand's indigenous populations by the likes of the Netherlands-based Forest People's Programme, or

Survival International. Moreover, the many academics, journalists, international activists, and development consultants who come to Jharkhand seeking to learn about the plight of the indigenous populations are too easily seduced by the city-based Jharkhandi activists. Together with the problems of understanding the many languages and dialects spoken in Jharkhand, and the difficulty of reaching areas that most people would consider remote, these outsiders' short trips into the rural areas are arranged by the activists. In the villages, they are inevitably met by the rural elites, who try to befriend outsiders while the poorest majority are very likely to shy away. One view of Jharkhand gets reproduced in the accounts that are heard globally, while many other views are never seen.[97]

But the bias toward reproducing particular perspectives does not stop here. It appears that even journals and publishing houses are more interested in the transnationally flamboyant indigenous rights activists than in their often rather dull rural counterparts. In Indonesia, for example, Tania Li protests that while we should pay attention to the rather drab folk who practice swidden agriculture, such as the Lauje, it was the dramas of the more prosperous and internationally savvy Lindy, articulating the indigenous position and protesting against a hydro-electric plant, that captured the imagination of reviewers of the early drafts of the article she submitted to *Comparative Studies in Society and History*.[98] There is, in some sense, circularity in the production of representations in which the voices of the marginalized cannot be heard. But scholarly democracy is not my only concern here. This book shows that the very actions of indigenous rights activists may be further marginalizing the rural poor.

THE DARK SIDE OF THE "THIRD WAY"

Claims to indigeneity have historically been made in terms of political representation and the state. This is often taken for granted by the activists. However, claims to the state may not always interest the people the activists represent. People exert, and seek to exert, differential influence within the state and development systems, and this book seeks to explore how and why certain groups exert their influence while others do not. The book shows how well-meaning, city-based indigenous rights activists may attempt to reclaim the state for the rural poor, while the rural elites—the descendants of the old landlords—maintain their dominance by intercepting the projects of democracy and development of modern India. Meanwhile, the poorest villagers, usually descendants of the tenants of the old landlords, experience an exploitative state with which they seek to minimize interaction and in whose shadows they seek to remain. Their reactions are not merely the result of cultural understandings of the state, but are also understandings based on historical experience and encouragement by rural elites seeking to colonize the local state.

This book seeks to understand, from the point of view of some of the poorest populations, what it means to live in a supposedly indigenous state. In so doing, it examines the social networks, forms of political representation, and economic structures that produce and subvert indigeneity as both an idea and a lived experience. As Jane Cowan, Marie-Benedicte Dembour, and Richard Wilson imply, it is not just the case that the language of rights might be constitutive of culture and associated identities, but also that the represented people may actually have concerns quite different from, and even contradictory to, those of their advocates.[99]

"The Dark Side of Indigeneity," may show that the local appropriation and experiences of global discourses of indigeneity can maintain a class system that further marginalizes the poorest people. This class dimension to the indigenous rights movement is likely to get erased in the culture-based identity politics it produces. In Jharkhand, the poorest adivasis often have very different perspectives and cares than those of well-meaning activists from urban middle-class backgrounds. I propose that the representations and arguments of the activists may inadvertently further marginalize the poorer rural people they are trying to help.

The following chapters focus on some of the key features often attributed to indigenous communities: their desire for an alternative form of governance, the need for development, their closeness to nature, and their attachment to the land. These attributes are not treated as self-evident but are explored as historically and politically embedded processes. The penultimate chapter examines a seeming alternative representation of indigenous people, in the shape of the Maoist revolutionary movement, a politics based on class rather than culture. The key arguments of each chapter can be summarized as follows.

Chapter 2, "Not Just Ghosts," focuses on the revival of indigenous systems of self-governance that are being promoted by indigenous rights activists. The chapter proposes that recent moves by the activists to eliminate the adivasis' so-called *jangli* belief in ghosts, in order to promote secular indigenous systems of self-governance, may undermine the local legitimacy of these very systems. The chapter shows that while Mundas want to distance themselves from the secular state, they valorize village authorities such as the *pahan* and the *paenbharra*, as well as intervillage entities such as the *parha*. The legitimacy of these indigenous systems of governance for the Mundas derives from the fact that they represent a sacral polity, a cosmology where the sacred and the secular are intimately connected, even identical. A corollary of this sacral polity is the promotion of egalitarianism, consensus in decision making, and mutual reciprocity and aid. Chapter 2 thus provides a commentary on how democratization processes in postcolonial societies may in turn build on postcolonial political ethics, which may be quite different from the norms of a bourgeois, Western political order. The suggestion is that the evidence from the Mundas elevates not the domain of religion but a cosmology of a sacral polity as the foundation for an alternative political order.

Chapter 3, "Shadowy Practices," focuses on the aesthetics of poverty. It looks at how state development resources meant for the poorest, such as Tapu's Mundas, get appropriated by historically dominant—usually higher caste—rural elites. Thus, it historically contextualizes the Mundas' desire to keep away from the state, as well as the importance they place on the idea of the alternative sacral polity. While this chapter explores the moral economy of rural elites' engagements with the state, showing the inadequacy of popular notions of corruption which are embedded in Western ideas of the state and civil society, the ultimate point is to show how participatory development efforts actually enable the reproduction of a local class structure that keeps the poorest firmly at the bottom.

Chapter 4 begins with the wild elephants that haunt the night in Tapu. The responses to these "Dangerous Silhouettes" by the Mundas, and their desire to chop down the forest the elephants live in, undermines the nature-loving, nature-worshipping imagery being reproduced by indigenous activism. Despite the fairly well developed scholarly critique of the so-called Indian eco-savage, its persistence in Jharkhand is destroying livelihoods and costing lives. In their attempts to domesticate the jangli adivasis of the poor rural areas, the urban, educated, middle-class indigenous rights activists have revived a Sarna religion as the emblem of the adivasis' inherent love of nature. The new state government made the elephant its national symbol, to show that in Jharkhand—"a land unspoiled by man or time," in the words of a roadside billboard—man and animal live in harmony with each other. Meanwhile, in Tapu and the surrounding villages, the Mundas' propitiation of their spirits with animal sacrifices cannot be reduced to nature worship, as poor adivasis spend night after night chasing away elephants that are killing people, destroying their homes, and consuming their crops. Elephants bring to the surface rural people's complex relationship with and understandings of their environment, showing the need to move away from cultural constructions of the environment and to focus instead on how representations of the environment are situated in, and emerge from, the sociopolitical context of the relationship between people struggling over resources.

Chapter 5, "Night Escape," focuses on another dimension of the cultural politics of the eco-savage: the production of an eco-incarceration when indigenous cultures are presented as rooted in their land, and the threat that migration produces to this representation. As Jharkhandi activists campaign against seasonal casual labor migration, this chapter shows that such migration to brick factories in other states gives the poorest adivasis not only the ability to cope with everyday livelihood struggles but also freedom from the social constraints at home. Many who migrate see the brick kilns as a temporary space of freedom to escape domestic problems, explore a new country, and experience love affairs forbidden at home. I suggest that the construction by Jharkhandi indigenous rights activists of this migration as a problem is as much about their ethnoregionalist vision of what the new tribal state ought to be, as it is about exploitation and poverty. Activists see migration to the kilns as both a threat to the idea of the connection with the land that adivasis allegedly have, and a threat to the purity and regulation of the social and sexual tribal citizen. This moralizing perspective creates a climate that paradoxically encourages many young people to flee to the brick kilns where they can live freely. In this way, the new puritanism at home, incarcerating and attempting to civilize the jangli adivasi, helps to reproduce the conditions for capitalist exploitation and the extraction of surplus value, while not focusing on the material issues of how the conditions of labor migration could be improved for the poorest workers.

Chapter 6, "The Terror Within," shifts the book's attention from indigenous rights activism to a class-based struggle inspired by Marx, Mao, and Lenin that claims to hold greater hope for the development and liberation of the poor of rural Jharkhand. This is the early spread of the revolutionary guerrilla Naxalite movement, the Maoist Communist Centre (MCC), labelled a terrorist organization by the Indian government. The chapter challenges conventional analysis of the Naxalites to argue that, in practice, at least in the early stages of expansion, the MCC's main support comes from the rural elites and not the poorer peasantry. Rural elites support the MCC not because of a shared ideology, but because it offers better protection for them to access the informal economy of state resources. Selling protection, the MCC enters a market previously controlled by the state. The MCC increases its control by making its targets believe that it is immensely powerful and frightening, as they extrapolate from its visible and invisible qualities, including its propensity for violence. Unveiling this market of protection, chapter 6 blurs the boundaries between the state and the terrorist in rural Jharkhand, showing the ways in which it is the interests of the rural elites, and not those of the poorest adivasis, that are served by the initial expansion of the Maoists.

In this critical and grounded exploration of indigeneity, my aim is not to promote an exposure of indigenous rights activism. We don't have to show them up, or argue that indigenous identity is created strategically and made into an invented tradition by maximizing goal-oriented actors who are pursuing their own ends. But we should pursue our careful and committed scholarship and highlight the need to pay attention to the voices that are not usually heard in transnational, or even national, forums, as well as the processes which lead to their marginalization. So as scholars and political actors, we should not hesitate to ask the questions: Who is representing whom, and how and why? Who and what are left out? And what are the unintended consequences?

2. *Not Just Ghosts*

DEMOCRACY AS SACRAL POLITY

10:00 A.M., 8 DECEMBER 2000

"Too much rice beer last night," I thought, feeling a bit dazed. I was sitting in the front of my house, playing with the dangly silver balls of the earrings I had bought in the Bero market. I couldn't help smiling to myself as I tried to decipher my notes from the night before:

> Dangly earrings in your ear.
> Dangly earrings in my ear.
> Move them, shake them, show them,
> Don't be shy . . .

Whose rice you eat, and who you eat it with, definitely does matter. I felt more accepted among the Mundas now. The joking and teasing and my attempts to sing the song about flirting with dangly silver-balled earrings had certainly helped. However, it was eating the Munda food with them, while celebrating the rice harvest at the Khalihani feast, which really broke the social boundaries between us.

"Alfa, Alfa!" Onga Munda popped his head around my door, making me smile. Since he always greeted me with such enthusiasm, I never bothered to correct his mispronunciation.

He smiled back at me—a distinctive smile that showed his missing bottom teeth and made his eyes small, exaggerating the deep wrinkles around them. "Come on. If you want to know anything about the Jungle Raj, you have to see the selection of the new village authorities, the pahan[1] and the paenbharra.[2] It only happens once every three years. Let's go."

I stuffed my notebook in a cloth bag, slung the bag over my shoulder, and followed Onga into the courtyard. His pink-checked lungi flapped in the breeze as he opened it to retie it more tightly around his bony waist. We walked to the edge of the Tapu fields, where the fluorescent green of the sal trees rose into the horizon. We were heading for the area where perfectly round circles, about four meters in diameter, had been covered with cow dung to make a level space in which to beat the rice grains from the stalks.

This is where we had been the night before. The outgoing pahan and paenbharra had sacrificed twelve small chickens to thank the village's spirits. The year's rice harvest had been good, and looking after the spirits now would ensure a fruitful crop in the coming year. As the smoke from the fires had risen and the moon had appeared, the rest of the village had trickled in for the feast—Mundas, Oraons, Lohras, Badaiks. Of course the sadans, who were mainly the higher-caste descendants of the landlords, had not come. Marking their superiority and purity vis-à-vis the Mundas, they never ate food cooked by the Mundas, let alone ate with them.[3] Large pits had been dug in the ground to cook the rice grown on the spiritual lowlands given to the pahan and the paenbharra for the period of their duty.[4] Under the weight of the stars dropping from a deep blue sky, the merriment of the Khalihani feast had taken place.

During the night, as Onga and Burababa helped cook the rice, I had asked them, "Why are the pahan and paenbharra so important to the village?"

"It's their duty to make sure the spirits are kept happy. They are the only people who can communicate with all the village spirits," Onga had said.

"And what happens if they fail?"

Flapping his hands in the air, and pretending to sound bewitched, he had replied, "The spirits will get very angry. There will be droughts, floods, and earthquakes. Disease will take hold of people. Crops and cattle will die." And then in a softer voice, and with a warning in his eye, he had added, "And if they really fail, people will die."

Characteristically calm and patient, Burababa had summed up: "*Beti* [daughter], you see, the pahan and the paenbharra are the spirits' representatives in the village. By feeding and caring for the spirits, they are the main protectors of the adivasis. At every festival in the agricultural cycle and whenever the spirits may get angry, the

Drinking and smoking at the Khalihani feast.
Painting by author.

The *pahan* sacrificing a chicken to the spirits.
Painting by Deepa Shah.

Cooking for the Khalihani feast. *Photo by author.*

pahan and the paenbharra must keep them happy by carrying out blood sacrifices and giving them lots of rice beer. When the hot weather approaches, before the hunting season begins, they must carry out a sacrifice for the hunting spirits. And they must lead the annual three-day hunt of Bisu Sirkar, at the end of which all the surrounding villages that belong to the parha [the intervillage authority] meet to discuss the area's problems. They must also protect the village from malevolent spirits, which come from outside, by exorcizing them beyond the village boundaries. When they look after the village spirits well, the spirits in turn give them the power to solve village disputes."

"What kinds of village disputes?"

"Accusations of thefts, of sorcery, of claims to land, of tabooed relations between men and women [adultery, incest, sexual relations between members of the same clan or of different tribes] — you know, all the kinds of issues you can imagine that need resolving in the village."

"What about sarkar [the state]? What about the courts — don't you use them?"

"Sarkar?" Onga had sounded alarmed. "What good is sarkar? Sarkar is only interested in our exploitation. We stay away from sarkar and leave any dealings with sarkari people to the zamindars [the landlords]."

I was deep in thought about these conversations from the night before when we approached the clearing. A dozen men were seated around a few aluminum and clay pots of rice beer. There were about ten middle-aged and old Munda men, one Lohra, and one Badaik. I copied Onga's actions, greeting each man individually by touching my closed hands with theirs.

"Sit here, on this pile of hay, beti," said Burababa, who was already there. A young Munda man gave me a cup made from a sal leaf, and poured in some rice beer. Copying Onga, before taking a sip, I tipped a few drops of beer onto the ground for my grandfather's spirit and those of other ancestors.[5]

Onga winced as he tasted his beer. "These days you young boys are not making good beer. There is too much water. It is not pure," he complained. Looking at the young man in disdain, he added, "There will soon be a time when you people won't even know what beer is!"

The others had been drinking for some time, and the conversation turned to their drinking. "If you drink so much, you won't be able to pee," said Somra to Mangra.

Budhwa laughed. "Won't he be able to pee? Not just that! If he drinks more, he won't be able to get his penis out. He will pee in his pants."

"So what if he pees in his pants? It's winter, the pee will keep him warm," teased Burababa.

Amid the raucous laughter, Onga Munda came to my side and drew my attention to a man attaching a winnowing basket to a bamboo pole.[6] "Get your machine out and get it ready to take some photos. You'll need them for your research."

"What are we waiting for?" I asked.

"The pahan has gone to the next village to look for a man with a light shadow that was light rather than dark. The spirit will only possess men with light shadows. You'll see," he said. "She will enter him through the winnowing basket, making him move and shake. She will direct him to the house of the people she wishes to make the new pahan and the paenbharra. When the spirit is happy, the man will stop shaking, as she leaves him to settle in the house whose head she wishes to declare the new pahan. The second time she does this, it will be the house of the new paenbharra."

The pahan returned, unsuccessful in his attempts to find a man with a light shadow. Someone said that another man who had married a woman from the village, and who was visiting his in-laws, also had a light shadow. The pahan went to look for him but came back, half an hour later, to report that he was in the forest grazing his in-laws' cattle. By then everyone was getting concerned.

"Shall we postpone the selection and have it tomorrow, so that we can get the man from the next village?" asked Somra.

"No, why don't we bring Fatra, who has just become a *bhagat* [spirit medium]? He is supposed to have a light shadow," suggested Budhwa.

"I don't think he is suitable."

"Why do you say that, Mangra?" asked Burababa. "When we've finally found someone, don't interfere."

The young bhagat, Fatra, was brought and blindfolded. Throwing rice at him,[7] the pahan chanted, "East, west, north, south. In my whole area, in your whole area, Sarna Mai, relieve me of my duties and find a new person to take responsibility." The winnowing basket held at the end of the bamboo pole started moving, and Fatra began to shiver. He walked off toward the main hamlet.

In the first house he entered, that of Mangra Munda, Fatra stopped shivering, and Mangra became the new pahan. Blindfolded again, Fatra was possessed once more and walked toward Onga Munda's house. Onga, who was hungry and had gotten tired of waiting, had by then left the group. He was peacefully eating in our courtyard when Fatra approached. Onga continued to eat, and inside his house, he was declared the new paenbharra.

I feel fortunate to have witnessed the selection of the pahan and the paenbharra, as well as the selection of their seven helpers later on in the day. It drew my attention, early in my fieldwork, to the importance of the Munda spirits and the cosmology of a sacral polity in what has been called traditional indigenous systems of governance. This is a polity that is divorced from the secular postcolonial state—not in the classic Dumontian sense of the Indian case, where the sacred encompasses the secular, but where the sacred and the political are indivisible. Around the world in recent years, there has been an increasing concern to protect, revive, and recognize indigenous systems of governance.[8] This interest resonates with ideas of democratic decentralization that are at the heart of good governance agendas promoted by multilateral and bilateral development institutions since the 1990s.[9] The interest also resonates with transnational demands for self-determination and sovereignty,[10] a language that has become a part of the international human rights discourse at the United Nations. It is articulated by indigenous rights activists who

Blindfolding the man with the light shadow for the selection of the *pahan* and *paenbharra*. *Painting by author.*

The man possessed by a spirit entering the house of the new *pahan*. *Photo by author.*

see in traditional systems a content and form for governance that are alternatives to what the activists argue are systems imposed by the West on the states in which they live.

In India, Jharkhandi indigenous rights activists are at the forefront of the revival of more authentic forms of adivasi governance.[11] Various names are given to these systems, depending on the tribe and the area—for instance, parha, *munda-manki*, or *manjhi-parganait*. Across Jharkhand, a range of organizations, such as the Bharat Jan Andolan and Johar, and independent activists are involved in reviving village-level political structures. Organizations such as the Jharkhand Pradesh Parha Raja and the Manjhi Parganait Manki Munda have been set up with the mission of rejuvenating transvillage indigenous systems of governance.[12] Some even call this revival a parha movement.[13] Such efforts are supported by the interest of Indian NGOs[14] in participatory development and traditional democratic institutions, as well as by the sustained effort of some scholars who are interested in evaluating the status of traditional systems of governance.[15] In the indigenous activists' models of Oraon and Munda adivasi systems of governance, the pahans and paenbharras are celebrated as village-level authorities, while the parha is resurrected as a structure of intervillage governance for groups of between twelve and twenty-one villages.[16] Reflecting on the selection of the pahan and paenbharra in Tapu, and my subsequent exploration into the significance of the parha, I was surprised that the recent revival of the parha, the pahans, and the paenbharras was discussed by the activists in almost entirely secular terms.

This chapter is about the contradictions between the representations of indigenous activists and what the traditional systems of indigenous governance of the Jungle Raj mean to the adivasis who live in the Jharkhand countryside. I show how and why, for the Mundas, the parha, pahan, and paenbharra represent an alternative political system to the secular postcolonial state. In contrasting these alternative political systems with the Munda desire to keep the state away, I argue that the legitimacy of the former is derived from the fact that they represent a sacral polity. This is a cosmology in which the sacred and the secular are intimately connected or are one and the same, and which promotes values of egalitarianism, consensus building, reciprocity, and mutual aid. I propose that recent attempts to elevate indigenous systems of self-governance to the purely secular political level may undermine their local legitimacy. In doing so, I also provide a commentary on how democratization processes in postcolonial societies may build on postcolonial political ethics which, in turn, may be quite different from the norms of a bourgeois Western political order. The suggestion is that the evidence from the Mundas does not elevate the domain of religion; rather, it resurrects the cosmology and values of a sacral polity as the foundation of an alternative political order.

"OUR RULE IN OUR VILLAGES"

The recent celebration of the pahan, paenbharra, and parha systems as alternative secular systems of indigenous governance is intimately tied both to a longer history of protection of tribal customary structures of governance and to more-concerted efforts to revive them. Colonial policies to protect adivasis by excluding tribal areas from the ordinary laws of British India, through the Scheduled Districts Act of 1874, were preceded by other protective measures in the Chotanagpur Plateau. Here, one of the first moves to protect customary structures, especially tribal structures of landholding, came in the form of the 1869 Chotanagpur Land Tenures Act, developed in response to the rebellions—the 1857 Sepoy Mutiny and the 1859–65 Sardar Movement—against changes in land tenure brought about by colonial rule. Under the 1869 act, a survey was undertaken to record the ancestral tribal holdings in Ranchi District. It became known as the bhuinhari survey because it recognized the special Oraon (and to some extent Munda) common ownership rights over the lands of the original settlers, called *bhuinhars*, and set out to demarcate these lands.[17] The bhuinhari survey also demarcated so-called service lands occupied by persons connected with the performance of village worship, such as the *pahanai* and the paenbharra land, as well as land given to their helpers, called *bhutkhetta* (land of the spirits). This survey thus gave formal recognition to village-level authorities such as the Tapu pahan and paenbharra and their assistants, the men who became beneficiaries of the bhutkhetta. Later Indian Civil Service surveys[18] on land tenure in Ranchi reinforced the importance of posts such as the pahan and the paenbharra and protected their lands from taxation.

The colonial officers who conducted these surveys drew a distinction between sacred and secular matters: the pahan was seen as dealing with the spirits, while another functionary, the *maheto*, was seen as presiding over secular matters. For example, G. K. Webster, a member of the Indian Civil Service who produced one of the earliest colonial reports on the pahan and the paenbharra, said: "No village can get on without this person (the *pahan*) . . . as he alone can possibly know how to appease the *bhuts* or spirits who delight in upsetting mortal arrangements . . . He has great influence even in all secular matters."[19] While these officials realized that the spiritual authorities could influence secular matters, the two domains of the spiritual and the secular remained distinct in most of their writings, and none of them allowed for the possibility that the pahan was the most significant village authority because he represented a sacral polity, a world where the political and the sacred were one conceptual realm.

This distinction between the secular and the sacred was endorsed by Sarat Chandra Roy, albeit with hesitation. A much quoted lawyer, an advisor to colonial administrators, and the man often described as the father of Indian ethnology,[20] Roy argued: "The function of the village *Baiga* (also called the *pahan*) is to propitiate the village deities, and of the *Pujar* (the paenbharra) is to help him at the public religious festivals. The *Maheto* is the secular village-headman."[21] However, reading between the lines of Roy's material, there is some uncertainty in his analysis of the division of roles of the secular and sacred functionaries. Roy argues that the position of maheto in fact developed only after landlords were introduced into Chotanagpur, in order to collect tax.[22] My own research in the Ranchi District Commissioner's archives—looking at the 1932 land settlement survey, still the most significant land record of the area—shows that in the 113 villages around Tapu, many did not have a maheto, and in those that did, it was either a hereditary position or a man chosen at the landlord's discretion. In Tapu itself, there was no maheto, but the sons of the original landlord in 1932 had taken the title Maheto, which suggests that they had taken over the tax-collecting function and thus felt it unnecessary to appoint a maheto. In light of the recent creation of the post of the maheto, Roy argues that "there is evidence to show that formerly the *baiga* or *pahan* was the secular and also the religious head of the village. To this day, there are Oraon villages in which there is no separate *maheto*, but the *pahan* acts in both capacities."[23] He adds: "Before [the development of the maheto], the *baiga* or *pahan* appears to have been the sacerdotal as well as the secular head of the village."[24] As I will show, today these uncertainties are ignored by the activists who have appropriated Roy's texts into their secular model of indigenous self-governance structures. I will argue that in fact Roy's hesitations are crucial to the analysis of the significance of the pahan and the paenbharra in Tapu.

In many of the colonial officers' reports, while the vitality of the village-level authorities was noted, the adivasi intravillage governance system, including the parha, was described as being in decay. After Indian independence, however, there was a concerted effort to revive the parha. The main impetus came from a new generation of non-Christian adivasi youth, trying to curb the success of the Christian-based Jharkhand Party.[25] The former were concerned that if a state of Jharkhand materialized, Christians would dominate it through the Jharkhand Movement, which was seen at the time as a gift of Christian missionaries. In 1947–48, two organizations were formed with the purpose of reviving the parha; one even started a weekly magazine called *Parha*. Although financial troubles apparently meant that the organizations lasted only three years, their activities inspired a later revival attempt by Kartik Oraon, a man recruited by Prime Minister Nehru to lead the Congress Party in the area.

Nehru had met Kartik in London in 1959, after the latter had received his engineering master's degree in that city and while he was working on the design of what was then the world's biggest atomic power station, the Hinkley Point Nuclear Power Station in the United Kingdom.[26] Nehru promised Kartik a job in the newly established Indo-Russian project of the Heavy Engineering Corporation in Ranchi. A year and a half after joining the Ranchi project as deputy chief engineer, Kartik quit this job and began full-time activities for the Congress Party. To achieve victory for Congress, Kartik saw his goal as uniting non-Christian tribals and Hindus against Christians in Jharkhand. That strategy was successful, and as the strength of the Jharkhand Party waned, the strength of the Congress Party in the area grew.[27] While no doubt there were many other factors, the reestablishment of the parha in Ranchi in 1963 was crucial to Kartik's local success.[28]

As I will go on to show, Kartik's rejuvenation of the parha came to be directly relevant for the people of Tapu and the surrounding areas. Here, the success of the Congress Party in gaining support was dependent on both the antistate rhetoric of the local Members of the Legislative Assembly and the promotion of what people interpreted as an alternative sacral polity, the parha. It is thus curious that in present-day Ranchi, indigenous rights activists, who viewed a short film I had made about the parha, claimed that the parha in Bero was corrupted by politicians and was not the "real thing." The real thing that they seek to promote is a totally secular vision of the parha.

In the discussion after the screening of my film, I tried to stress the fact that the parha was important to people in villages like Tapu not just as an alternative form of government, but also because of its spiritual relevance, and precisely because one could not separate the spiritual from the political. But one activist said: "Well, these superstitious views don't have a place in adivasi society today. You have to realize that the parha that we have to revive is a confederacy of village governments, whose heads will be elected by the democratically elected village heads, just as they were in the past."

Another activist added: "Their function is to preside over inter- and intra-village disputes. And today they must also engage in looking after natural resources, for instance protecting the forests, as well as other broader social issues, such as preventing migration to the brick kilns and enforcing the prohibition of the consumption of liquor. This is how adivasis must better themselves. It is belief in ghosts, the need to give them blood sacrifices, and such superstitious views that are keeping the adivasis jangli [wild, savage, and backward] today."[29]

These recent secular and sanitized visions of the function of indigenous self-governance are propped up by the backlash from adivasi advocates against the seventy-third Indian Constitutional Amendment Act, which came into being in 1992 and made provision for decentralized government in the form of village-level *panchayats* across the country.[30] The adivasi advocates argued that the decentralized governance of panchayat elections would undermine the special protection that tribal areas should enjoy under the Fifth Schedule of the Constitution. In response to the backlash, the Indian Parliament appointed a special committee of members of Parliament and experts to make recommendations on the salient features of the law for extending panchayats to the Scheduled Areas. The committee was chaired by Dilip Singh Bhuria—an adivasi MP who was supported by a former officer of the Indian Administrative Service, B. D. Sharma, in a campaign called Our Rule in Our Villages. He argued that adivasi society's own representative system of governance should be legally recognized as the primary system of tribal governance. In December 1996, this proposition was passed in the Provision of the Panchayats Extension to the Scheduled Areas Act. The act gave special powers in adivasi areas to village-level authorities that it called *gram sabhas*. While these provisions included the powers to resolve disputes through customary methods and to conserve and protect customs and traditions, there was no recognition of supravillage structures such as the parha, the gram sabhas had no power to challenge forest and police departments, and the issue of land acquisition remained relatively unaddressed. Most important, however, when analyzed vis-à-vis the local importance of the sacral polity, the discussion of customary practices was entirely on secular terms and was, of course, positioned within the framework of the state bureaucracy.

For a range of reasons,[31] panchayat elections have not yet been held in Jharkhand, but the principle of the new amendments are welcomed by many city-based, middle-class indigenous rights activists as an opportunity to revive the traditional structures of governance, seen now as alternative political structures. In January 2002, I joined a meeting in Ranchi led by B. D. Sharma to address the formation and empowerment of gram sabhas. At least fifty men were present, adivasis who had traveled all the way from the neighboring states of Orissa and Chhattisgarh. They were mostly Christian, Sharma told me after the meeting was over (and as he flipped through two of the books he had written on tribal affairs in India, making me feel compelled to buy them!).[32] By then I was not surprised that the spiritual importance of the customary leaders had not been mentioned once, let alone the concept that they might embody a different notion of politics than that presented by the postcolonial state: a politics representing a sacral polity in which the sacred and the secular were one conceptual realm.

I realized that this concept had been at the heart of one of the most important political battles in the Bero area that I had witnessed, in June 1999. This concerned the hosting of the *parha mela* which represented, on the one hand, the commitment of contending members of the State Legislative Assembly (MLAs) to protect their poor adivasi voters from the processes of the state and, on the other hand, their dedication to resurrecting the sacral polity of the parha.

THE PARHA MELA

2:00 P.M., 3 JUNE 1999

Just before returning to England after a preliminary phase of this research, I got caught up with about fifty thousand people in the merriment of a spectacular festival happening on my doorstep in

Bero (where I was then living). A central focus was a group of men dancing in a colorful and dramatic procession, carrying across their shoulders people who sat astride colorful wooden elephants and horses and waved huge white flags. The parade circled the market square, and the people on the elephants and horses dismounted and ascended a specially erected stage. Meanwhile, other people danced to the beating of village drums and to the rhythm of more modern Nagpuri songs blasting from loudspeakers. Small stalls selling plastic toys for children and deep-fried snacks, sweets, and tea lined the fringe of the crowded market square. Vendors from the surrounding villages sold rice beer and alcohol distilled from the mahua flower. For this annual festival, people came by foot and by specially organized public transportation (buses, tractors with trailers, trucks, and jeeps) from villages as far as thirty kilometers away.

"The festival's purpose is to unite all the people of the area in one place and at one time to celebrate and respect the parha," said Ajay. Then only vaguely aware of the rich social and political landscape around me, I was surprised when he and others pulled me away from the dancing and took me on a two-kilometer walk to the village of Baridih, where almost the same festival was in motion with a similar mass of people. Concentrating on trying to impress my friends with how quickly I could learn the dance steps, I made only a vague note of the fact that our swaying to the rhythmic beating of drums at both destinations took place against a backdrop of two local politicians, in two different locations, making fierce speeches against each other.

However, when I returned to live in Tapu and witnessed the selection of the pahan and the paenbharra in December 2000, I knew I had to revisit the local history and significance of the parha mela. It became clear that the June *parha jatra* (or parha mela, in Hindi) is the symbolic focus of the battle for power between two Oraon tribal men who preferred to go by the surname Bhagat. Karamchand Bhagat controlled the Bero *mela* (festival), and Vishwanath Bhagat the Baridih one. Of further interest is that both men had been the local MLA, a position reserved for Scheduled Tribes—a result of the Indian government's affirmative action policies, which reserve a certain number of seats for Scheduled Tribes or Castes, allocated in proportion to their population in that constituency. The mela was the single most important event of the year for the two Bhagats, and each man spent vast amounts of time, energy, and resources to get as many people as possible to attend *his* event. The number of people at a mela was a sign of the MLA's strength in terms of local allies and followers, and hence in terms of determining his relative legitimacy. The number of attendees was also important in securing outside patrons (for example, higher-level politicians who determine an MLA's position within a party). The history of battles over the mela reveal the significance the MLAs placed on promoting and reviving the notion of the parha in order to secure the adivasi vote.

Bero had historically hosted its small annual village festival on the first Thursday of June. In 1967, however, the day before the Bero mela, a police shooting in a nearby village killed six adivasis, and the government imposed a total curfew in the area, prohibiting the mela. Karamchand Bhagat, having had an argument with the local Bihari Block Development Officer, mobilized more than ten thousand people to break the curfew. Honoring the strength of the parha, Karamchand made sure that from then on a celebration took place on 3 June every year in Bero—the parha mela.

In the years preceding the 1967 mela, influenced and supported by Kartik (Nehru's Congress leader in South Bihar), Karamchand was resurrecting the parha in the Bero area. Although unable to use Kartik's anti-Christian rhetoric in Bero, for fear of alienating the substantial Christian population (approximately 15 percent), Karamchand revived the parha for electoral support. Two years before the 1967 mela, he initiated parha meetings to resolve disputes. And in 1967, the year of the first parha mela, he became the MLA representing the Congress Party, displacing the Jharkhand Party, which had won the previous three elections in the area. Karamchand maintained this seat in four succeeding elections, each year using the mela to promote the unity and strength of the parha.

Kartik died in 1981, and Karamchand lost his Congress candidacy in 1985 to Ganga Bhagat, who had networked effectively within the party. In June that year, Karamchand fell sick and was hospitalized, and Ganga hosted the mela. The following year, while Ganga announced that as MLA he would host the mela, Karamchand declared that the right to host the mela belonged to the person who began it. In compromise, they hosted the mela together, but the battle continued in 1987. Ganga argued the authentic mela date was the first Thursday of June, and not 3 June, so that year Ganga's mela took place on the first Thursday, while Karamchand's occurred the following day.

Two melas in Bero were held on consecutive days until 1990, when Ganga lost an election to Karamchand (then representing a different party, the Rashtraya Janata Dal). One of Ganga's supporters, Vishwanath Bhagat, decided to stand for the next election, representing the JMM. Vishwanath realized that the symbolic importance of hosting the mela would help him to displace Karamchand. The problem that year, however, was the first Thursday of June was also 3 June.[33] The question was who would host the Bero mela: Karamchand or Vishwanath?

Battling against Karamchand's considerable power as MLA, Vishwanath could not secure the Bero venue. He therefore hosted a separate mela on the same day at the same time, but in his own village of Baridih, two kilometers from Bero. Since 1990, therefore, two competing parha melas have been held on the same date, at the same time, in two different villages, Bero and Baridih. Following Karamchand's actions many years before, Vishwanath and his JMM workers began a campaign for strengthening the parha. The number of people attending the Baridih mela increased each year, and in 1995, Vishwanath Bhagat was elected MLA. By 2000, it was impossible to tell which mela was better attended.

THE PARHA VERSUS THE STATE

By the time I started investigating the history of the mela, Vishwanath and Karamchand had established arguments against each other to attract the crowds. Karamchand accused Vishwanath of initiating the second mela only to win votes. Moreover, Karamchand claimed that because Vishwanath had secured the support of only one *parha raja* (the head of a parha), Simone Oraon, Vishwanath had tried to destroy the traditional, sacred system of parha raja selection. Karamchand accused Vishwanath of using the principles of the modern state's democratic elections to establish a counterfeit second raja in another parha. Karamchand claimed that democratically chosen rajas had no legitimacy, since the authenticity of the raja was dependent on his hereditary position. Vishwanath, in defiance, argued that democratic election of a raja was an age-old tradition—one that preceded MLA elections. Indeed, in his explanation, he carefully disassociated the idea of democracy from the state. Democratically electing rajas, according to Vishwanath, was an authentic, homegrown, traditional custom.

Vishwanath, in turn, accused Karamchand of attempting to destroy the parha by disrespecting its gods and goddesses. He claimed that the mela's wooden horses and elephants were religious symbols of the village they belonged to and, therefore, only spiritually endowed people could ride them. Vishwanath accused Karamchand of placing not only ordinary people like himself on the sacred symbols, but also three former chief ministers of Bihar, all Bihari high caste or Muslim representatives of the state. Vishwanath argued that letting these outsiders ride the gods and goddesses was the ultimate sign that, instead of protecting the parha, Karamchand had become corrupted by self-interested politics of the kind associated with the expansion of the state. Vishwanath further accused Karamchand of replacing the parha flags waved in the parade with flags of a political party. In response to the first accusation, Karamchand argued that it did not matter who rode the horses and elephants. In response to the second, Karamchand did not legitimize his actions, but he did not repeat them at future melas.

The most striking aspect about these allegations is that each MLA accused the other of not protecting the parha from outside forces most often represented as intimately linked with the state. (Karamchand coupled democratic elections of the rajas with the state, while Vishwanath associated chief ministers, political party flags, and self-interested politics with state processes). While Vishwanath separated the state from democracy by arguing that the latter was an authentically traditional custom, both MLAs used a discourse about the parha to legitimize their authenticity in protecting the parha from the state. They sought to publicly separate the state and the parha. They depicted the state as producing a politics of self-interest, division, corruption, pollution, and immorality of an outside world. In contrast, they marked the parha as authentically indigenous, spiritually endowed, organic, and representative of unity, purity, morality, and a lack of self-interest.

In fact, this theme of separating the idea of the state from that of the parha had been a central part of each MLA's first strategy for election.[34] Karamchand represented both the initiation and the success of the first 1967 mela as being the parha versus the state. He argued that through the first mela, the state was defied by the parha because the parha breached the state's imposed curfew, and because the mela was a symbol of protest and resistance to the police shooting. When Vishwanath became MLA, he asked villagers to view him as a servant who would protect and strengthen the parha. He accused Karamchand of being corrupted by the state and thus weakening the parha. A fundamental part of Vishwanath's campaign was strengthening two parhas, consisting of twelve and twenty-one villages, respectively, and hence called "twelve" and "twenty-one" parha, by ensuring regular parha meetings were convened in which village disputes were settled. When I moved to Tapu, Vishwanath sought to regain legitimacy as the protector of the people through a campaign to rid the area of elephants. As I argue in chapter 4, elephants were almost a metaphor for the state, because many Mundas blamed the state for increasing the forest cover and bringing destructive wild elephants to the vicinity. Threatening letters were sent by the parha to the district commissioner, and road blockades were organized during which Vishwanath's workers handcuffed forest guards. To understand why Vishwanath and Karamchand were using an antistate, proparha rhetoric to legitimize their authority, and ultimately to win election to state office, it is pertinent to explore imaginings of the state and the parha held by the majority of the local people, the descendants of the tenants of the old landlords.

KEEPING THE STATE AWAY

Great excitement in Tapu preceded the 2001 mela. The pahan and paenbharra collected fistfuls of rice, oil, and spices from every house, as well as other donations people wished to make, for the feast at the end of the mela for the guests who came from outside the region. Onga Munda gave an additional half-kilogram of his best *gongra*, a vegetable like a zucchini. Somra Munda gave a kilogram of onions. Indeed, many of the old Munda men were proud to give some of their best crops to the parha. The four Munda and Gope houses of Tapu, which had each hired a space to set up a small plastic tent to sell sweets, deep-fried snacks of lentils and rice, and tea on the Baridih mela grounds, prepared their wares and secured some labor from the village to help them on the mela day. Many of the Munda women, and some Badaik men, spent the days before the mela brewing rice beer and mahua wine to sell in the clearing in the forest where many routes to the mela from different villages meet. Some of the younger Munda men were recruited by Vishwanath as volunteers on the day of the mela, to do odd jobs for Vishwanath and his supporters. A few of the migrants from the brick kilns returned in time for the mela. Young unmarried Munda women borrowed each other's saris for the day and teased one another about the boys they hoped to dance with at the mela. Only the female descendants of the landlord households would stay at home and wait for their husbands to bring them sweets. Most of the Tapu people were going to Vishwanath's mela. In Tapu, the most important factor influencing Munda attendance at a particular mela is the relative legitimacy they attribute to one MLA (candidate) over his rival. Understanding the basis of MLA legitimacy shows the importance of Munda imaginations of the postcolonial state vis-à-vis the parha.

In Tapu and the surrounding area, the state is seen as a recent and outside invention that has become an increasingly potent form of danger to adivasi society. Thus, given a choice, most of the Mundas would prefer to have nothing to do with sarkar and expect nothing from it.[35] With its officers and development projects, the state takes on an ominous, almost Kafkaesque quality for the Mundas, encompassed in the term "sarkar." Whenever a state jeep arrived in Tapu, for example, whereas landlord descendants of the village rushed to greet the visitors, the Mundas would steer clear. Somra Munda once said: "In the olden days, when *sarkari* [state] people arrived in the village, women would rush into their houses, sweep the children in, and close the doors, and men would even hide in the forest." This fear of the state when officials appear has also been noticed in the neighbouring state of Chhattisgarh.[36] Moreover, scholars of adivasi areas in western India have noted that, historically, officials of all sorts—whether from the revenue department, the forest department, or the police—were regarded with fear.[37]

Munda mistrust of the state is not, of course, based on some kind of abstract imagination. Jharkhand's history is marked by the oppressive and exploitative treatment of its population by various governments. It is widely accepted that both the colonial and the independent states proved to be very exploitative of poor adivasis living on the Chotanagpur Plateau. Ranajit Guha's *Elementary Aspects of Peasant Insurgency in Colonial India* discusses the terms of this dominance and subordination in the colonial period. These included adivasi alienation from the land, changes in livelihoods through loss of forests, and the double effect of taxation and the rise of moneylenders, resulting in indebtedness.[38] The Santhal-Hool (1855), Birsa Ulgulan (1895), and Kol (1831–32) insurrections[39] were peasant protests against this subordination. Moreover, the colonial period saw the forced displacement of thousands of people by labor contractors to West Bengal, the Andaman and Nicobar islands, Assam, Bhutan, and even Burma, where they worked on indigo and tea plantations and building railways and roads.[40]

These exploitative experiences of the colonial state carried on into the period after independence, in the form of the oppressive visions and policies of Hindu high-caste Biharis.[41] Dominating the state apparatus, these high-caste Biharis had very little respect or understanding for local ways of life and proved themselves to be extremely exploitative.[42] As late as the 1980s, the most significant experience with the state that the Mundas had was with the police. In the late 1970s, a murder case in a nearby village had resulted in the arrest of several Mundas in Tapu, who had all been tortured by the police. The soles of their feet had been whipped until they bled, and one old man still limps as a result. This experience was repeated in the aftermath of a murder in Tapu in the late 1980s, when several people were jailed, and their families were crippled by the legal costs that were negotiated by the landlord descendants.

The other significant immediate experience with the state was with excise officers, whom local people associated with the police, and who came to the village to beat those selling rice beer and mahua wine.[43] In Tapu, alcohol was important for every Munda festival and family ritual occasion, and each Munda household brewed rice beer and mahua wine for domestic consumption. While this domestic consumption was not prohibited in Jharkhand, the sale of alcohol was.[44] And although there were only a couple of individuals (from the Badaiks community) who regularly brewed alcohol for sale in the surrounding villages, inevitably everybody sold excess alcohol created for domestic consumption to needy neighbors, especially at the time of festivals. Thus, while the Badaiks created special hiding places near the forest for their brew, and others dug holes deep in their fields for their pots of brew,[45] crackdowns on the sale of alcohol by excise officers drove the fear of the state into every Munda household. This fear was further enhanced when one Badaik man was caught selling alcohol and jailed for several years.

While Mundas clearly feared the state, they were also unclear about what the state really was. For instance, there was a lack of clarity about who exactly was included in the category of sarkar, as it contained not only forest officers and police, but often also labor or building contractors, as well as NGO workers. There was also uncertainty about when and how sarkar had come to the area. Some speculated that the *Angrez*, the British, had brought it.[46] Others thought that, at the time of British rule, the local maharajah might have been a part of sarkar. Most, however, agreed that sarkar was a recent invasion, an increasingly visible and powerful threat to the Mundas, and that in former times, in the absence of sarkar, tribal society had been united and therefore stronger. This was a time when the parha had been strong.

In contrast to sarkar as a destructive source, therefore, the parha was imagined as an alternative, authentic, adivasi political vision. The parha derived its legitimacy not from the idea that it was authentically adivasi, nor from the idea that it represented a solely sacred realm, but from the idea that it represented a sacral polity. To the Mundas, the parha represented an idealized politics, inseparable from the sacred realm, and contributing to a non-self-interested, united, and more harmonious world.

The parha was the essence that united and protected adivasis—an essence that had, in recent years, been weakened by sarkar. One common example of the weakening of the parha was the rise of the modern courts, which were seen as trying to undermine the dispute-solving function of the parha. Moreover, the courts were extortionately expensive, and places in which one was inevitably cheated by mediators and lawyers. Most important, though, state court decisions lacked spiritual legitimacy and were controlled by outsiders, not local people.

In another common example, the state had taken over the rights of the forest, potentially imprisoning those who did not obey its rules. Indeed, this became a growing frustration in Tapu because of the increased crop raiding and damage to houses that elephants caused, which I discuss in chapter 4. The Mundas wanted to kill the elephants, as they would have done in the past in the annual parha hunt. However, the state protected the elephants over the people. Moreover, the Mundas could not chop down the forests which the state had made them regenerate, but which they felt had attracted the elephants.

In fact, the state was seen as becoming increasingly sophisticated in its ability to exploit Mundas, as was evident in its most recent camouflage as Block Development Officers. While the forest officers[47] and police, who fined and locked up Mundas, were exploitative and violent in visible ways, the block officers were seen to disguise their destructive capacity in the language of acting in the interest of the poor. Bero Block Development Office staff were in fact extremely prejudiced against adivasis. The most common attitude among the staff was that the adivasis were jangli and beyond development. For their part, Mundas showed a lack of interest in having ration cards which would give them access to government-subsidized provisions, being on Below Poverty Line (BPL) lists for state development schemes, or in having electricity or running water.

"What about all the *vikas* [development] going on in the area, what about the roads that are being built?" I asked Burababa one day.

He laughed. "Roads only bring *chor* [thieves]."

There is a sense in which his cynicism is justified. In Tapu, the only motor vehicle was a scooter owned by a landlord descendant. The new roads in the area were little used because of the shorter, faster village and forest trails to the market and other villages. Moreover, roads were seen as being built and used by *thekkidars* (contractors) and *dalals* (mediators), whom Mundas regarded as corrupt and dishonest outsiders.[48]

One inherent obstacle to legitimacy in the Mundas' eyes for the Block Development Office was its divisive and self-interested politics, which failed to take account of the Munda ethos of consumption. Take, for example, the office's selective distribution of housing grants to people identified as BPL, under the Indira Aawas program. Despite the fact that many people in Tapu were eligible, few participated. Indeed, even after the intervention of an NGO, which gave the housing contracts to the four families it considered the poorest in Tapu, they—Mahelis in this case—were reluctant to accept them. Five years later, not one of the families had built new houses. The NGO organizers explained to me that this was yet further evidence that these people have no interest in their own development and only care to drink. However, they missed the point that Maheli reluctance to build new houses was symptomatic of not wanting to create public distinction between themselves and the rest of the village.[49] Unless sarkari resources were distributed to all, the Mundas also usually showed little interest in them. The potential to acquire material resources from sarkar was seen as a sign of its inherently destructive politics; by giving to some, but not to all, sarkar differentiated among people, enhancing the potential for division among Mundas.

Where the Mundas were beneficiaries of sarkari resources, closer investigation often revealed that the resources were given through the influence of rural elites, who hoped to pocket some of the BPL resources in the process. Most of these resources were not in use, as shown by the numerous empty Indira Aawas houses dotting the Bero landscape. Where they were used, strikingly the Mundas believed that the resources came not from sarkar, but from the elites. On other occasions, such as in seeking compensation for damage to houses and crops caused by elephants, albeit always through the encouragement and mediation of the village elites, the Mundas accessed sarkari resources for what they saw as compensation for damage created by sarkar.

In the face of this weakening of adivasi society by the state, the Mundas thought it was important to strengthen the parha. At the intervillage level, the Mundas attributed the waning strength of the parha sacral polity in recent years to the waxing power of sarkar. It is true that some of the younger generation, educated and aspiring to join the village elites, had more contradictory understandings of sarkar and often looked down on the ideas of their parents and other relatives, attributing the ideas to illiteracy. Their kin, however, explained the youth's disenchanted attitudes as further evidence of sarkar's increasing power to mislead the new generations. In fact, many older people explained that by grabbing those who came to or aspired to engage with it, sarkar brought an amoral, self-interested kind of politics into the village, further dividing it.

Seeking the Munda vote, both Karamchand and Vishwanath promoted Munda passion about the necessity of the parha mela as a space to celebrate, and from whence to resurrect and strengthen the parha. In seeking Munda support, these former MLAs sought to become the legitimate protectors of the parha by reproducing the notion of the dangerous outside state. Hence, they promoted a very particular understanding among Mundas of the role of MLAs. Unlike block development officers or forest officers, the MLA was not seen as a functionary of the state but as a person who remained a part of Munda society. Indeed, the Munda elders of the village commonly explained to me that the MLA was like their servant, and it was his job to protect them from the state. In order to do so, the MLA was expected to know state representatives, to take a limited part in state processes (such as elections), and to wield considerable influence over the state in order to keep it at bay. Contrary to the assumptions about people's participation in democratic practices, as put forward in much of the contemporary literature on democracy and good governance, Mundas supported an MLA in order to have less, not more, access to the processes of the state.[50] In contrast to the state, the continued presence and significance of the Tapu pahan and paenbharra symbolized the possibility of a sacral polity where all aspects of life were legitimized by the spirits. In some ways, then, the resurrection of the notion of the parha, pahan, and paenbharra sacral polity can be seen as a Munda alternative to the state. It is to the values embodied in this sacral polity that I now turn.

THE VALUES OF THE SACRAL POLITY

The first important aspect of the sacral polity is that it embodies democratic values. In a fascinating article, Stephan Feuchtwang criticizes Chinese urban intellectuals for not recognizing that traditions of divine selection of self-organization, around an incense burner, might pass most of the tests for a form of local democracy: "not the exercise of choice, but yes the exercise of voice, local sovereignty, possibly universal qualification for leadership when women are included, and certainly universal judgement of legitimacy."[51] He argues that for these intellectuals, as for anthropologists, what is in the countryside is often referred to as "culture" and "community," while "civil society" and "democracy" are used only for institutions of local government and elections introduced by the urban central government as an electoral political system based on Western models.[52] Feuchtwang's commentary should be taken seriously in an analysis of traditional forms of governance in rural Jharkhand, which I argue need to be seen as alternative and legitimate forms of democracy. The selection of the pahan and the paenbharra takes place through egalitarian principles. The divisive politics that Mundas associate with state voting procedures are absent in principle; instead, the randomizing device of a spirit traveling through the village via a blindfolded medium means that any household could be chosen.[53] The heads of the households chosen do not have an indefinite responsibility but change every three years. These authorities are held responsible for the prosperity of the village in the period of their duty, and they are judged by other villagers on their ability to sustain good fortune and on their generosity.

The second important aspect of the sacral polity is that it represents the values of mutual aid and reciprocity. For their duties, the pahan and the paenbharra are given special land to farm. This is the land from which they feed the entire village three times a year. It is also the land from which needy families are given rice in times of hardship. Values of mutual aid and reciprocity are replicated beyond the functions of the pahan and the paenbharra and among Munda families more generally. For instance, Mundas engage in voluntary associations called *madaiti* and exchange their labor in times of hard work. The most obvious example is the rice transplanting season, described in more detail in chapter 5, where a household's rice is sown with the help of the labor of one person from every household. There is no payment for such labor. Rice beer and mahua wine, and sometimes a meal, are served at the end of the day. No accounts are kept for the labor exchanged. The values of interest, saving, and utility are absent in such systems.

The third important aspect of the sacral polity is that, in principle, dispute resolution and punishment takes place through consensus. The pahan and the paenbharra are to preside over any dispute concerning Mundas in the village. Such dispute resolution takes place in village councils attended by all the elders of the village, and to which the pahans and paenbharras of neighboring villages are also welcomed. Although the pahan and paenbharra have a final say in the decisions taken, settlements are arrived at through discussion, negotiation, and consensus. The ultimate punishment is to expel a person from the village, but it is much more common that a fine is paid.[54] The fines are not fixed but are negotiated, based on the material circumstances of the culprit. A person who is struggling to make ends meet, for example, will have to give less than someone who is better off.

Promoting the values of egalitarianism, consensus in decision making, reciprocity and mutual aid, the pahan and the paenbharras function as the spirits' representative on earth. Their function can be equated neither to that of the Brahman priest, nor to that of the king of traditional India[55] — whose position was approximated by the maharajah and his zamindars in the area, as discussed in the next chapter. Unlike Brahman priests, the pahan and paenbharra do not play any role in ritual cleansing, and their presence is not essential at marriage or funeral ceremonies, which are conducted by the concerned families. (Brahman priests have never been present at any adivasi ritual occasion in Tapu.) The pahan and paenbharra receive no gifts for their duties. Although their special powers derive from the spirits, they are in no sense regarded as more pure than any other Munda family. Moreover, their powers to propitiate the spirits do not derive from their purity vis-à-vis other people, but from their ability to protect people from danger by looking after the spirits. Their role is different from that of a traditional Hindu king, even a divine one,[56] because while they are responsible for dispute resolution and the maintenance of social harmony in the village, they do so through consensus with other elders and not with the stick, the *danda*, which is part and parcel of the monopoly of violence of a traditional Hindu king. Moreover, unlike the traditional king, the pahan and paenbharra are selected every three years, and in principle the elder of any house could be chosen to fill the role.

Rather than approximating the role of the king or the priest of traditional India, the pahan and the paenbharra are closer to the idea of a chief priest who not only presides over both secular and sacred matters but who, moreover, marks the existence of a sacral polity where the sacred and secular exist in one conceptual realm. This is the kind of polity that interested the famous French scholars Marcel Mauss and Louis Dumont in their project to understand how the domains of religion, economics, and politics have become separated in Western ideology.[57]

Unfortunately Dumont's wider comparative project of situating India in the context of other societies such as Melanesia and Western Europe has generally been downplayed by scholars of India, so that his arguments are often regarded in a specifically Indian context as addressing solely mainstream Hinduism. Jonathan Parry's "Mauss, Dumont, and the Distinction between Status and Power"[58] is one exception that importantly places Dumont's work in the broader project of comparative historical sociology, continuous with that of his teacher Mauss, to which it undoubtedly belongs.[59] It is from Parry that I take the term "sacral polity" to describe situations where the political, economic, and religious were one conceptual realm.[60] My use of a sacral polity in this book is thus not in relation to Dumont's mainstream Hindu ideals (of the sacred hierarchically encompassing the political) but to his comparative project, showing that in some societies, such as in Polynesia, the sacred and the political were completely intertwined.

Dumont tried to show how India marked a transition between such sacral polities as those found in Polynesia, ancient Egypt and Sumeria, and the Chinese empire, where the sovereign was the priest par excellence,[61] and those regions of the world like France and the United States, where the political, economic, and religious were autonomous realms. In contrast to Polynesia, where Dumont, like Mauss, showed status and power to be combined, with the king also being the chief priest, in India, Dumont argued, status had come to encompass power, religion to encompass political economics, and the Brahman to encompass the king. In fact, Dumont believed that sacral polities (of the sort found in Polynesia) had also been a feature of ancient India,[62] but had been replaced by a system in which the political-economic functions had not only been split from the religious ones, but the latter had also encompassed the former. The pahan and the paenbharra of Tapu show that a sacral polity is not just a feature of ancient India or Polynesia. It exists in some form today in some parts of India, and it is certainly valued by some people, in this case the Mundas of Tapu.

DEMOCRACY AS SACRAL POLITY

In *The Coming of the Devi*, which explores adivasi assertion in western India, David Hardiman points out that in their studies of adivasi rebellion, secular-minded historians have consistently ignored the religiosity of adivasis.[63] He shows that in western India in the 1920s, the political actions of the subaltern classes, the adivasis, were necessarily suffused with religion. By not recognizing the importance of the spiritual in adivasi spaces when alternative forms of governance are resurrected, today's secular-minded indigenous rights activists may be making mistakes similar to those of past secular-minded historians.

Recognizing the significance of the parha, the paenbharra, and the pahan among poor adivasis in rural Jharkhand makes it clear that there are at least two related problems concerning the local legitimacy of traditional indigenous systems of governance being promoted by urban-based, middle-class indigenous rights activists. First, the systems remain within the framework of the postcolonial state. And second, they promote a secular vision of alternative governance structures, thereby relegating the spiritual importance that adivasis invest in these structures to a belief in the supernatural. These two issues are particularly important given most poor rural adivasis' mistrust of the state. Moreover, the issues highlight a crucial fact: the local legitimacy of indigenous systems of governance derives from the possibility of politics intimately connected to the sacred realm of the Jungle Raj, to which Mundas are proud to belong, and which cannot be reduced to superstitious beliefs in ghosts.

In recent years, some anthropologists and historians have argued that we must pay attention to the ways in which Western models of the state and power are inappropriate for postcolonial societies. In Africa, for instance, some scholars have argued that democratization processes in Africa should build on African political ethics which may be very different from Western models of power,[64] and anthropologists have shown the importance of African idioms of witchcraft and sorcery in modern processes of politics and the state.[65] The implication is that we have to move away from essentializing popular political values and postcolonial political institutions as being similar to those in the West,[66] or as flawed imitations of mature Western forms,[67] and instead understand that they may provide the foundation for alternative political orders.

Following this line of argument, some scholars in India have argued that secularism is a Western idea and as such is bound to remain an "alien cultural ideology."[68] This thesis on what has been called the inevitable Indian crisis of secularism has been most forcefully proposed by the Indian sociologist T. N. Madan. Following Dumont, Madan argues that secularism in South Asia can have little currency because—unlike in the West, where the sacred and secular are independent—in India, political power was always subordinated to and encompassed by religious authority. Furthermore, other critiques of the Indian state suggest that the nation should reside in the resurrection of the virtues of the local, the subjugated, and especially a notion of community which entails a morally purified space of true tolerance, derived from religion and beyond the political community.[69] This is a valorization of community that Thomas Blom Hansen has called "anti-politics": "the production of culture (religion, tradition, ritual practices) as something elevated, perennial and pre-political."[70]

The evidence presented here shows that the legitimacy of an alternative political order for the Mundas lies not in the elevation of "anti-politics," but in a cosmology where the political and the sacred are indivisible. In the Munda view, the valorization of "anti-politics" entails a limited and particular vision of politics as a morally questionable and dangerous realm. While for the Mundas, politics associated with the state was dirty, self-interested, divisive, amoral, and exploitative, they romanticized a different kind of politics associated with the legitimate village authorities of the pahans and the paenbharras, and the idealized intervillage parha. This was a non-self-interested, nondivisive, and moral politics endorsed by the spirits.

These values do not inherently make Mundas prototypes of what some authors have called "society against the state,"[71] as evidence of a collective desire among nonmodern ethnographic subjects to fight the emergence of the state. The Mundas are our contemporaries, and their understandings of the state result, in part, from their historical experiences of it. The persistence of these values, of course, also need not undermine the role of political mobilization of indigenous governance systems in the nineteenth and twentieth centuries. The values associated with the pahan, paenbharra, and parha are to some extent regenerated by this political mobilization and also represent a longer history in the area.

The Munda view shows that, in the foundation of an alternative political order, Louis Dumont and Marcel Mauss provide the most relevant analytical departure because they analyze the possibility of the political, economic, and sacred realms combined into one indivisible conceptual realm. Rather than reinforce the arguments of those who may claim that democratization processes in India should build on a notion of culture and community that is free of the potentially dangerous realm of politics, the Munda view points to the importance of the notion that indigenous systems of governance are locally significant because they embody an idea of politics which is indivisible from the spiritual realm. If we take this concept seriously, then, we may also take seriously what has been argued for other parts of the world (most notably China): that some divination processes, such as the spiritual selection of the pahan and the paenbharra, may be legitimate forms of democracy. We have to treat such forms of democracy, revolving around a sovereign notion of a sacral polity, as intimately linked to the language of power and politics and not just reduce them to the realm of culture and religion. Rather than build on the norms of democracy emanating from a bourgeois Western secular political order, perhaps an alternative postcolonial ethics should build on the concept of democracy as emerging from a sacral polity—a sacral polity embodying values such as egalitarianism (every person has an equal chance to bear the responsibility of authority), consensus (major decisions are made, and disputes resolved, through open discussion and negotiation), and reciprocity and mutual aid between people.

While I want to insist that we take seriously the Munda vision of democracy through a sacral polity as the foundation for an alternative political order, in the next chapter, I show how the processes that led to the Munda demonization of the secular state in comparison to their idealization of the parha sacral polity are not just a result of their response to the historical experiences of the state. Munda imaginings also point to the importance of the reproduction of class in the social production of cultural imaginings of the state. In rural Jharkhand, middle-class elites whose lives and livelihoods are intimately entwined with the state, and who therefore have vested interests in the state, want to limit the number of people accessing the material resources of the state to better capture those assets for themselves.

The rural elites' access to these resources is partly dependent on the Mundas' having no role in mediation with the state. Enhancing the reproduction of Munda imaginings of the state as distinct from, and separate to, the parha,[72] the rural elites simultaneously resurrect notions of the traditional parha. A stronger idea of the state has evoked stronger ideas of the parha.[73] And it is to the exploration of this local political economy that the next chapter turns.

3. *Shadowy Practices*

DEVELOPMENT AS CORRUPTION

5:00 P.M., 21 JANUARY 2001

"But how are you going to save Rs 10,000 building that road?"[1] I asked Dharmesh, as I gave him some tea in a tall steel glass and settled down opposite him on my mud floor. I had invited him over when I bumped into him on the trail which connected the village of Tapu to a hamlet by the river. He had been dripping sweat over his pickax as he worked alongside the adivasi laborers he had recruited from the village in order to turn the trail into a mud road. The road was one of the rural development projects of the Ministry of Rural Development. The scheme was being implemented in the area via the ministry's most local office, the Bero Block Development Office, which was responsible for the surrounding 114 villages. Dharmesh had been chosen as the village-level contractor.

Before Dharmesh could reply, I added, "It seems to me that your cousins Neel and Anand have been rather clever with this project. They knew they could not get chosen as contractors this time since the rest of you [the sadans of Tapu] would create a big commotion if they continued reaping the benefits of sarkari resources. So instead they put forward a condition that none of you could argue against—the contractor had to give Rs 10,000 to build the Hanuman Temple. Together with all the bribes and percentages you will have to give the block office staff, how are you meant to make a personal saving under such conditions? It's hardly surprising, don't you think, that, unlike all the other projects, nobody else in the village volunteered to be the contractor for this one?"

"You watch me," said Dharmesh, "I have my eye on that Honda motorbike. I'll make the money with ease. First, there is the usual saving on labor costs. I'll give the adivasis who are working as manual labor RS 50 a day instead of the government rate of RS 51.50. And, of course, they will all sign, with a thumb print, that they have worked three weeks when in fact I will only pay them their due for the one week they will have worked."

I wasn't convinced. Dharmesh, who couldn't have been more than thirty, was quite a straightforward young man, not the cunning, plotting, scheming type; but he clearly wanted to show off. I persisted. "But how much money will you save from such small measures? You're clearly struggling—otherwise you wouldn't have to work as manual labor on your own road."

"The real savings will come from the three culverts. On the official plans they've estimated these at RS 33,000, but all I'll need to buy them is RS 16,000. And then there is the mud. The estimate says ten trucks. I'm going to use seven, and of lower quality."

"What if the supervisor comes to check what's really been going on?"

"But they never do. They're far more interested in making sure I give them their dues. And, on the off chance that the block officers come to the village, I'll just give them a few rupees to keep their mouths shut."

"So how did you learn about how to save money, deal with the block office, negotiate with the officers, and give them their percentages? It's clearly not easy. These things have to be learned. It seems that Shiv has learned from the MLA Vishwanath Bhagat and his workers, and Neel has learned from the NGO worker who stayed in their house for a couple of years. What about you?"

"To me it comes naturally. I'm cleverer and better than all of them," said Dharmesh boastfully.

Hearing a shuffling noise, we turned our heads to the wooden doorway. Rajan was standing there with a beautiful red-breasted, blue-headed cockerel on his left arm. With his right hand, he was gently stroking the bird's arched neck. He was a splendid sight in his spotless white vest and a crisp green lungi that stretched right down to his ankles.

With a hint of mischief in his voice, Dharmesh asked Rajan, "How's

Building Dharmesh's road, a project of the Bero Block Development Office. *Photo by author.*

the training going?" He was making fun of his older cousin, who loved rearing cockerels for the cockfights in Bero bazaar.

Rajan ignored him and—in his characteristically relaxed manner, with his head tilted to one side and his weight on one foot—said, "Your mother's been looking for you everywhere. You've got to go and tie your cattle up when my brother brings them back from the forest. Come on, go and do your duties."

Dharmesh left, and I went out to admire Rajan's cockerel. A much more serious and reserved character, Rajan looked down on his cousin's happy-go-lucky attitude. He did not approve of Dharmesh's latest flirtings with the Block Development Office, which he saw as "dirty." He had been applying for state jobs for the last five years, in the hope that he could follow in his father's footsteps and become a clerk. His lack of success, and his lack of desire to try the alternative route to making a living through brokering development funds, had made him slightly bitter in his attitude toward some of the other young sadan men.

Neel and Shiv were passing by; seeing Rajan and me, they walked toward us. As they joined us, Rajan asked me, "Has Dharmesh been bothering you again? Has he been boasting to you about his road contract?"

"He is quite foolish," interrupted Neel. "We were very willing to help. After all, we are far more experienced than he is, but he refused to take any advice from us. He insisted on doing it all by himself."

"The problem is his pride," reflected Shiv. "He could have made a lot of money on the road. But now, together with the fact that he has to contribute to the village temple, it looks like he will have to put money from his own pocket into the road!"

Almost exactly a year later, I found myself standing at the end of the road with Dharmesh, looking at adivasi laborers unearthing sal saplings that were growing through the mud. Apparently there was a new project to construct a new road going from the main village to the riverside hamlet. It was to be built along exactly the same route as the one Dharmesh had used the year before! Not many people in the village knew much about it—apart from the fact that they could work on it as laborers. This time the project had come through an MLA development fund, and the contractors were from Bero. The debates over contractorship had taken place at the regional, Bero level, rather than at the village level.

"Well," sighed Dharmesh, "At least this time there is no bad feeling in the village over who gets to be the contractor. I'll find some other way to buy that motorbike."

THE AESTHETICS OF POVERTY

The sadans I describe here make up about 20 percent of the village's population and are largely the descendants of the former landlords, or zamindars. Together with the landlord descendants from other villages in the area, they form rural elites that are usually higher caste (although the elites also include a few tribal families who used to collect revenue in the area). At first glance, to an outside observer, the differences between these sadans and the Munda adivasis, working as manual laborers on Dharmesh's road, may not be very apparent. The sadans also live in mud houses and have neither electricity nor sanitary facilities in their houses. They also fetch their water from the village wells or groundwater pumps, go to the forest to collect firewood for fuel, farm their fields, and sometimes even perform manual labor for pay. These similarities mark what has often struck me as an aesthetics of poverty—that is, the seductive visual imagery of poverty, which makes it easier for NGOs and state development projects to legitimize why these rural elites are the main beneficiaries of resources coming into the village in the name of the poor. You can

Dharmesh's road a year later. *Photo by author.*

be sure, for example, that most of the rural elites will be registered on the government's BPL list and on the so-called red card lists of the Public Distribution System for the poorest people, while most Mundas will not.

However, a deeper analysis of the rural area that moves beyond an aesthetics of poverty—and that begins to address poverty not simply in terms of material resources but also as a form of systematic sociopolitical exclusion from the development process—may draw the observer's attention to some marked differences. For instance, the sadans usually have larger plots of irrigated land and more cattle than do the Mundas. Sadan houses often have walls that are two feet thick and contain beds, chairs, and sometimes a table. Every sadan household will have at least one bicycle, and although at this point only Neel's brother owned a two-wheeler (a scooter or a motorbike), many sadan young men aspire to buy one. The sadans are likely to have a family bank account. All their children will attend primary school at least. Their women wear longer saris than Munda women, cover their heads in public in front of strangers, and never openly drink alcohol. A sadan man might own a wristwatch, and he will wear a shirt and trousers and shoes in public. Brahman priests officiate at sadan weddings and funeral ceremonies, sadans pray at the village Devi Temple and now at the Hanuman one as well, and they consider the propitiation of the village spirits as mere exorcism. But perhaps the most important difference for the purpose of this chapter is that whereas the Mundas seek to keep outside authorities such as the state away, the sadans maintain their livelihoods vis-à-vis the Mundas through direct or indirect benefits from the developmental machinery that infiltrates the rural areas, most often in the form of the state.

Jharkhand is a center of attention for governmental, nongovernmental, bilateral, and multilateral development efforts for its doubly marginalized indigenous populations. They are marginalized because they live in a state which contains one of India's poorest populations: in 1997, 63 percent of its 26.9 million people were thought to live below the poverty line,[2] with 78 percent in rural areas; and only 40 percent of villages are accessible by road, and only 15 percent have electricity.[3] And they are doubly marginalized because they are generally thought to be so lowly as to be placed outside the caste system. Examples of development efforts include the major Indo-British Eastern India Rain-fed Farming Project, funded since 1995 by the Department for International Development (DfID) of the U.K. government and based in the state capital, Ranchi.[4] Since 2000, this project has been run by the Gramin Vikas Trust, an autonomous trust established by a national cooperative-sector organization that manufactures and markets chemical fertilizers. DfID continues to fund the trust through the wider Poorest Areas Civil Society Programme in Jharkhand. The World Bank also has a pilot program in the region, the Jharkhand Participatory Forestry Management Project. And more generally, the NGO industry has exploded in Ranchi. But of course the majority of the development resources for India's poorest indigenous populations in the rural areas still comes through the official state machinery via the block-level offices. These offices distribute funds from both the state government, which places a high priority on the participatory development of its poorest populations,[5] and the central federal government.[6]

In this chapter, I show how and why rural elites—like Dharmesh and some of the other landlord descendants—appropriate these state developmental resources coming into the area for the alleviation of poverty, and how this appropriation is part and parcel of their attempts to maintain their historical local dominance.[7] I focus, in particular, on construction programs implemented by the Bero Block Development Office, such as the building of the road by Dharmesh. Many observers may call these rural elites' engagements with the state corrupt, but I prefer to think of their practices in terms of access to the "informal economy of the state"[8] because corruption conjures up loaded images of immorality, when actually these practices are often embedded in a local moral economy.[9] This chapter, then, will next analyze the moral reasoning of rural elites' engagements with the informal economy of the state. Questioning the view that corrupt actors are rational economic individuals who are maximizing personal gain, this chapter explores the varied reasons why rural elites participate in so-called corrupt activities. The chapter moves on to historically contextualize these rural elites' engagements with the state: it explores the transformations in the local political economy, from a dependence on land to a dependence on the state, through which rural elites have sought to maintain their dominance over the majority of the rural poor, the tenant descendants. In this changing context, the chapter stresses the importance for the rural elites of capturing the local economy of the state by blocking others' access to it. This results in the rural elites' contributing to a Munda perception of the dangerous state, a Munda reluctance to engage with the state, and a Munda desire to resurrect the alternative sacral polity. Therefore, this chapter considers how participatory developmental efforts may be filtered through a local class structure that keeps the poorest firmly outside the material benefits of such development.

THE "SCHOOL OF SCANDAL"

3:00 P.M., 15 APRIL 1999

Indu locked the metal door of our small brick house in Bero, and we stepped out onto the dusty road. The temperature was at least 108 degrees Fahrenheit, but it felt cooler outside than it was under our low, corrugated-iron roof, despite the fact that we had covered it with hay to keep the heat down. I had not yet discovered the many benefits of living in a mud house. I covered my head with my scarf, as Indu put up her umbrella for protection from the beating sun. She did not offer its shade to me, and I kept my distance from her as we walked. We picked our way across the dirt road to the Bero Block Development Office. Entering its walled compound, we stood under the mango trees for a few minutes to enjoy their cool shade, and the smell and weight of the ripening fruit above our heads.

"Look Indu, *that* is what the block officers call the 'School of Scandal'!" I pointed to the flagpole in front of us and the cemented area at

The Bero Block Development Office. *Photo by author.*

its base, where some of the block officers sat in the evening to gossip. I was trying to break the ice between us because Indu had been quite upset the night before, when I had recounted to her my conversations with some of the officers at the "School of Scandal."

The officers had talked about many things, but what I told Indu about was what I had found most interesting. The issue was why nobody was interested in the program we were then researching, called the Development of Women and Children in Rural Areas (DWCRA), through which women were encouraged to build small self-help groups to lift themselves out of poverty.[10] In contrast, rural development construction programs received the most interest, from both the block office staff and the rural elites who spent much of their time hanging around the office.

One of the most popular was the Jawahar Rojgar program,[11] which primarily brought in rural development construction projects such as roads, community buildings, ponds, check dams, and bridges through allegedly grass-roots agendas (the villagers were supposed to decide which projects should be built). These were also supposed to be implemented through participatory means (the villagers had to elect a fellow villager as the contractor), and they employed village labor. In these projects, it was routine for block officers to take illicit commissions through a system of percentages, or "pcs." The money initially came from the district office to the head of the block development office. The village-level contractor received the money in installments, for which a series of documents had to be signed by various officers. The percentages were taken during the process of signing these documents, especially by officers in the technical and the administrative wings of the block office. Thus, in the technical wing, for example, the junior engineer could expect to take 10 percent, the assistant engineer 3 percent, and the executive engineer 1.5 percent. The administrative wing included the block development officer, who could expect to take 5 percent; the supervisor and the head clerk, 3 percent each; the cashier, 2 percent; and the assistant clerk, 1.5 percent.[12] If the project could be completed for less money, the percentages could be higher. Altogether, approximately 30 percent of the money for any project went to the block staff.[13] These so-called systems of mediation were significant in making construction projects a high priority for the officers.

But these programs were also the center of attention for the rural elites. As part of the participatory development mandate, through which villagers themselves chose which projects they needed, public petitions for particular ones were brought by the rural elites to the block office.[14] The officers would select only some of the proposed projects, and those that were promoted by influential elites, especially those backed by an MLA or an MP, were given preference.[15] When a project was selected and the money for it arrived, a contractor from the village was supposed to be chosen through a public meeting at the village level. However, these meetings often did not take place, as interested and influential members of the rural elites would fix the outcomes with the block officers. When they did take place, they were dominated by members of the rural elites, who would often be in competition with each other.

The choosing of a contractor at the village level was a highly politicized affair for many reasons, which I will outline below. One significant reason was that although contractors got paid an average of Rs 50–60[16] a day for a project, all the money came in checks addressed to the contractor, and he determined its expenditure. Thus potential contractors could expect to siphon off up to 10 percent of the total cost of the project. As Dharmesh later showed me, such cuts were possible by using materials of poorer quality, digging shallower foundations than proposed, or counting twice the number of laborers who actually worked.[17]

"And so," I concluded to Indu, "the one we have set out to look at, DWCRA, is of no interest to anybody because there is no money to be earned in it. And we can't understand why none of the DWCRA groups exist despite the fact that the files show that there are fourteen, why the ladies extension officer is never here, why no additional village-level worker has been posted, or why I found the DWCRA manuals for the Bero office crumbling away in the back rooms of the New Delhi Ministry where they had been for nine years — if we don't understand how DWCRA is situated within the other programs, in which systems of corruption are a routine affair."

Indu blew up: "Why are you doing this? Why are you coming from outside to discover the terrible facts of our country? We already have such bad publicity around the world. So why are you interested in our India and making worse what is already bad? Surely you will tell all your professors at the London School of Economics about all this. Why should they be interested? This is our India, and not yours."

I listened quietly to this outburst and then had a long conversation with her about globalization, nationalism, and how the world's problems couldn't be solved if we treated countries in isolation — and what were national boundaries in any case? But even I was not wholly satisfied with my response.

We were both twenty-four at the time. I was thinking of doing a Ph.D. I had come to Ranchi in January for a temporary research job, and since I had no reason to return to London until the doctoral program started in September, I had decided to stay on, move to Bero, and hang out in the block development office. This was where I hoped to explore the relationship between the policy and practice of well-meaning development programs for the poorest people, designed in New Delhi but implemented at the local level by such block offices. I had met Indu in Ranchi, we had liked each other, and she had agreed to come and live with me in Bero. It was the first time she had left her parental home, and the first time that I had left the country where my parents were based to live on my own for several months. We were excited by the adventure of discovering the fascinating workings of the block office, but we were also struggling to make sense of the multiple and contradictory emotions that came with these new experiences.

A year later, when I found myself walking the cold corridor above the sign "Our Dream Is a World Free of Poverty," hung in the sparkling glass atrium of the World Bank in Washington — where I was struggling to write a report on decentralization and corruption—I was still wrestling with the question of why it was important for me to study what most people would call systems of retail corruption. The World Bank, like many international development agencies, was at the time particularly concerned with good governance. This focus was due to the fact that initial hopes of achieving strong government in many postcolonial states, through development and progress, had faded. In postindependence Africa, governance was often interpreted as resembling a return to "the heart of darkness,"[18] of which a central feature was the "criminalisation of the state."[19] In Russia, the spread of democracy since 1991 was often associated with a spread of "corruption, opportunism and crime."[20] India was supposed to be gripped by a crisis of corruption, a cancer of corruption, a pathology of corruption, rotting the core of the state.[21] At the time, Jharkhand was still part of Bihar, and Transparency International, the leading global NGO devoted to combating corruption, had not only ranked India the 72nd most corrupt nation in the world, it had called Bihar as the most corrupt state in India.[22] I was deeply dissatisfied with the brown-bag seminar I gave at the Bank, in which my complex ethnography had been forced into a dry, sterile, but flashy PowerPoint presentation under the supervision and encouragement of my bosses. In the end, it seemed that my presentation was an exposé of systems of corruption in Bihar—at least, that is what the audience seemed to be interested in as they asked questions while eating the lunches. "But surely," I thought, "the point could not be simply to expose what was going on in India or in sub-Saharan Africa?"

I found an antidote to my discomfort in the sobering arguments of Jonathan Parry, who says that perhaps the crisis of corruption in India is not, as most have claimed, a symptom of the weakness of the state but actually a sign of the extended reach of the state and the values of its universal bureaucratic norms, to which people have become increasingly committed.[23] But there is also the question of why, despite the huge public scandals in the West,[24] does the proliferation of accountability and transparency teams committed to controlling and curing corruption center on what is still sometimes called the third world? Transparency and accountability have become catchphrases of neoliberal globalization, tools through which not only the Western model of the state but also the market economy spreads across the globe.

At the Bank, corruption was seen as an obstacle to the developmental efficiency of neoliberal forces. While definitions of corruption were widely debated, the Bank's position was that corruption was any form of misuse of public property, office, or mandatory power for private gain.[25] Corrupt people hinder the developing economy by using public resources for goals other than the official ones. There is a moral dimension to this argument: public servants should work for the common good, without being diverted from that end. The corrupt actor can hence be understood as a rational economic person, usually of doubtful morality, who misuses state resources for private gain.[26]

When I came back to live in Tapu and got to know people like Dharmesh, Neel, and Shiv, I slowly began to understand the roots of my discomfort with the World Bank perspective. If viewed from the perspective of combating corruption, these young people struggling to rise in the social hierarchy would essentially become amoral, profit-seeking individuals pursuing their private gain and conducting their shadowy practices in the twilight zone[27] between the state and society. But from the point of view of these young men, there is a much more complex relationship between economy and morality. For them, what we might call corrupt practices are based on a moral economy, are not indulged in just for private gain, and are embedded in social relationships and understandings.[28]

THE MORAL ECONOMY OF THE TWILIGHT ZONE

The first thing that struck me about Dharmesh's seeking to make cuts on his culverts, mud, and labor costs was that all the other sadans expected him to do so. For Neel and Shiv, for example, the issue was not whether he would make the cuts, but whether he could do it well enough to save as much as he expected. One might think that perhaps these sadan men did not know that such pocketing of money from development programs was illegal. While the rural elites and sometimes even the local officers were often uncertain about the precise boundaries between legal and illegal actions, in the case of cuts from block development programs, the situation was different.[29] Money earned from the savings—called *do number paisa*, or money of a second order, to distinguish it from *ek*, or first, number work and money from, for instance, farming or manual labor—was thought to involve illegal activity, *do number kam*. The point is that for the officers and elites alike, illegality did not equate to immorality.[30] Instead, in the Bero area, illegal activity was legitimized through a moral discourse which showed a general lack of commitment to the state as it manifests itself locally.

In rural Jharkhand, the state is thought to be incapable of fulfilling the promises it made as a servant of the people, the guarantor of a certain social order, and a power above partial interests. It is recognized to be administered by people who have their own personal agendas, and whose vision of the common good may be far removed from that of ordinary people.[31] Moreover, engaging in illegal practices is legitimized locally because most development programs are seen to be inappropriate for the rural areas, given that they are designed by New Delhi officials who know little about local conditions. For instance, why would a village in rural Jharkhand need a community hall for village meetings? Or, more problematically, why should development programs target the poorest adivasis, who are too jangli to care about or know what to do with the programs? In fact, many members of the rural elites actually legitimized their activities by arguing that they were reappropriating state resources for more useful purposes, even referring to themselves to outsiders as *sevaks*, or social workers.[32]

The second thing that struck me about Dharmesh's experience with the road contract was that the custom of engaging in corrupt practices did not mean that there was no moral debate about these activities. While the projects themselves were often considered of little importance, morally charged discussions regulated who got a contractorship and the way in which the contractor's cut was distributed. For instance, while landlord descendants such as Neel saw contractorship as their hereditary right, other men wanting to join these elite networks took the more democratic approach that all educated young men should have the opportunity to be a contractor. Faced with this rising conflict over contractorship, Neel and his family used Dharmesh's road contract to introduce in a new politics of redistribution whereby contractors of block development projects had to contribute to the betterment of the village by purifying do number money into *ek number* funds. In Dharmesh's case, this meant helping to build the Hanuman Temple they had begun to erect in the middle of the village. This was a moral argument that no contractor could contest. More generally in the area, as the number of potential village contractors rose, there was an increasing trend toward rival contractors' condemning each other for using public money for individual ends. As a result, competing village elites have started to pressure contractors to divert their cuts to other common village causes, in particular as donations for religious celebrations.[33] Increasingly, a new moral discourse around money siphoned off from construction contracts has emerged that, in many ways, appears to mirror the relationship between short-term and long-term exchanges as described by Jonathan Parry and Maurice Bloch.[34] Wealth acquired from potentially individualistic short-term exchanges of do number kam can be converted into the long-term religious capital.

A third important issue is that all the practices involved in the informal economy of state resources were not equally condemned. The giving and taking of *chai-pani* (literally, tea water);[35] the *pagdi* (bribe); and the pc (percentage) — which match Parry's useful distinction among the gift, bribe, and commission — were all differently evaluated in moral terms.[36] Gift giving was regarded as the least reprehensible activity, not only because it was part of a broader social system of maintaining relations between people, but also because it was considered a transaction that was willingly engaged in. In contrast, the bribe was rarely voluntary on the part of the donor, and thus its giving was sometimes accompanied by resentment. Furthermore, the bribe's negotiability engendered feelings of unethical practice, especially if one person had to give more than others. The commissions, the third form of payment, were a fixed, nonnegotiable percentage of the value of a development project given by contractors to different officers involved in its implementation. As a result, the percentage was expected and arranged in a manner that was so matter-of-fact that it was rarely considered morally wrong. Indeed, it was in the logic of treating pcs as the norm that acts which deviated from what was considered normal, or fair, were deemed morally wrong. For example, if an officer tried to take more than his allocated percentage, he was typically regarded as greedy. If an officer did not take his or her allocated percentages, he might be regarded with respect — not because he or she was acting legally, but because people who are not greedy are usually praised. In a similar vein, if a contractor tried to get away without paying the commission, he was considered immoral. This would also hold true for those that tried to avoid paying because of caste or kinship relations with the officer concerned. Thus morality, in the discourse of corruption, was often judged in the context of values such as caste, negotiability, gift giving, hierarchy, and greediness.

My point is that Dharmesh, Neel, and Shiv were not morally dubious characters but were acting within locally established norms which did not correspond to the rule of law, which were evolving, and against which deviations were morally evaluated.

THE LURE OF THE TWILIGHT ZONE

So what were the men's motivations for engaging in the informal economy of the state? The World Bank perspective would have it that corrupt actors are rational economic individuals who are maximizing personal gain. In this vein, I will show in more detail that since the abolition of zamindari in the 1950s, direct and indirect state benefits have been a central means through which many descendants of zamindars have attempted to maintain their wealth and patronage status. However, while their objective may be to obtain material benefits from the state, being a contractor is not solely about financial gain, and the twilight zone has other lures.

Dharmesh, for instance, hoped to buy at least a motorbike from the cuts he made on the road, although he did not manage to do so. However, controlling a bright shiny machine with a revving engine was only part of the attraction of gaining a contract. Like Neel and Shiv, he too wanted to be a worldly actor, hobnobbing in the streets of Bero, wining and dining in its restaurants—becoming a particular kind of man. Securing contracts was also about a new, exciting, and challenging lifestyle in the elite networks in Bero and away from the more mundane environment of Tapu. The challenge was to become accepted among a new group of men acquainted with state activities and state officials, men who were in the know and had developed the skill of being in the right place at the right time.

Of course, becoming accepted was one thing, and acquiring status was quite another. Whereas in the village, as descendants of landlords, status came with birth, in the new community of worldly actors in Bero, young men had to earn their credibility and position in a new and bigger field. Tension and conflict over state resources were rife. Block development office contracts were few, there was stiff competition, and thus securing one was difficult.

The young village men negotiated relations with the more experienced older men based in Bero, who had greater leverage over state officials, and who were usually working for a political party and thus seeking village-level workers. The most prominent of these Bero men, who were members of Scheduled Tribes, would also attempt to win seats in the legislative assembly every five years. If one supported a particular candidate and was close enough to that candidate, the assumption was that the candidate's success would later influence the distribution of government development contracts in one's favor.

Becoming accepted, acquiring status, and securing a contract required skill and tactical ability to perform and do politics. To be successful, one had to be shrewd, intelligent, and also willing to engage in "dirty" activities.[37] "Dirty" because they involved not just cunning alliance building, but also violence, secrecy, caution, and the potential to betray one's allies if they became a threat. Doing politics was dangerous. While many young men of landlord descent tried it, not all were able to sustain their involvement in political networks for more than a couple of years. For many, as turned out to be the case for Dharmesh and Shiv, doing politics was a transitory and transient activity—an experience of a particular stage in life, after which one settled down to a more peaceful village or town existence.

In much of the literature, these men are called mediators, intermediaries, or brokers, and they are seen as blurring the boundary between the state and society[38] or perpetuating patron-client relations,[39] and sometimes as more positive forces of civil society, creating order in the fragmented politics of the postcolonial state.[40] In the next section, I will describe more specifically how the men mediate the relations between the poorest peasants and the state. Here, I want to clarify that these mediators are by no means uniform, and there is much difference and hierarchy between them. For instance, at the village level, Neel was much more experienced, better connected in Bero, and very calculative, while Dharmesh was young, in some ways naive, and merely trying his luck in this new domain of worldly actors—with not much success. And although for Dharmesh, being a broker became a transitory period of his youth which he gave up after marriage, for Neel, it became a way to secure a business in Bero and become a distributor of food for the poor through the public distribution system. There was also a significant difference between such village-level mediators and those based in Bero, who were usually older, far more experienced, and often involved in more than one project at a time. For these men, brokerage of state resources was an ongoing source of activity—albeit a subsidiary one, alongside a more stable source of income, such as owning a shop.

In summary, then, the financial utility of pocketing illegal money from block development projects was not the only reason the rural elites wanted to participate in the twilight economy of activities that some would call corrupt. Instead of solely being a rational way to maximize income, engaging in these practices also served the men's nonmaterial interests of becoming accepted, acquiring status among a particular group of people, and experiencing the challenge and fun of doing politics.

FROM LAND TO THE STATE

While there is certainly a moral economy to practices which some would consider corrupt, this moral economy is based on a political economy in which the rural elites try to colonize interactions with the developmental state, and keep the poorest villagers firmly out of the state system.[41] For example, since the building of the first mud road in Tapu, every single block development contract has gone to the sadan men, and none of the Mundas have been beneficiaries of rural development construction programs. The processes which make certain actors into such brokers has generally been acknowledged to be very poorly understood.[42] In the Jharkhand case, I show below that the rural elites' colonization of state resources must be understood historically, in terms of the evolving relations which serves today to maintain a kind of patron-client alliance between the sadans and the adivasis.[43]

The Mundas had been brought to the village by the zamindars around the end of the nineteenth century, probably in the 1890s. At this time, a Brahman sold Tapu for Rs 2,200 to an Ahir (a cattle herder and dairy farmer). As was more generally the case in the area, the Brahman had been collecting tributes from several villages under his control, first for the Mughals and later for the British colonial government. Tapu, however, was an isolated village in difficult and inhospitable forest terrain. Thus it was not a desirable property, and the Brahman was pleased to sell it to the Ahir. The maharajah of the area gave the Ahir the title Odhar to mark the new status he granted to most of the Hindu settlers, from whom a class of zamindars emerged.[44] Like neighboring zamindars, the Odhar populated the village with his own troop of servants from elsewhere. Herdsmen, cooks, farm laborers, weavers, basket makers, and spirit controllers came to Tapu.[45] The Odhar leased them land to live off, and the servants became his tenants. By 1932, the village land records show that there were twenty men who eventually brought their families to Tapu. These men were ten Mundas, brought to control the village spirits and to work as laborers; an Oraon, who was famous for controlling a particular malevolent spirit; a Khan henchman, who collected taxes; two Maheli drummers to keep evil spirits at bay in festivals; four Ahirs, who were cattle herders and laborers; and two weavers — a Parn[46] and a Chic Badaik. In return, they had to pay the zamindar tax, usually in rice. After 1932, more people were brought from neighboring villages: a Lohar blacksmith, another Maheli, an Oraon, and a Pramanik barber, who presided over Hindu rituals and supported a Brahman priest who came from another village when required. Apart from the Pramanik, all these tenants would have been defined by the present government as Scheduled Tribe, Scheduled Caste, or Muslim, and — as noted earlier — today their descendants make up 80 percent of the village's population, with the Mundas the dominant group, at 40 percent. Even as late as 2008, the tenant descendants treated the zamindar descendants with a certain degree of deference, saying that it was the zamindars who had brought them to the village and given them land to cultivate.

In the period of zamindari, the Mundas considered the landlords rich and believed they had a herd of horses, as well as stores of rice and pots of silver hidden under their mud floors. Although the landlords in the area had varying reputations, people in Tapu say that most relationships between tenants and landlords were similar. The landlords had brought them to the village and had given them land. In return, they had to pay a tax and attend to the landlord's every need, regardless of their occupation or other demands on their time. "If they said you had to go and fetch them firewood, you had to do it immediately," Onga recounted, "and if you didn't do it, you'd be punished with the zamindar's *lathi* [stick] and his *chapal* [slippers]."[47] The landlords set the village rules, the most significant of which was that the tenants were not allowed to harvest their rice before the landlords' rice, which often meant that tenant crops rotted in the fields. Such practices established and reinforced, in Tapu and the surrounding villages, a patron-client hierarchy in which tenants were the servants of landlords. It appears that this structure did not significantly change with the abolition of zamindari in 1952 but, as the experiences of Tapu demonstrate, continued well into the late twentieth century. For instance, the practice of not harvesting tenants' rice until after the landlord's own crop existed in Tapu until the mid-1990s.

In addition to this control of the village population, the landlords also mediated all the relations with the state. The first courts and police system in the area were established by the British in 1834, through the South West Frontier Agency.[48] These institutions were in Ranchi, a six-hour walk from Tapu, but people told me that the police used to come to Tapu occasionally to eat and drink with the landlords, one of whom was notorious for having said: "The police are indeed my dogs."

In the early 1950s, the Nehruvian government sought to eradicate the intermediaries between the government and the tillers of the soil. In Bihar, this precipitated a string of legal acts and amendments, as landlords sought to challenge any change to the status quo. Finally, in November 1952, the Bihar government placed a ceiling on the amount of land an individual could own—effectively abolishing zamindars. This took effect on 1 April 1953, and was incorporated in the Bihar Land Reforms (Amendment) Act.[49] The act provided for compensation for the zamindars and redistribution of any land above the ownership threshold. Those who had previously been the landlord's tenants became the owners of the land they tilled, paying the state a yearly tax equivalent to the rent that the landlord had charged.

This process of zamindar abolition has sometimes been portrayed as one of the most successful projects of the Nehruvian era.[50] Yet in Tapu, there is little evidence to show that such transformation occurred during the years following abolition. In fact, while the tenants had become local owners of the land they tilled, they did not come to fully understand the implications of this change until much later. In practice, even in 2007, the landlord descendants helped state officials collect rent from the former tenants. In this context, it is understandable that many former tenants believed that they were still paying the landlords and, furthermore, that they perceived the functionaries as representing an alien authority that the landlords nevertheless had long been in contact with. The Tapu landlords did not even have to hide the legal implications of the 1953 act, as the status quo was reinforced by the extremely limited access their former tenants continued to have to knowledge about the state-led transformation. For instance, the only newspaper to arrive in the village was the one that came to my house; the three televisions in the village were in the houses of landlord descendants; and the first radios were bought by younger Mundas only at the start of the new millennium. Thus, Tapu exemplifies how changes to legal ownership can often, in practice, have little impact on the social structure of an area.[51]

However, to the landlord descendants themselves, the legal implications of the early 1950s land reforms were of immense importance. They understood that the change, if fully implemented, would speed their material decline. Legally, they had to give most of the forests and *ghairmazrua* land (land with no right of occupancy) to the state, and they had to sell surplus land above the ownership ceiling. As was the case in most of the villages in the area, they were able to offset some of their potential losses at the time by *benami* (spurious) transfers. They also divided land strategically among family members, so as to keep as much of the land as possible under the de facto control of their families. Nevertheless, it was clear that the landlord descendants would lose much of the land they previously controlled. Moreover, with time, the demographic expansion of their families would mean that there was less land for each individual.[52]

To maintain their status, the landlords knew that their families could no longer solely depend on their land. They encouraged their sons to gain an education and seek resources outside the village. At this time, following Indian independence, government expenditures on development were beginning to transform the landscape. Roads were being built and development offices set up, and the state bureaucracy was expanding. In time, these institutions came to Jharkhand, and it was through them that the landlord descendants sought to sustain their livelihood and status. They had various strategies. Some of them got jobs in the government bureaucracy, especially in the development offices, and were posted to other regions. Some married rich women. Others started an open-pit mining industry in Tapu.

Starting in 1965, the road from Ranchi to Bero and beyond was being paved by the government's Public Works Department. This was the first of numerous paved roads in the area for which gravel was needed. Contractors from Ranchi, the private suppliers to government projects, came to excavate the blue gneissic stone from the common land in Tapu and chip it into gravel. This gave the landlord descendants in Tapu the idea to chip the stone themselves. Despite the fact that the 1950s land reforms had made these ghairmazrua lands public property, many people in the village still saw them as belonging to the landlord descendants. By 1975, one of the descendants was supplying his own stone directly to road-building projects and was employing many of Tapu's Mundas in his stone-excavation site during the dry months of the year. The profits he made attracted other immediate relatives. When I arrived in 2000, five landlord descendants were excavating stone from Tapu, using for labor tenant descendants from Tapu and sometimes neighboring villages.

Other landlord descendants sought to benefit from the different development resources coming into the area. In the mid-1990s, the Eastern India Rain-fed Farming Project of the Indian government and the U.K. Department for International Development targeted the village. The project community officer stayed in the house of a landlord descendant, and as a result, landlord descendants were the main beneficiaries of the various seeds, wells, and pumps brought in by the project. Moreover, because the project stressed building links with the state, it also led to a strengthening of links between the local government forest office and block development office and the landlord descendants. Beginning in the mid-1990s, as Tapu became the target of more state development resources in the form of construction contracts, some of the landlord descendants developed a monopoly of resource control in this sphere. In short, the developmental state in its various forms (whether through jobs, construction contracts, the proliferation of a stone-chipping industry, or development programs) came to replace land as the source through which the landlord descendants attempted to maintain their material lifestyles as rural elites vis-à-vis their former tenants.

From the Munda perspective, however, things did begin to change, and for more reasons than land reform. Tapu is not the same as it was in the late 1980s or even in the early 1990s. The relative material wealth of the landlords has significantly diminished. Whereas once the landlords had horses, both Mundas and landlord descendants now have bicycles. However, rather than the legal land reform, the Mundas remember a battle over land between two zamindar brothers, which began in 1932 and on which a lot of money was spent, as the beginning of transformation in Tapu. Changes also became more evident to the Mundas as new relations between landlord and tenant descendants became apparent in the surrounding villages. The market for both land and labor had become more accessible to the Mundas. The landlord descendants also became more eager to sell land, as many of them became increasingly short of resources, and some Mundas had saved money from their earnings in the tea plantations of northeastern India. Thus, as detailed in chapter 1, whereas in 1932, the average landholding of a zamindar was four times the size of an average Munda landholding, sixty years later, it was only one and a half times the size.

A further factor in this process of transformation was that during the 1960s, local produce markets opened up, and former tenants found it easier to sell their surplus produce. For those who had no surplus produce in the dry months, there were opportunities to work as day-wage laborers outside Tapu, in the farms of the wealthier former landlords of neighboring villages; in the stone-chipping businesses; or as manual laborers on various government development programs, building roads, dams, and bridges. In addition, if they wanted a bit of fun and adventure away from the constraints of village life, villagers could go away for six months of the year to work in the brick kilns of Bengal, Uttar Pradesh, and sometimes Bihar. Indeed, many people from neighboring villages started doing this in the 1970s. Thus, the landlords were no longer the main source of livelihood for the Mundas living in Tapu. There were alternatives, both locally and outside the area. The Mundas farmed their own land and began to keep all their produce for their own consumption or sale. They stopped putting the former landlords' needs above their own.

As a result, the economic structure in Tapu has changed significantly. Landlord descendants are still quick to remind Mundas of the generosity of their forefathers, through whom most of the Mundas acquired land. Most Mundas still acknowledge this and, in some ways, continue to feel indebted for it. Moreover, some Mundas experience new types of indebtedness created through the patron-client relations of employment and state mediation. Indeed, most of the few Munda families who remain totally dependent on the landlord descendant families continue to drop everything when the landlord descendants call. However, the number of such families is now small: of the forty-three Munda households in Tapu, only about nine (20 percent of the Mundas) are more or less dependent for their livelihood on members of the old landlord lineage.[53] A direct consequence is that those who have become more independent, through their own fields or alternative sources of income, not only complain about the landlord descendants in the privacy of their own houses, but they also no longer publicly behave like the landlord descendants' servants. In fact, while I was in Tapu, some of the landlord descendants often complained about how hard it was to get laborers: "These days everyone does as they please, they follow their own mind."

PRODUCING THE DANGEROUS STATE

In this context of changing relations, it has become more important than ever for the landlord descendants to control access to the state and its resources as a means to maintain their patronage status vis-à-vis the Mundas. It is thus significant that most Mundas had kin employed in the stone-chipping enterprises. Block development projects also provided a means through which landlord descendants could contract with village laborers in the construction process. In most cases, laborers felt indebted to the contractors, perceiving them to be the patrons of projects on which relatively higher salaries are earned.[54] Indeed, laborers usually saw the block projects as being owned by particular contractors, rather than by the state. And even though as villagers, the laborers had a vote in who became a contractor, the process of voting largely remained within, and reinforced, village hierarchies—to the extent that laborers felt indebted to the elected contractors. Moreover, Munda families who accessed state resources (such as the BPL benefits of subsidized kerosene and grain) did so because one of the landlord descendants mediated the supply. Mundas thus often believed that these resources were coming from the landlord descendants, not the state.

State resources, especially those from the block office for development for the poor, were most often captured by exclusive networks of state officers and rural elites. This exclusivity, and the misinterpretations it encouraged about the roles and practices of the state, may have been central to local control of state resources by members of the elites. It often appeared to me that, in front of Mundas, some of the sadans sought to perpetuate, perhaps even exaggerate, the narrative of state exploitation, playing on Munda imaginings in order to reinforce and further the elites' control of the local government.

Some authors have argued that brokers play a role in the fantasies of state power.[55] I was struck by this idea when, early one morning in Tapu, as all the men of the village gathered on the hill outside our courtyard for a meeting called by Darshan, Popat Yadav, and Neel Odhar, two uniformed forest guards arrived in the village unannounced. They were greeted by the landlord descendants and promptly went with them to find Somra Maheli, a tenant descendant, who had not come to the meeting. A quarter of an hour later, the officers and the landlord descendants returned with Somra. One of the officers was shouting and holding the shivering, horrified Somra by the ear. It turned out that the forest guards had been informed, by some unnamed source, that Somra had been cutting trees in a part of the forest where that was not allowed. After bellowing at Somra in front of the group, the foresters took him to their offices in Bero, where he sat for a few hours, was threatened with a large fine, and was eventually released.

The peculiar thing about this visit was its timing. It almost seemed as if the officers came to the village knowing that they would have an audience and a stage on which to perform. Indeed, I later found out that Neel and Popat had informed the forest officers of Somra's alleged crime and had asked them to come to Tapu at a time when he would be humiliated in front of the villagers. It is highly probable that they hoped that this would drive a fear of sarkar into those present. Indeed, while both Neel and Popat appeared to take great pleasure in the event and later laughed about it, back in our courtyard that day, Neel stressed to Etwa and Somra Munda how unnecessary it was for sarkari officers to behave in that manner. In fact, Neel even argued that the officers were really only interested in poor people's soshan (exploitation).

The performance of state exploitation is a crucial means through which the sadans maintain their local control over the state. I have often seen adivasis trying to get land revenue documents, caste certificates, or signatures from officers, and being given an endless runaround until they are eventually convinced that they need their village patron to get the job done. Consider the example of Wahib, a Muslim tenant descendant in Tapu, whose house was destroyed one night by three elephants, a subject I turn to in the next chapter. Neel convinced Wahib that he could receive compensation from the state, but that Neel's uncle would have to deal with the corrupt officers. Since the uncle was out of town, Neel helped the illiterate Wahib write an application. However, the officer in charge threw the papers in Wahib's face, shouting that the application was unacceptable. Neel's uncle returned and laughed at Wahib's attempts, asking him if state officers could really be expected to treat the poor differently. He said that only some people had leverage over these officers, and that if Wahib found him free in the market the next day, he would look after Wahib's application. Neel's uncle was known to wine and dine officers in his house, and Wahib believed he could get the job done. Wahib thus followed the advice of Neel's uncle and eventually received a check through him, from which he took a cash percentage for some officers and money for a new suit for himself.

Thus, while some of these landlord descendants would quite willingly joke to me in secret about the stupidity of adivasi beliefs about the state, in the presence of adivasis, these elites perpetuated the notion of a dangerous state, an exploitative monolith that it was better to stay away from. They realized that it was important to reinforce and even exaggerate the narrative of state exploitation. Capturing the local economy of the block development office, for example, was made easier by creating a network of personal ties between state officers and village elites from which others were excluded. This exclusion was brought about by taking every opportunity to stress the cultural differences between honest, innocent, ignorant, illiterate, insiders (the tenant descendants) and corrupt, exploitative outsiders (the state and its agents). Keeping others misinformed about the roles of the state was key to being able to control its resources and the way in which they were accessed. The control of block resources by these officers and village elites was essentially based on their control both of the idea that the state functioned for the public good and of the localized practices of the state. Thus part of the reason why adivasis today continue to see the state as irredeemably foreign and polluted, and therefore to be avoided to a significant degree, is that in the local political economy, it has been in the interest of other villagers to propagate and reinforce such a view.[56]

GODS, SPIRITS, AND THE STATE

While Tapu village elites do stress the exploitative and oppressive images of the state to the Mundas, I do not want to suggest that Mundas are merely ignorant and malleable. The flip side of this political economy that underpins cultural imaginings of the state is, as I have argued in the last chapter, the resurrection and desire by Mundas to protect the parha, the pahan, and the paenbharra as the basis for an alternative sacral polity of the Jungle Raj. In this respect, Mundas do feel a moral superiority over the sadans because of their exclusive ability to be guardians, bearers, and controllers of the sacral polity. Indeed, the sadans' ancestors had had to bring Mundas to the village for this purpose. Yet the Mundas regard the sadans with a degree of skepticism and inferiority since they know the sadans see the village spirits as mere nuisances to be appeased, they see the Munda ability to appease them as low and polluted functions of mere exorcism conducted by jangli people, and they prefer to believe instead in Hindu deities, whose ceremonies are presided over by Brahman priests. In taking charge of what they see as a superior sacral polity, the Mundas thus leave the inferior and dangerous functions of mediation with the secular state to village elites. However, I believe that things were not always this way, and that a specific set of historical transformations have led to the present situation.

There is some evidence to show that before the zamindari period, the Mundas and the Odhar landlords were sociologically closer, because the Ahirs were the cattle herders of Oraon and Munda villages.[57] Given this social proximity between the Ahir landlord of Tapu and his first tenants, the landlords of Tapu were, I suspect, eager to rid themselves of their lowly title. Indeed, by the time the British surveyed the village in 1932, as pointed out in chapter 2, the sons of the original Ahir landlord had taken the title Maheto, a name more generally given to a functionary whose specific role was to deal with outside authorities. The Maheto title of the landlords in Tapu was succeeded by the Odhar title, given by the Ratu maharajah to distinguish the status of his landlords. Today, some of the direct descendants of the landlords in Tapu still use Odhar to distinguish themselves from the indirect descendants of the landlords, those who are the children of daughters and hence cannot rightfully claim Odhar as their title. However, both these lineages of descendants, as well as the Ahir tenant descendants who had taken the Gope title, now also call themselves Yadavs for official purposes, as this clearly categorizes them as Other Backward Classes, giving them access to the potential benefits from affirmative action policies. Given the original closeness of the Ahir to the tribals, it is possible that they too believed in spirits rather than in gods and goddesses. However, as the Ahir acquired landlord status, they became more closely connected to the Hinduized world of the maharajah and his other zamindars.

With this higher status, the Gopes, Yadavs, and Odhars sought further distinction from their tenants by defining themselves as Hindu. They acquired gods — Ram, Hanuman, Durga, and Shiva — that also became known by the more generic term of *bhagwan*, or God. These gods needed temples or shrines. And with these gods, the landlords also adopted Hindu rituals and festivals. The Hinduization of the landlords' sacred world thus was contrasted to what they now see as the supernatural beliefs of the Mundas. Whereas in the past the pahan, the paenbharra, and the bhutkhetta beneficiaries were central to the landlord world, Hinduization reduced these functionaries, in the eyes of the landlords, to the lowly level of exorcism of potentially harmful spirits that was fit only for the jangli people. In this process, the importance of the Munda sacral polity was erased. It was replaced by the secular status of the landlords, as the dominant caste at the village level, and the maharajah, as king at the intervillage level, encompassed by the absolute superiority of the spiritual plain in which Brahman priesthood was of a transcendent nature.[58] The superior sacred function, of the landlord descendants, officiating at the rites of the sacred world, came to be performed by the Brahman priest,[59] while the Munda sacral polity was reduced to the exorcism of evil spirits, not only inferior to the worship of Hindu deities but controlled by jangli adivasis.

Yet the sadans today remain very aware that part of their local dominance depends on creating a divide between a temporal-material world of the secular state, with which they alone interact, and a sacral polity over which Mundas preside. Thus they do not interfere with the selections of the pahan and the paenbharra and their spiritual lands, and their young men are very involved in the organization of the parha mela, recognizing that this is a vital tool through which they can gain the support of the adivasis to vote for their chosen MLA. However, by acknowledging and demarcating a domain in which Mundas become superior—the control of the spirits of a sacral polity—the sadans create a hierarchy between this and their own role as mediators with the state. In this hierarchy, the latter are roles that Mundas are happy to leave to the landlord descendants. Mundas see these roles as diametrically opposed to, and therefore inferior to, the higher domain of the sacral polity of the Jungle Raj that they command. Thus, because the landlord descendants appear to value and support, but do not interfere with, the sacral polity of the Mundas, their material connection with them remains secure.[60] The control and reproduction of these Munda imaginings of the secular state vis-à-vis the sacral polity is therefore crucial to the reproduction of a class of rural elites, who are able to maintain their material dominance today over the poorer adivasis in large part through mediating access to the developmental state.

CROSSING THE SHADOW LINES

While most members of the rural elites in the Bero area are sadans, there are also a few members of Scheduled Tribes who have joined these elites, and who are mainly descendants of the old revenue-collecting families of the area. These educated Scheduled Tribe elite families have generally also sought to distinguish themselves from the poorer adivasi villagers. They have purified and Hinduized some of their practices and beliefs, and many have become Tana Bhagats. A sect which grew in the late colonial period, under the leadership of a Jatra Oraon, the Tana Bhagats believed in a supreme God and wanted to free Oraons of so-called evils such as witch hunts, the belief in spirits, animal sacrifice, drinking liquor, and eating meat. All the former MLAs of the area (the seat is reserved for Scheduled Tribes), who fought to have control of the parha mela, as described in the last chapter, went by the surname Bhagat. The vote of the rural adivasis was crucial for the MLA candidates. Hence, like the sadan elites in Tapu, these Scheduled Tribe elites also encouraged further Munda separation of the idea of the state from the parha in order to mobilize the support of the poorest adivasis. Unsurprisingly, anthropology was a large influence on their cultural politics.[61]

Karamchand Bhagat, while studying for his B.A. in anthropology at Ranchi University, had read accounts of the "lost" tribal traditions in the works of the anthropologists S. C. Roy and L. P. Vidyarthi. He used these accounts as models in reestablishing the parha in the Bero area in the 1960s. Ganga Bhagat was also well versed in the idea of using traditional tribal customs as a political tool. Working on his B.A., in economics and psychology, Ganga often studied at the library set up by Roy in his house in Ranchi, called The Man in India Library. Later, at the Tribal Welfare Research Institute, Ganga was a research assistant to the anthropologist Rekha Olip Dhan, an experience that he says was fundamental to his political career. Vishwanath Bhagat, though not as formally influenced by anthropologists as the others, had read the works of Vidyarthi and was particularly interested in collecting tribal songs and myths. Vishwanath argued that for a regional sentiment to be mobilized, one had to arouse people's feelings for local language, culture, tradition, and race that were visibly different from those of the nation, thus supplanting national sentiment. Vishwanath said his application of this idea to the promotion of the parha enabled him to defeat Karamchand in an election.

These rural elites understood that the goal of monopolizing state resources was enabled by, if not dependent upon, the perceived authenticity of the parha and the foreignness of the state. The protection of the parha and its mela became important symbols for this purpose. The MLAs produced their own legitimacy by recreating the imagined boundary between the state and the parha. The production of a stronger idea of the state in turn evoked a stronger contrasting idea of the parha.

While sadan village elites were treated with a degree of suspicion by Mundas, both Karamchand and Vishwanath, as Oraons from humbler backgrounds, were at first seen as protectors of the Mundas from the state. However, managing the two different ideas of the state held by the Mundas and the sadan elites entails an inherent contradiction for these MLAs. In seeking to please his sadan supporters, the MLA is seen by the Mundas as betraying them by becoming corrupted by the material resources and politics associated with the state, and thereby crossing the shadow lines between Munda and sadan societies. The danger this poses is great because often the success of each MLA candidate rests on his capacity to devalue the other's ability to protect the parha—claiming his opponent has been corrupted by the state, has become a man of the outside world and therefore a danger to the parha.

Indeed, Vishwanath challenged Karamchand in precisely these terms. Vishwanath claimed that nearly thirty years of contact with outsiders had polluted Karamchand, who—living in a two-story brick mansion, being driven by a chauffeur, and dressing like a politician in white *kurta-pyjama*—was no longer a simple villager. Vishwanath argued that Karamchand, having corrupted himself, was destroying the parha. After Vishwanath became an MLA in 1995, however, he was faced with the same problem of appealing to both the sadan rural elites and the Mundas. In his time in office, he too built himself a large brick house, bought two cars, and started wearing kurta-pyjama. He lost the 2000 election in part because the Mundas had come to believe that, like Karamchand, Vishwanath had gone over to the other side and could no longer be trusted to protect them.

The person who most successfully negotiated the boundary between the state and the villagers in the Bero area was Simone Oraon. He was the raja, or intervillage authority of the "twelve parha" (a cluster of twelve villages forming a parha), a position that was considered by Mundas, alongside pahans and paenbharras, as a representative of their spirits. In front of the endless stream of visitors from the outside world—NGO representatives, state officers, missionaries, and journalists from Delhi and beyond, Simone showed off his repeated nominations for an "International Man of the World" book. Successful at acquiring contracts from the block development office, Simone acquired resources for a tractor, irrigation canals, and a dam. However, despite his significant interaction with the state, his legitimacy as a parha raja has never been challenged by Tapu's Mundas.

There were several reasons for his seeming immunity. He was careful to show that any resources acquired from the state were for communal, not personal, use. One of his strongest assets, one that no MLA could acquire, was his spirit-endowed status as a parha raja. He knew this and was quick to take every opportunity to highlight aspects of his life which were attributable to the spirits. Among these were several famous claims that he had survived two falls into wells, two dam collapses, and a tiger chase as a result of his spirit-endowed status. His legitimization by the spirits as a parha raja meant that, unlike ordinary villagers, he had the power to engage with the state and not be harmed by this interaction.[62]

With the exception of Simone, MLAs in this part of India were seen as servants who could not claim the legitimacy endowed by the spirits. Indeed, if an MLA tried to do this, he would be accused of trying to destroy the sacral polity—as Ganga Bhagat (a former MLA) was when he claimed that he should become the permanent pahan of his village since the spirit kept entering his house. In fact, by 2007, most Mundas in the Bero area were disillusioned by the MLAs. There was once great faith in Karamchand, and then in Vishwanath. However, as Burababa then explained, "Now, the men who stand as MLAs are too easily spoilt." MLAs everywhere in India are in danger of being accused of becoming fat cats and distant from their voters. However, this is a particular problem for MLAs in this part of Jharkhand, because they must not be seen to materially differentiate themselves from the majority of adivasis who live in the surrounding villages. In the last MLA election, there was a very low voter turnout, and the rural elites attributed Dhan's victory to his capture of the electoral booths and bogus votes.[63] It is difficult to know the precise implications of this low interest in voting. One possibility is that there is a growing belief among Mundas of the MLA's inability to protect the parha as the imagined heart of tribal sacral polity. This may in turn lead to a declining importance given by Mundas to the parha and, paradoxically, a more ambiguous vision of the possibilities of state interaction. But the opposite may be likely—that Mundas will try even harder to retain their distance from the state, further enabling the appropriation of state resources by the rural elites.

THE POLITICAL ECONOMY OF SHADOWY PRACTICES

In this chapter, I have focused on how state resources for the development of poor rural areas get appropriated by historically dominant, usually higher-caste, rural elites. The chapter has historically mapped the local political economy in order to further contextualize the Mundas' desire to keep away from the state, and the importance they place on the idea of the alternative sacral polity. I have also explored here the moral economy of the rural elites' engagement with the state, showing the inadequacy of popular assumptions about corruption. However, the ultimate point of this chapter has been to show how participatory development efforts enable the reproduction of a local class structure that keeps the poorest firmly at the bottom.

Since the 1990s, as a result of the top-down critique of development, programs of poverty alleviation have been focused on "putting the last first,"[64] and on the participation and empowerment of the world's most marginalized populations. Participation has become almost a panacea for development, through which poor people should build social capital to reduce their marginalization. However, in recent years, this new focus on the grass roots, on village communities, has been shown by many scholars to be a romanticization on the part of policymakers, which essentially depoliticizes development—or, to use James Ferguson's phrase, makes it an "anti-politics machine."[65] It does so by not taking into account the fact that poor rural populations are heterogeneous, characterized by inequalities of power emerging through complex interrelationships between people, and embedded in broader structures of power and social transformation.[66] Poverty, some scholars have argued, needs to be seen in a relational context and understood through both the social relations that produce it and the ways in which some people have control over and further marginalize less powerful others.[67] This is an important critique of development in the context of India's doubly marginalized forest-fringe communities because, as I have shown, the resources coming into areas like Jharkhand, in the name of participatory development for its poorest indigenous populations, are mediated by rural elites who can easily produce the aesthetics of poverty that are required of worthy beneficiaries.

Observers might see this mediation of state resources as evidence of a weak civil society, as a sign of the proliferation of the supposed cancer of corruption raging through rural India. However, to a certain extent, Partha Chatterjee is correct to point out that many popular terms used to describe everyday localized practices of governance, such as "civil society," are really categories of a bourgeois political order which have an extremely limited meaning in much of the non-Western world.[68] In India, it does not make sense to insist on localized practices' respecting the rule of law, the equality of law, the protection of private property, or the freedom of contract because most people are not bourgeois and simply do not negotiate claims against the modern state in this way. Chatterjee suggests instead using the term "political society" to describe the way in which localized subjects operate on a set of norms which are often quite contrary to what the larger principles of governance would dictate. This chapter has looked at the shades and textures of such a political society in relation to the debates around corruption, morality, and the state.

Understanding the actions of those who make up a political society in their own terms is important, because we are faced with an increasingly powerful international development discourse condemning corruption in the developing world, treating it as somewhat pathological. Several points emerge that have relevance beyond the Jharkhand case. First, the monetary aspects of corrupt activities may be eclipsed by a whole range of other motivations, governed by a set of moralities, for engaging in those activities. Economic action is indeed governed by a pattern of moral rights or expectations.[69] Second, the discourse of corruption may itself be a tool through which potential opponents are defeated. Third, the institutional dualism at the heart of moralistic good-governance discourses on corruption, which forces people to separate personal agency from the state, may well be less honest than an open acknowledgment of their interdependence.[70] While it might be accepted that the idea of the state should be impersonal in order to serve the greater common good, it is also accepted that the state after all consists of real people doing things to and with each other, and often designing policies and development programs without having any idea about their relevance to the people they should allegedly serve. The moral setup of everyday life does not necessarily mesh with official or dominant rules and moralities. Fourth, what is legal is not necessarily considered the most legitimate. Often, state norms may be ignored because of their perceived inadequacy to make the state a public body working on behalf of the common good. Thus, the analytical power of the Jharkhand case cannot be reduced to promoting culturalist arguments about corruption—for example, that different cultures perceive economic practices in different ways, and we need to respect this. Instead, I have argued that the Jharkhand case promotes an understanding of corruption which takes into account the complex interrelationships between, on the one hand, how people reason about their corrupt practices in the wider socioeconomic context of understandings of the state and, on the other hand, the various moral and political economies that affect social action.

However, the Jharkhand case also shows that Partha Chatterjee's concept of political society needs refining. Political society is not uniform, nor does it have a hegemonic moral economy. And in Jharkhand, it is certainly different for different classes of society. As I have shown here, we need a fine-grained analysis that unravels the different, and interrelated, moral economies. For example, the majority of the rural poor, primarily adivasis, want nothing to do with the state, do not believe that the state acts for the public good, and do not want to know about the practices of the state. They resurrect an alternative cosmology of a sacral polity instead. These are not merely cultural imaginings of the state. They result from a political economy of historical experience with the state (analyzed in the last chapter) as well as ideas encouraged by the village elites, in whose interest it is to promote the idea of the state as alien, dangerous, and so beyond the moral pale that adivasis ought not to engage with it. Perpetuating such views of the state, the rural elites are better able to prevent the rural poor from interacting in the public sphere as well as in the moral economy of state development programs on the same terms as the elites themselves. In this sense, as Thomas Blom Hansen says, we do need stronger ethical standards than those Chatterjee's analysis of political society seems to allow.[71] The rural elites in Jharkhand are in fact ensuring that well-meaning development efforts for India's poor indigenous populations are reappropriated within a local class system that bars the poorest adivasis from access to the state. Ironically, as shown in the last chapter, this political economy is also encouraging the resurrection of Munda imaginings of a sacral polity from which an alternative political order could emerge.

4. *Dangerous Silhouettes*

ELEPHANTS, SACRIFICE, AND ALCOHOL

8:00 P.M., 13 DECEMBER 2000

"It's really dark, Etwa. I know your goats didn't need to be here in the day. But it would be good to have some daylight now for me to write field notes. Can't we carve out a small window into the mud wall?"

"Are you sure that is a good idea, Alpa? I agree that we have to repair the broken mud-roof tiles and replace some of the split bamboo on which they rest. Dada baked some tiles in the hot weather, and he will give us a few spare ones. I think you should also build a cooking hearth so that you don't have to use that expensive gas tank and worry about filling it in Bero every few days. But a window, I'm not sure about. The floor-to-ceiling mud walls keep the house cool in the summer and warm in the winter."

"But Etwa, there are big holes higher up in the wall in any case. It looks like you ran out of steam and forgot to put through them the logs that would let you to store hay."

Etwa's eyes grew distant, and he stared vacantly at the ceiling. About five years ago, when he was in his early twenties, he and his mother had built this large, two-roomed house with a front room. When it was nearly done, Etwa's mother had developed a high fever. She had tossed and turned on the mud floor for several nights and then died, leaving Etwa all alone. Although his cousins lived in the other houses in our courtyard, Etwa had no immediate siblings, and his father had died when he was very young. Aggrieved and disillusioned, Etwa continued to live in the tiny, one-roomed house next

Lighting the fires that keep elephants away. *Painting by Seema Shah.*

door and left the larger, incomplete house for his goats. That is, until I came along and persuaded him to let me live there. Etwa hadn't lost steam; he'd just lost the desire to live in that house after his mother's death.

Remembering this history, I told myself that I had offended him and brought back sad memories. "How insensitive of you!" I thought to myself, trying to figure out what to say that would make Etwa feel better. Suddenly, the still of the night was broken by what sounded like exploding fireworks. A few minutes later, there was a second explosion of cracks and bangs.

Outside the house, somebody shouted, "Etwa! Wake up! Have you gone to sleep? Don't you know that the elephants are destroying Wahib's house?" I opened the door as people flooded into our courtyard. Some carried *mashals*, branches with a kerosene-soaked cloth wound around one end and set alight.

"Quick, Alpa, give me that old rubber tire. I can light that," said Etwa, rushing toward me.

"Yes, yes. And take these as well." My hands were shaking as I tried to insert the batteries into my two flashlights.

Etwa joined the group of young men rushing past our house with their glowing mashals raised. They raced down the slope, skirted the pond, and ran toward Wahib Khan's house, drumming and shouting. They were mainly Mundas.

I joined the women and children on the ridge overlooking the valley outside our house. "Light the fires, light the fires!" shouted Somra's wife to her daughters. "When are you going to light them, when the elephants are here?" We huddled around the small heaps of hay set alight.

"There, there—there they are!" said Mangri, standing up and pointing into the dark night. "Where? There? That's just a *ber* tree!" replied Sanicharwa, poking at the hay with a twig to keep the flames alive. I tried to focus my eyes, looking for the dangerous silhouettes, and watched the lights of the mashals as they snaked toward Wahib's house. Then the line of flames suddenly went out.

THE MANY WAYS TO SHOOT TO KILL

That night, I could not sleep. It was not just that I was afraid of the elephants, but also that I could not stop reflecting on my evolving relationship with those dangerous silhouettes that haunted the night in Tapu. Until I was sixteen, my parents and I lived in Kenya. Most weekends, my sisters and I would plead with our father to take us to one of the numerous national parks in the country—a relatively inexpensive leisure experience for Kenyan nationals promoted by the government. These were spaces of that nostalgic African wilderness—nature as it first was—teeming with wildlife. We'd wake up at 5:00 in the morning or even earlier, scramble into the car, and eagerly await our arrival at the park, singing songs written by our gap-year American teachers that anticipated the sunrise over the savanna:

There's a one-ton, two-horned giant in the sun,
It's a three-toed, four-legged rhino on the run,
For he's all too rare, so do take care,
To shoot him with your camera but never with a gun.

We joined European and American tourists who paid thousands of pounds to sit in open-topped jeeps to travel into the dusty sunrise in search of game. The climax of most such journeys was to see a large cat make a kill—a cheetah or, even better, a lion or a leopard attack a wildebeast, gazelle, impala or some other minor species.

My favorite animal of the big five, as they were called, was either the rhino or the elephant. I had read and reread *To Save an Elephant*, produced by the Environmental Investigation Agency,[1] and my favorite artist was the wildlife painter David Shepherd. Little did I know then that many years later, when I found myself living in a mud hut in what many people would call remote rural India, elephants were going to return to terrorize me.

By the time I left Kenya, it looked like I was going to turn into an avid conservation and animal-rights activist. One route was to pursue an undergraduate degree in geography. But in my final year at Cambridge, I chose an optional course on Africa, taught by Professor Bill Adams, which made me question the nostalgic image of wilderness Africa and what I thought I missed most about life in Kenya.

I also read the work of David Anderson and Richard Grove[2] and realized that I had fully embraced a very particular Euro-American idea of the environment—which prioritized protecting a special kind of Eden overflowing with wildlife, where Euro-Americans could rediscover their lost harmony with nature, in a place that was devoid of Africans. A nature without people.

The institutionalization of this idea of nature, of course, has a long history, as I recognized in 2005 when visiting Yosemite National Park, in the western United States. The first national park in the world, Yosemite was formed in 1872 as an island of wilderness which represented the last remaining place where humans had not fully infected the earth—a place of escape, a refuge to be protected and recovered. Reading the thought-provoking work of William Cronon,[3] I realized that the more one knows about the history of particular national park wildernesses, whether Yosemite in the United States or Amboseli in Kenya, the more one realizes that wilderness is not quite what it seems. Far from being the one place on earth that stands apart from humanity, wilderness is, quite profoundly, a human creation, and its seductive images of untouched nature may say more about the unexamined longings and desires of its producers than about the so-called preservation of the natural world.

John Mackenzie's chapter in Anderson and Grove's book showed that the European desire to conserve the wildlife and habitats of Africa was intimately connected to the European interest in exploiting the continent's natural resources.[4] Current wildlife preservation policies have their roots in concepts of hunting in Africa. From the 1850s to the 1880s, hunting in Africa was a huge part of the colonial economy, especially through the flow of ivory. Europeans employed Africans to hunt elephants and acquire ivory, the profits from which helped finance other colonial missions. With a visible decline in game numbers toward the end of the 1880s, the hunt became a symbol of white dominance, manliness, chivalry, and sportsmanship. Through so-called protective legislation, such as the 1886 Cape Act for the Preservation of Game, Africans were entirely excluded from hunting, as licenses were priced well beyond their reach. Hunting became a white man's preserve. In the twentieth century, this demarcation of the privilege and power of the new rulers of Africa developed into notions of conserving wildlife and attempting to stop all African interference with animals.

In some ways, I thought to myself, lying awake in Tapu as I listened for the elephants, the sport of killing big game was replaced with the sport of watching big game kill. Now the action is once removed—as a tourist, one consumes the kill through an intermediary, another animal, without questioning the fundamental violence of our participation in this form of consumption. There are many ways to shoot to kill. The point is that paradoxically the same view of nature which lies behind the Western drive to conserve it also lies behind the Western drive to exploit it. Conservation and exploitation are both ways of dominating nature, of bringing it under human control.

However, with the looming threat of climate change, and as public attention focuses on the protection of natural resources—especially water, forests, and wildlife—more than ever conservation and the environment are major global businesses. The Discovery Channel and National Geographic have arrived in India, encouraging particular understandings about what constitutes the natural world and the threat it faces. Doordarshan, India's public-television channel, now broadcasts *Earth Matters*, and the educational curriculum is legally required to include instruction in environmental awareness.[5] The audience is middle-class Indians, who increasingly reflect the concerns promoted by a well-meaning global environmental agenda. The ecological romanticism at the heart of these concerns is underpinned by the evolutionist idea that first there was nature, and then man's technological advances progressively altered and often destroyed it. That is the idea of nature that, as Raymond Williams has famously argued, was understood as being all that was not man, neither touched by man nor spoiled by man.[6] The resulting promotion of national parks has gained enormous international currency, not just in Africa but also in Latin America and South Asia. Wildlife sanctuaries and national parks have a long history in India,[7] but they

A road sign in Ranchi City for attracting tourists to Jharkhand.
Photo by author.

are receiving renewed interest. In 2001, for example, the Jharkhand State created its first elephant reserve in the Saranda Forest, in Singhbhum District. The elephant was made the state symbol of Jharkhand and, on a Ranchi road sign aimed at tourists, its image appears alongside the slogan: "Welcome to Jharkhand, a land unspoiled by man or time."

But this global environmental move is often a way for states to increase their own control over productive natural resources. A detrimental result, as Nancy Peluso argues most powerfully, is that conservation ideology can be used by developing states to justify coercion and violence in the name of conservation.[8] This violence is claimed to be legitimate because it is for the global good and can help a state control those who challenge its authority. It is difficult to argue against the moral high ground of actions taken to preserve the world's biological heritage or national security. One of Peluso's examples, elephant protection in Kenya, shows how Masai nomadic pastoralists were gradually moved into fixed settlements and away from their old land in order to preserve the wildlife because nobody believed that the Masai could coexist with the region's wild game—even though they had done so for thousands of years. The environmentalists appeared to be the heroes, and the local people were seen as overpopulating pests. The game reserve authorities restricted Masai seasonal migration with their cattle. When this principal means of livelihood was threatened, the Masai responded by killing rhinos and elephants; in the 1980s, they were alleged to be collaborating with ivory poachers.

Meanwhile, although national parks were justified by moral arguments based on the need to conserve wildlife for the world, it was actually economic factors that were key to the development of game reserves at the expense of marginal communities such as the Masai. Kenya's tourism was contributing about 20 percent of the country's foreign exchange. In the 1980s, global environmental groups collaborated to create CITES, the Convention on International Trade in Endangered Species, and by 1991, its members had signed a declaration to ban the trade in raw ivory in order to protect the elephant. Nancy Peluso's well-made point is that the moral high ground produced by these treaties resulted in very detrimental consequences for marginal communities like the Masai because essentially, in the names of conservation and the environment, these global moves justified the violence of the state against them and the expansion of state control over their territories.[9] In Kenya, for instance, as a result of the CITES ban, I remember that the government armed rangers with automatic rifles and helicopter gunships. In two years, more than a hundred poachers were killed—most of them without a trial or even a chance to talk to officials. Like the military, the rangers were licensed to shoot to kill.

THE SILVER LINING

Thinking through these arguments that night in Tapu, I was filled with the same mixture of emotions that I had felt in 1997. On the whole, I felt frustration and disappointment with myself when I realized I had wholeheartedly bought into myths about the African wilderness. But then the glimmer of a silver lining was provided by those anthropologists who had evidence that the way forward was to see indigenous people not as enemies of the environment, but as people who may have ways to protect it. Inspired by Bill Adams's Africa course, I went the same year to the Cambridge Africa Studies Centre to hear Melissa Leach present a seminar on her groundbreaking work with James Fairhead in Guinea.[10] Their argument began with the fact that the driving force behind much environmental policy in Africa was a set of powerful, widespread images of environmental change—the received wisdom that is supported by the dominant science agenda. Overgrazing, desertification of arid lands, the wood-fuel crisis, removal of pristine forest, soil conservation, population growth—I knew all the problems.

In Guinea, Fairhead and Leach examined an impressive range of archival material to reveal a consistent bias in reporting by foreign observers of the region who, whether writing in the 1980s or in the 1890s, all noted that massive deforestation must have occurred fifty to seventy years before they wrote. Fairhead and Leach said that such deforestation narratives described a pattern of received wisdom for which there was actually little evidence. They analyzed oral histories and remote-sensing information and aerial photographs of past and present vegetation states. Based on this evidence, they proposed that where change had occurred in the last forty years, forests had actually increased: local inhabitants used a variety of techniques to encourage the development of islands of forests around villages, and thus had produced new forests in ancient savanna. Through this challenge to the received wisdom about the West African landscape, Fairhead and Leach drew attention to the need to respect local resource-management strategies, rather than see them and their related population pressures as causes of deforestation.

With the establishment of this new paradigm, indigenous people started to emerge as the natural partners in the global ecological imaginary, because they were now considered to have deep environmental knowledge of the habitat around them. They were now the guardians of information about how best to protect the environment.[11] In treating seriously indigenous concepts of the environment, ecological anthropology has produced a voluminous literature on the facts that different cultures have different understandings of the environment,[12] the nature-culture dualism must be deconstructed,[13] and it is a modern creation[14]—with some anthropologists even arguing for the so-called perspectivist position that some indigenous groups, such as the Amazonian Indians, see the original condition of both humans and animals as humanity, rather than as nature or animality.[15] Others have seriously questioned the boundary between an autonomous nature outside human endeavor, to show that people and the environment are mutually dependent.[16] As indigenous people appear to be the harbingers of a potential global eco-community, perhaps we should listen to the arguments of anthropologists such as Hugh Brody, who—drawing on the example of the hunters and trappers of the Arctic—says the best way to protect the animals and the land on which indigenous people depend is plain: leave it to them.[17]

THE INDIAN ECO-SAVAGE

Edenic bliss may have had a longer history in India than in Africa of being associated with tribal populations who were considered both as savages and as protectors of nature, living in harmony with and even worshiping it.[18] The hope provided by the notion of the eco-savage gained a particular purchase through environmental historians and eco-feminists in India. The best known of this work focused, in particular, on the Chipko Movement. Emerging in the 1970s in what is now the state of Uttaranchal, this movement caught the international imagination because of the captivating imagery that came to be seen as its symbol of resistance—poor tribal peasant women hugging trees.[19] Although, as scholars have argued, the struggle was probably focused on articulating policies and conditions for generating local employment opportunities and fostering regional economic development,[20] Chipko became celebrated internationally as an eco-feminist environmental movement that was recovering traditions. The women of Chipko were allegedly protesting the development trajectory of the modernizing Indian government, which had destroyed local ecologies and ways of life, and were calling for environmental protection and alternative paths to development.

A series of public intellectuals internationally promoted the Chipko story as evidence that rural Indian women were nature's true custodians[21] and depicted a golden age in precolonial India. During this time, traditional indigenous communities were natural conservationists who lived in socially harmonious and environmentally sensitive ways. This age was destroyed with the onslaught of colonialism, science, and development.[22] Much important work criticizes these arguments as somewhat romanticized and producing a "standard environmental narrative"[23] or "new traditionalist discourse"[24] that is deeply problematic. However, the golden-age rhetoric matches the current transnational idea of contemporary indigenous communities as eco-savages, natural conservationists, the living remnants of India's cultures that once naturally preserved the environment. The idea of a golden age also appeals to the indigenous rights activists who seek to protect today's adivasis by showing them as living in harmony with nature and worshiping it.

Images of environmental bliss in precolonial communities, and their isolated and threatened contemporary successors, have been combined with a critique of the modernizing, Western-influenced development strategies of the centralized state. In particular, there has been some criticism of previous state-driven forestry programs by various intellectuals.[25] These debates are reflected in the efforts by the Indian Ministry of Environment and Forests to involve knowledgeable local communities in Joint Forest Management (JFM).[26] This increased focus on local communities is prompted by the reemergence among international developmental and environmental activists of a concern for community empowerment and local participation.[27] Indeed, the representations of indigenous people as forest dwellers are now big business in Jharkhand, as NGOs and bilateral and multilateral developmental agencies flood into the new state. In 2004, the World Bank proposed a Jharkhand Participatory Forestry Management Project, to devote approximately $60 million to "improve the livelihoods of poor forest-dependent communities by increasing their access to and control over natural resources."[28] Indigenous communities are simultaneously viewed as those who have the answers to development dilemmas, and those who have to be protected and helped.[29] Despite the fact that some academics question the role of ecological romanticism, a perceived decline of the control of indigenous communities over their environment and the need to return this power to them has infiltrated the public imagination, having been reproduced by many journalists, environmentalists, activists, and development workers.

The 2000 separation of Jharkhand, the so-called land of the forests, from Bihar within the Indian federal union went hand in hand with a renewed interest in "ecological nationalism"[30] from Jharkhand's indigenous rights activists. This centered on the region's nature-loving, nature-protecting indigenous communities, enshrined in images essentializing adivasi religion as nature worshiping. While the cultural identity of Jharkhand's indigenous populations was thought to emanate from various sources—their "simplicity, truthfulness, mythical life, simple rituals, equality, freedom, hunting, dance and music"[31]—the forests, part of the new state's name, became one of the most important symbols of Jharkhand. The forests were argued to be an expression of the spirit of Jharkhand's exploited indigenous communities, inherently in tune and in love with nature.[32] Indigenous people's relationship with the forest was stressed as one of the most important unique aspects of Jharkhand, something that was not present to the same extent in neighboring Bihar. Indigenous rights activists have created a Jungle Bachao Andolan (Save the Forest Movement) and mobilize around the protection of their jungle, jamin, and jal.

"The adivasi youth of the new generations are forgetting the names of plants found in Jharkhand, even the most common ones," complained one of the activists, standing in front of a map of Jharkhand in the Ranchi City office of the Save the Forest Movement. "These are the areas where we have formed village committees to patrol and protect the forests and learn about its uses," he said, pointing to dots spread out across the map. "The forests are a central pillar of adivasi identity, and we can't let them forget that."

Fearful of the Hindu nationalists who seek to incorporate adivasis into mainstream Hinduism,[33] Jharkhandi activists have also been promoting a separate indigenous religion comparable to Christianity, Islam, and Hinduism that is sometimes called Sarna and sometimes Adi-dharam.[34] The latter literally means the beginnings of the religious beliefs of the adivasis, and the former, a sacred grove of trees. Supported by scholarship proposing that tree worship has a long history among Indian tribal populations,[35] with sacred groves being preserved as untouched primary forests because of the people's deep religious sentiments,[36] Jharkhandi activists argue that central to the concept of Sarna dharam is the worship of nature, showing the naturalistic base of Jharkhand's indigenous communities.[37]

"Did you hear about the villagers in Bero Block who got together to lift out a baby elephant who had fallen into a well?" one activist asked me in February 2007. "The villagers returned her to her mother, who thanked them by trumpeting. You see, this is the classic example of how adivasis live in harmony with nature." Such examples are common in globally celebrated accounts of the supposed cultural disposition of indigenous people to protect nature,[38] and of the need to preserve this environmentally harmonious cultural heritage. The indigenous rights activists argue that the government, dominated by exploitative outsiders collaborating with contractors, has demolished the region's forests for commercial purposes, and now control of the

The sacred grove in Tapu. *Photo by author.*

forests should be returned to Jharkhand's indigenous populations, who have always lived in harmony with nature.[39]

In my bed in Tapu that night of the elephant attack, I kept tossing and turning, mulling over these issues. We do need to rethink our conventional wisdom and respect other ways of living in the world. In our environmental and conservation policies, we do need to seriously consider the proposition that Western middle-class ideas of nature and the environment are the product of particular social and historical circumstances and may have detrimental consequences for marginalized populations, from whose knowledge systems and relationships with the environment we can learn. But doesn't the idea of indigenous people representing the core values of the eco-community say far more about a generic stereotype that is currently in vogue in the international public sphere than it does about the diversity and complexity of indigenous peoples' relationship with their environment? The potential dangers of this popular idea have been outlined with great clarity and wit by Beth Conklin and Laura Graham in the Brazilian context, where eco-conscious celebrities like Sting joined hands with the Kayapo. However, once the Kayapo had had some success in claiming land rights, they—perhaps understandably—rushed straight into the arms of the market economy, granting timber companies contracts to cut down hardwoods.[40] In

India, Amita Baviskar shows a widening gap in Madhya Pradesh between the higher-caste, middle-class activists who seek to preserve the purist model of adivasis as practicing sustainable eco-development and protecting their natural resources, and the emerging tribal leaders who, like the Kayapo, want a share of the benefits from resource-intensive industrialization.[41] Aren't indigenous communities shot through with unequal power relations, aren't they internally stratified, and isn't it anachronistic to call them natural environment conservators?[42] Government rules often assume that resource management by communities is autonomous and traditional, and many notions of community might be nothing more than the products of officials and politicians.[43]

In Jharkhand, it seems that the image of the celebrated eco-savage is costing lives. Neither the government nor indigenous rights activists seem to care at all about the poor adivasis in villages like Tapu, who despair as by day they try to repair the damage wrought by the wild elephants, and by night they try to chase away the dangerous silhouettes. They are not allowed to kill the elephants or to cut down the forests which have brought the elephants there. But nobody wants to hear their fears today, when indigenous people are supposed to be nature lovers and nature worshipers.

THE STATE AS AN ELEPHANT

Three elephants had attacked Wahib's house from separate directions, leaving three elephant-sized holes. What we had heard that sounded like fireworks had been the snapping of the bamboo and wood framework, and the crashing of roof tiles as Wahib's roof fell down. Wahib's ducks were in a flap, and his goats had watched the elephants eat most of his harvest of about thirty kilograms of rice and fifteen kilograms of wheat, which had been stored in the front room of the house. Wahib and his wife had tried to hide their petrified children in the back room and had then stood paralyzed in the doorway between the two rooms.

The elephants had calmly walked away when the villagers from the main hamlet had come toward Wahib's house, making a commotion. The animals then visited the next village, destroyed another house, were chased away from there, and returned to Tapu to eat potatoes in one of the fields. This was their usual pattern. In the daytime, the

One side of Wahib's house, destroyed by elephants. *Photo by author.*

Elephant damage to crops in Tapu. *Photo by author.*

elephants rested in the sal forest; at dusk, seeking more food, they ventured out either to the fields to feast on the crops, or toward the houses, where husked rice and grain were stored. Experts on the Indian elephant have argued that most of the damage to crops by elephants takes place because of rogue males.[44] I found no evidence of that in Jharkhand, where herds of animals made their way through crops. As the attack on Wahib's house showed, the damage to houses was often done by entire families of elephants, calves included. When the elephants were in the forest near one set of villages, they would be chased from one village to another until they eventually moved further afield, to a different set of villages—perhaps eventually returning to their starting point. Nobody was sure exactly how many elephants there were, and although I never saw a herd larger than six, others had sighted twelve and even sixteen animals together.

Over the next year in Tapu, one woman was kicked by an elephant and received severe back injuries, four more houses were destroyed, and many crops were eaten. In the hamlet by the river, people got tired of chasing elephants night after night. In the villages immediately surrounding Tapu, nine people were crushed to death—including Bhim Mahato, a man brought by the government from West Bengal to the Tapu area because he had a national reputation for chasing elephants away. This raised the total number of elephant deaths in Bero Block since 1987 to 60, and in Jharkhand State since 1995 to around 230.[45]

In Tapu, the former tenants, the majority of whom were Mundas, suffered the greatest share of the damage inflicted by elephants. Their houses were usually the ones attacked because they were located on the outskirts of the hamlets and thus the most exposed, while they protected the interior houses of the landlord descendants. The Mundas were also the most affected by the elephant attacks on crops, not only because their fields were usually on the edges of the forest but also because—unlike the landlord descendants, whose livelihoods came from multiple sources—the Mundas' income came from manual labor and crops from their fields.

After chasing the elephants away that night, Etwa came home in despair. He said, "In the neighboring areas, the Naxalites [left-wing guerrillas] have taken over the jungle, and here it is the elephants. Sarkar [the state] made us protect the jungle. This jungle has attracted the elephants, but sarkar does not allow us to kill the animals.[46] Sarkar has made us suffer."[47] Over the next year, I heard more frequently the complaint from the Mundas that elephant destruction had become one more example of the dangers of the expanded reach of the state.

"Chopping down trees?" I asked Mangra one day. "But how will you live without the forest?"

"After all, not so long ago there were no elephants here because there was no forest. It is only recently that the protection of small plants has resulted in the growth of the jungle, attracting the elephants. We've managed before, and we can manage again."

"No forest?" I was puzzled.

Listening to the stories that some of the older Mundas in Tapu tell today, it appears that their ancestors recalled a time when Tapu was surrounded by trees with trunks wider than their arms could circle, but the village was not then visited by elephants. These older Mundas say that over time, the forests increased and decreased, but around the 1970s, there was barely any forest around Tapu (although the hamlets and their peripheries still had mango, jackfruit, tamarind, and other useful trees). Some say that this serious depletion of trees was a result of the deals struck between zamindars and outside contractors to take away trees as timber. However, I was surprised that most of the middle-aged and younger Mundas believed the recent trajectory was one of aforestation, not deforestation, contrary to the conventional representations of environmental change in Jharkhand—which, in the words of Melissa Leach and Robin Mearns, is a "lie of the land."[48] These younger generations recall recent times of sparse forest, and they are concerned that the forest has regrown as a result of government policy.

In the last two decades, on the orders of forest officers and the landlord descendants, Mundas had to prevent other villagers from venturing into the Tapu forest for fuel and timber. Moreover, there were also regulations on the Mundas' forest use. They were only allowed to use certain branches for fuel and could no longer freely cut trees to build houses and plows. While the trees were protected, the Mundas were left powerless to kill the wild elephants that damaged their crops and houses—a powerlessness imposed by the state.[49] When the livelihoods of Mundas, dependent on the crops in their fields and their mud houses, are being destroyed, it is not surprising that the more skeptical, like Etwa and Mangra, now ask why the state made them protect the forest which has attracted the elephants. They wonder whether this is yet one more case in which, as Etwa said, "It is the officers, together with the descendants of the village landlords, who reap the benefits—and we who have to suffer."

Given the advocacy of Ranchi-based indigenous rights activists, who sought to promote indigenous people as nature worshipers, I was also surprised that Etwa's and Mangra's attitude seemed to show a lack of care for the forests rather than a worship of them.

"But what will you worship if you don't have the forests?" I asked Mangra.

"The spirits that live in the trees can be moved, as long as they are well looked after in their new homes. After all, that is what our ancestors did when they first cleared this area for settlement. And, after all, it is the spirits that we worship, and not the forests."

I understood this point more clearly when I witnessed the festival of Phagun, or Fagua, as it was called in Tapu. In constructing Sarna religion as nature worship, Jharkhandi rights activists argue that the spring festivals such as Sarhul and Phagun mark the welcoming of nature in its new form, or the arrival of the new year.[50] Since Jharkhand's independence, large celebrations of Sarhul in Ranchi, Jharkhand's capital, have begun on a fixed date each year as a marker of adivasi religion that is not subsumed by the Hindu Ramnami or Muslim Moharram, which happen around the same time.[51] The activists call the rituals of the Sarhul and Phagun celebrations by the Hindu term *puja*, and, in an effort to domesticate what they consider the jangli practices of their rural counterparts, they offer coconuts, flowers, and water in the urban festivals, instead of the villagers' offerings of alcohol and animal sacrifices. Although these are efforts specifically created to keep the spread of Hindu Nationalism at bay, such attempts to civilize adivasi religiosity are ironically similar to the arguments of the extreme right-wing Hindu Nationalist BJP that Jharkhand's tribals are merely fallen high castes whose proper status should be restored by converting them into real Hindus through Sanskritization — that is, the adoption of upper-caste values by lower castes in order to increase their status.[52] However, since the explicit cultural goal of the activists is to form an adivasi religion that is not Hindu, David Hardiman is correct in observing that we cannot call their activities Sanskritization, as this concept does not include the challenge to upper-caste power by those lower down in the caste hierarchy.[53] Nevertheless, in Tapu and the surrounding villages, these festivals had an altogether different significance. Not only were all such festivals on different days each year and celebrated on different days in each village, but the symbolism of the festivals was also far removed from the worship of some autonomous nature with mere flowers and water.

3:00 A.M., 28 MARCH 2002

Mangra was clearly angry. On the orders of the pahan, he had been trying to wake up the Munda young men for the first part of Fagua. Eventually a group of young men gathered outside our courtyard, rubbing their eyes. A branch of a *sember* (*Bombax malabaricum*) tree, with three other branches forking off it, was brought by two of the men and planted in the soil. At its base, the pahan and the paenbharra broke an egg. The branches were covered in hay, two braids of hay were placed over this pile, and the heap was set alight. As the braids caught fire, Mangra and another young man—each carrying one braid—ran to the fringe of the forest, to two rocks in opposite directions. The flaming pile of hay fell to the ground as the pahan chopped off the planted branch. When the fire died out, the remaining part of the stump was slit at the top to insert a sember bud that was left to flower and then blow away.

With its use of leafy branches, hay, and flowers, the festival can easily be interpreted as being about the worship of nature. However, as I came to understand in Tapu, this small affair represented a reliving of the time when the Mundas first settled in an area. At this time, in order to prepare land for settlement, they burned off and cut down the forest and rehoused the spirits that had lived in the cleared patch. The pile of hay on the branches thus represented the forest, and the braids of hay, the spirits. In fact, the braids were called *chendis*, the same name given to some of the spirits of the village. Hence, as the forest was set alight, the two young men rehoused the braids of hay, or the spirits.[54]

But this was only the beginning of the ritual. At dawn of the following morning, only several hours later, I accompanied three unmarried men through different parts of the forest and fields belonging to the village. We went to eight sites, marked either by a tree or a rock; each was the residence of one of eight different chendis. The first and last of these sites were where the two braids of hay had been taken when the miniature forest was set alight early the previous day. In the past, the young men had performed this ritual naked; these days, despite the urging of the older Mundas, they refused to do so out of embarrassment, and they wore lungis around their waists instead. At the sites, the men washed the spirits and gave them rice, rice beer, *sindhoor* (vermilion), and a cotton thread. Whereas the ritual burning the day before had recreated the initial deforestation to make the settlement, these visits to the rocks and trees marked the initial stage of a sacrifice to the spirits who had to be appeased, since they had been displaced.

On our return, a tepee-like structure, made of a framework of branches covered with hay, was in place in the hamlet. A young, unmarried man, who had just taken a bath, crouched inside it. There, he acted as if he was about to sacrifice a frog by enacting the first stages of animal sacrifice and trying to make the frog eat rice. But, in fact, he let the frog escape and broke an egg instead. At the same time, the symbolic forest—the tepee—was set on fire, and the man ran out.[55] To one side, a mixture of cow dung and *erendi* fruit was boiled, then distributed on eight large leaf plates and several smaller ones laid out along a path. People were prohibited from visiting the area for another day. Then the rest of the festival was celebrated, with an abundance of rice beer.

It is difficult to understand all the symbolism of these latter rituals, as the Mundas explain parts of them by saying only, "We do it this way as it has always been done this way." However, the mixture on the plates was food for the spirits and their invited guests. And if one believed the rumors about this part of the ritual, in the past, the young man in the tepee was the human sacrifice to appease the displaced spirits. When human sacrifice became taboo, the frog came to represent the human,[56] and the breaking of the egg that followed the release of the frog the surrogate sacrifice, and the tepee on fire the symbolic cooking of the human to appease the displaced spirits.[57] Today, animal sacrifice is the central ritual component of every festival in Tapu and on all inauspicious occasions, such as sickness or crop failure. If blood sacrifices were not performed, the spirits would bring disease, famine, and even death. To the Mundas, the festivals were not about worshiping some autonomous nature, as conceptualized by Jharkhandi activists in the form of trees and flowers; rather, they were about appeasing spirits that are intimately a part of their environment.

The concept promoted by indigenous rights activists of adivasis' worshiping nature with flowers and water is therefore a purified and commodified representation of nature that is at odds with the realities experienced by many villagers.[58] For the activists to acknowl-

Rituals of the Fagua festival in Tapu. *Photo by author.*

Preparing rice beer for the Fagua festival in Tapu. *Painting by Deepa Shah.*

edge that these nature-worshiping rituals are in fact rather bloody, that they are centered around appeasing spirits with rice beer and through animal sacrifice, and that the original sacrifice was probably that of a human, is all too close to colonial ideas of the jangli tribal in need of civilization. In fact, a central part of the purification of adivasi rituals as they are promoted in the cities by the activists is that—like the missionaries who were their predecessors in the early twentieth century[59]—they are actively encouraging a move away from the allegedly barbaric practice of animal sacrifice and instead promoting the cracking of coconuts, while at the same time substituting water for rice beer.[60]

In fact, the Mundas' attitude toward the forest was always more complex than merely inherent love. The forest was often feared. Certain parts of the forest (and the fields) were avoided, especially at night. Particularly so were the areas inhabited by malevolent *churels*, the unhappy spirits of women who had died suddenly. In the hottest months of the year, children, in particular, avoided certain areas of the forest for fear of being kidnapped by the pahans of neighboring villages, who were waiting for victims to sacrifice to the spirits.[61] The interpretation given to me was not that this was the time of the year when the Hindu goddess Kali was most thirsty,[62] but that these were the months of initial deforestation for settlement, when the spirits required sacrifices for the violence of their original displacement.

While the evidence from Tapu encourages a more sophisticated reading of nature worship than that proposed by the Jharkhandi activists, there is no doubt more to be said for the argument that the livelihoods of the Mundas are dependent on forest resources. There are, however, certain important caveats to note. First, it is true that wood from the forests is important as fuel, for the making of plows and other tools, and for the building of houses—roof frameworks and doors, in particular. It is also true that leaves from the forests are important as plates and cups. However, the first point to note is that this does not make the Mundas natural conservationists.[63] The second point to note is that although most Mundas wonder how life can be lived in England without forests, a few were quick to point out that "if only we had electricity and brick houses, we could do away with the forest."

And what about Munda dependence on other parts of the forest, often referred to as nontimber forest products? It is true that a multitude of fruits, seeds, leaves, flowers, mushrooms, and vegetables form an important supplement to the village diet (of Mundas and

Collecting firewood in Tapu. *Photo by author.*

others), especially for families who grow only rice or who have low yields from cultivated crops.[64] However, it is also true that many, though not all, of these products are actually found on trees in the hamlets, fields, and forest margins, and that it was not often that Tapu villagers ventured far into the forest in search of the evening meal. Only some men and women in Tapu knew where to find many of the more specialized products.[65] Furthermore, the forests were not thought of as starkly distinct from the crops in the fields,[66] or in opposition to the village.[67] The Mundas saw the forest as part of a landscape continuous with the fields and, like the crops in the fields and trees in the hamlets, were, over time, both cut and protected by them.

The Mundas' relationship with their environment is too sophisticated, and sometimes too adversarial, to allow for a simplistic reading of them as worshiping nature or living in harmony with it. It is thus hardly surprising that when faced by the everyday threat of elephants to their livelihoods, they feared the forest, the space frequented by the animals, or that many of the younger Mundas advocated chopping the forest down to keep elephants from venturing into the vicinity. In fact, in the neighboring village, state forest guards threatened a group of men who were cutting down some sal trees.

SAVAGE ATTACK

12:00 P.M., 20 FEBRUARY 2007

I was in the Ranchi office of the Principal Chief Conservator of Forests and Wildlife. Peering at me across the large, empty, shiny wooden desk sat a burly, bald man, who wore a smart suit and had a sparkling scalp. This was the top man for forests and wildlife in the entire State of Jharkhand. I sat up straight in my chair, smoothed my hair, and repositioned the scarf across my shoulder, feeling rather disheveled in the huge, white room, faced with his domineering presence. I had asked to see him because I was frustrated that my friend Shiv had still not received the Rs 33,000 that he was due from an attack by a wild boar in the Tapu forest more than three years before. After discussing the case of Shiv, we moved on to more general discussions about the problem of the wild elephants in the Bero area.

"People from the villages just have to learn to live with the elephants. There is no other solution," he said adamantly.

"But how is this possible when the elephants are tearing down their houses and eating their crops every night?" I asked.

"There are four important things they must do." He looked at his fist and opened his fingers one by one. "First, they must learn how to chase the elephants. Second, they must not keep rice in their houses. Third, they must learn how to worship Ganesh Devta. And fourth, they must stop drinking rice beer and mahua wine."

My jaw dropped. I was stunned by his comments, especially his last two statements. I could not believe that he was openly reiterating the kind of prejudice against the adivasis that I was so used to hearing from the sadans of Tapu.

When I pointed out to members of the elites of Tapu that in fact it was the Mundas who suffered the worst elephant damage, their answer sometimes was that this was hardly surprising, given that the Mundas do not pray to Ganesh, the elephant god. But, most often, their response was that the elephants attacked people who were drunk and houses that stored mahua wine and rice beer. It might be true that elephants enjoy wine and beer. However, I was struck by the fact that such comments were a savage attack on Mundas and starkly reflected the prejudices of these purified, Brahminicized and Sanskritized castes toward those they considered lower in the social hierarchy.

As I argued in the last chapter, the rural elites' attitude toward Munda development—or, rather their underdevelopment—was that they were jangli. Apart from their lack of sexual control, discussed further in the next chapter, which resulted in overpopulation, one of the most dominant aspects of this jangliness was their allegedly copious drinking. The elites of the village, who generally aspired to move up the social scale by Sanskritizing and Brahminicizing, or emulating upper-caste values, claimed that drinking alcohol was morally wrong and ritually impure. In fact, not one of the houses and people I knew that had been attacked had been storing or drinking alcohol at the time. Moreover, as I described in chapter 2, in Tapu, drinking homemade brew was a central and respectable part of Munda ritual life: their deities needed alcohol to be appeased, it was common to pour a libation before starting to drink, and men and women of different generations openly drank together. Mundas were proud to belong to the Jungle Raj and enjoyed ways of life that were different from those of the village elites. Nevertheless, Munda ideas of their own practices were suppressed by the village elites, who perpetuated the view that those who suffer the most are those who are the most jangli. Moreover, as an example of the savageness of the Mundas, I was once told that the high number of adivasi deaths due to elephant attacks was the result of adivasis' leaving marginal family members in front of the animals!

The elites of the village—the sadans, the descendants of the landlords—told a different story than the Mundas' to scholars and NGO workers about the elephant invasions. Elaborating a neo-Malthusian trajectory that begins with elephants and humans living in harmony with each other, the sadans claimed that forest depletion caused elephants to invade habitable land. The elites place the blame for deforestation squarely on the jangli Munda—the majority in the area, who had overpopulated and overused the environment, and therefore were suffering the consequences. "It is we, the sadans, who have created a Forest Protection Committee here in the village. It is we who make sure that these jangli people don't cut the trees in the forest. If it wasn't for us, there would be no forest in this area," said Popat Odhar, when I asked him about the Forest Protection Committee, of which he was president. The sadans took the credit for the subsequent forest maintenance and protection, claiming that they had ensured that the Mundas copied their actions. In this account, elephant damage was the result of deforestation by a jangli Munda majority to be corrected by their patrons, the elites of the village.

Why the elites of Tapu wanted to appear as patrons of the local environment can be explained to a significant degree by their desire to maintain their mediating role between the state and the resources it feeds into the local areas through forestry and development programs. Presenting themselves as protectors of the local environment and at the same time blaming the Munda majority for the violent consequences of damage to the forest, these elites are able to augment their own legitimacy, vis-à-vis their Mundas competitors, as the worthy and deserving beneficiaries of state resources.[68]

As shown in the last two chapters, while the Mundas kept away from the state, after the abolition of zamindari, the elites of the village maintained or developed their dominant material position, vis-à-vis the majority of the villagers, through intimate links with the state. They were the chairpersons and executive members of the village Forest Protection Committee, recognized by the government under the JFM program. They colonized the resources coming into the village through the forest department: kerosene, firecrackers (to help scare elephants away), and, in later years, a gas tank and solar panels intended for the common good of the village, could be found in their houses. When Neel Odhar gave Wahib five liters of kerosene and firecrackers after the elephant attack on Wahib's house, Wahib believed these had come from Neel's household resources rather than the forest department. When Neel gave Dhuta Rs 1,400 to help pay the initial Ranchi hospital costs after his mother had been kicked by an elephant, Dhuta thought that this money had come from Neel, and not from the village Forest Protection Committee. Later, when Dhuta's mother received compensation from the forest office, the money arrived via Popat Odhar (Neel's uncle), who took Rs 1,000 for the forest officers and Rs 1,000 for himself from the first installment of Rs 8,300.[69]

After an Oraon woman from the neighboring village was trampled to death in October 2001 while picking mushrooms in the Tapu forest, some of the rural elites of the area laid the body (minus the head and one arm) in the middle of the national highway in Bero. They mobilized the adivasi villagers of the surrounding areas to stop traffic, and a line of trucks soon stretched as far as the eye could see. Barefoot men in lungis, asked by the landlord descendants to come with their bows and arrows, sticks, and spears to reproduce the barbarous imagery of adivasis, led the protest on one side of the road, with women and children behind them. On the other side of the road stood the rural elites, dressed in trousers and shirts, the spokespeople of these adivasis. A few hours later, when the district forest officer had arrived from Ranchi, two landlord descendants criticized the government for not caring about the poor adivasis who were being victimized by the elephants. The elites were careful, however, to distance themselves from their barefoot fellow villagers, telling the officers that these adivasis were so angry that they would stay on the road for several days. When the block development officer and the forest officer finally each gave Rs 5,000 as immediate compensation to the family of the dead woman, the elites allowed the crowd to disperse, and the traffic blockade was called off. Later that night, some of the more politically active landlord descendants were merrily drinking away some of their cut from this compensation, and they conjured up a plan to form a Chase the Elephant Front.

Some Mundas were aware of the contradictory faces of these village elites—acting as the Mundas' patrons, while hijacking resources in the name of the poor. For example, the Mundas recognized that the landlord descendants and state officials colluded to pocket state monetary compensation for elephant damage. However, most Mundas also saw such compensation as part of the dirty business the state did in the name of development, in which they did not want to be involved. Indeed, there was much discussion about how, although it was impossible for a Munda to kill an elephant without going to jail, certain landlord descendants, together with state officials, were selling illegal ivory for great sums of money.

In April 2002, while grazing cattle in the forest, Jogo Munda and Ramsee Yadav stumbled across two pieces of an elephant tooth. A few days later, forest guards arrived in Tapu and threatened to arrest Jogo if he did not give up his share. Ramsee, the landlord descendant, was ignored by the guards, and a rumor circulated in some Munda households that he was selling his share hundreds of miles away, in the city of Benares. The Mundas speculated that the landlord descendants had informed the forest guards about Jogo's find and that they, in cahoots with the guards, would sell off both pieces of the tooth and keep the profits.

So when the politically active landlord descendants from neighboring villages appeared to speak on behalf of the poor and formed what some might describe as a social movement, the Chase the Elephant Front, creating further road blockades to make the state pay compensation for elephant damage, the more skeptical Mundas said that this performance did not reflect any genuine concern for poor villagers. Despite the fact that the rural elites who formed this movement explicitly stated during long meetings that their activities were not political, the Mundas saw such endeavors as being linked to the dirty world of politics and the state, a way for the rural elites to get their names in the newspapers to be recognized by politicians and state officers in Ranchi, so as to become part of their big world.

ELEPHANTS AS NATURE OUT OF PLACE

In this chapter, I have focused on how the production by indigenous rights activists of the eco-savage—the nature worshiping, nature-loving adivasi—may be costing lives. Trying to domesticate the jangli adivasis, indigenous rights activists have revived a Sarna religion as the emblem of the adivasi's inherent love of nature. The new state government made the elephant its symbol, to show that in Jharkhand, man and animal live in harmony with each other. However, as I have shown, in Tapu and the surrounding villages, Munda propitiation of their spirits with animal sacrifices and plenty of alcohol is not and cannot be reduced to nature worship. Moreover, in fact, poor adivasis spend night after night chasing away elephants that are killing people, destroying their homes, and consuming their crops.

Lévi-Strauss long ago argued that animals are "good to think with."[70] In Jharkhand, wild elephants bring out contradictory ideas about the forest and people's relationship to it. This makes the elephants good to think with about notions of the environment. The Mundas of Tapu, the elites of the village, and the Jharkhandi activist accounts have three interrelated but different explanations of the problem of wild elephants and the related history of forest use in the area. Analyzing these accounts, it appears that the way in which different people construct their environment cannot be simplified to a causal relationship with culture, but instead is affected by how their representations impinge on their livelihoods, which in turn is dependent on the relationship they have with other people around them. We need to move on from cultural constructions of the environment and show how representations of the environment are rooted in material reality[71] and are situated in, and emerge from, the socio-political context of the relationships among people struggling over material resources for their livelihoods.

While the rural elites and the Jharkhandi activists stress a trajectory of forest depletion, they blame different people for the depletion of the forests. The sadans blame the jangli Mundas, who are potentially their direct competitors for state resources. By appearing to be the real protectors and patrons of their villages, these elites legitimize their mediating role with developmental agencies, such as the state, to secure control over resources coming into the rural areas. The urban-based, educated activists—whose own livelihoods as journalists, writers, NGO workers, and representatives of indigenous communities to foreign donors are centered around the protection of nature-loving indigenous people—blame outsiders for forest depletion. Despite these differences, both the rural elites and the Jharkhandi activists are interested in further protecting the forest. The Mundas, however, who face the violence of the elephants most directly, are far more interested in the time when elephants were absent from the area. The younger generations argue that this was the case thirty years ago, when there were no forests, and they attribute the elephant invasion to collusion between state officers and the village elites, who encouraged the protection of trees that in turn attracted elephants. To some Mundas, a possible solution is thus to cut down the forest. While they may advocate this action, it is not a practical solution, as the Mundas are materially dependent on some forest products, especially wood for cooking in the absence of electricity and gas. Nevertheless, forest conservation policies in Jharkhand have ironically led to a Munda perspective that attributes the destruction done by wild elephants to growth of the forest, a direct reflection of the expansion of state control in the area.[72] The elephants have become almost a metaphor for the dangers of the state.

Can Munda voices be heard today, when, internationally, people are increasingly concerned with putting the use and abuse of the environment under close surveillance? Does aligning the rural poor with nature encourage them to be placed outside the world of politics—the politics of representational and development dilemmas from which the poorest people should be protected? Promoting representations of forest-dwelling indigenous people as part of a cultural and political struggle for indigenous rights should not, as some have argued,[73] be read in Gramscian terms of a struggle for hegemony in the cultural and political arena. Instead, it may actually represent a passive revolution[74] of the urban, educated, middle-class activists, who have little support from the poorest rural masses. Such representations should also be seen as big business in Jharkhand.

It is hardly surprising, then, that the elephant-human conflict in the rural areas of Jharkhand has not become a priority on the agenda of indigenous activists. The everyday life of the poorest villagers in rural Jharkhand, such as the Mundas of Tapu, often undermines indigenous rights activists' representations of them. Since their own livelihoods and causes are dependent on simplistic, culturalist representations of Jharkhandi villagers, the activists are often more comfortable living in cities like Ranchi. From this base, they are able to create the fetishized representations of Jharkhand that are underpinned by the cultural difference of its indigenous people, symbolized by their closeness to nature. The activists are hence able to domesticate as nature worship what they see as the jangli imagery of alcoholic and bloody sacrifices to the spirits. And they cautiously flirt with the development industry that is increasingly pumping money into the rural landscape for the preservation of the oppressed, nature-worshiping indigenous populations and for the protection of their forests.

While the indigenous activists seek to reproduce an image of adivasis living in harmony with nature, even using examples such as an elephant's being removed from a well to support this, the Mundas in Tapu have a very different interpretation of such events. "Of course the baby elephant had to be removed from the well. Otherwise not only would the water be poisoned, but the herd would attack the village," said Etwa. The elephants produce a range of responses that raise a complicated set of issues concerning indigenous people's sophisticated relationship with their environment. Elephants are inconveniently nature out of place.[75] By enticing the Mundas to chop down the forest, elephants jeopardize the activist constructions of the adivasis and the environment. In its most fetishized representation, indigenous culture is authentic only when it retains its links with nature. Elephants bring to the surface rural people's complex relationship with and ideas of their environment that threaten the myth of their love for and worship of nature. Environmental protection and ecological romanticism are remote concerns for the Mundas, as they feel that their livelihoods are at risk because of, and not in spite of, the forest.[76] Ignoring people's relationships with each other and the politics of their struggle for livelihoods enables the reproduction, rightly questioned by many scholars, of the fetishized ideal of nature-loving indigenous communities. In Tapu, it is not deforestation but aforestation which some use to explain the threat of elephants to the poorest villagers. But such perspectives will remain buried in the current global environment, where there is a strong incentive to reproduce ideas of indigenous communities that are essentialized as loving nature. Indeed, representations of nature-loving indigenous communities are in danger of becoming a new variety of Orientalism that serves the agenda of its proponents, rather than the varied demands of the people it claims to speak for.

4:00 A.M., 28 FEBRUARY 2007

I sat up straight in bed. I had just heard the sound of leaves being dragged close to my ear. I sat still for a moment. There was the sound again, just on the other side of the mud wall.

"Etwa, Etwa, wake up! They're pulling down Jubu's banana tree."

Once more the familiar ritual of chasing the elephants began. I got out of the house just in time to see two large, muddy brown silhouettes walk away in the moonlight, heading into the forest.

Seven years after Wahib's house was broken, the situation in Tapu for the poorest villagers is worse than ever. Fourteen more houses—15 percent of the village's houses—have been damaged. Far more crops—almost everyone's crop—have been damaged every year. The wheat, peas, and potatoes were eaten; other crops such as onions, coriander, or mustard were trampled. In a village where the poorest people live off their fields, this is a huge amount of damage—not just in terms of the labor lost or the cost of the inputs, but in terms of everyday food consumed in the households. People still chased the elephants night after night. Many people have now stopped farming as much wheat as they used to, and those who do raise significant amounts of it spend two extra hours every other night spraying their fields with a mixture of elephant dung and phenol, which appears to keep the elephants away. As the person in Tapu who designed this ingenious solution of manually spraying the fields with dung commented, "nobody would like to eat something that smells like their own shit." Crop compensation, firecrackers, or injury or death compensation are mere bandages to cover the slow death of the rural poor in the Bero area. From the poorest people's perspective, since they can neither kill the elephants nor chop down the forests, the only solution is to remove the elephants from the Bero area.

We gathered back in our front room after Mangra let off a few firecrackers. Fifteen minutes later, we heard more being fired by people in the next village. It was too late to go back to sleep, but too early to do anything else. I had returned to Tapu after giving a lecture at the Asian Development Research Institute in Ranchi to about sixty people—mainly indigenous rights activists, politicians, wildlife specialists, academics, forest department officials, and NGO workers. My talk had focused on the problem of wild elephants, and I was exasperated by the fact that the discussion afterward seemed to have been captured either by the indigenous rights activists, who used the platform to propound their nature-worshiping views, or by those whose attitudes seemed to reflect what the forestry official had told me in Ranchi: "I am a forester. My interest is in the protection of wildlife and biodiversity. You are an anthropologist. Your concern is man. You won't find my views palatable."[77]

I recounted to Etwa and Mangra the fact that as a result of this lecture I had just seen a Jharkhand Forest Department film, "a true story," according to the film, about two elephants who had strayed from the "forest" (by which was meant the villages around Bero) in April 2004 and who were "lovingly" rescued from Ranchi City—after they had visited the gardens of the large industrialist Birla and even the governor's house, and before being sent back to the "forest."[78]

At this point, Etwa laughed. "The elephants are themselves so fed up with the situation that they decided to go to Ranchi to make their voices heard. They're saying 'If you don't care about the villagers of Bero, now at least listen to us whom you have made your state symbol. Take us somewhere else where we can live more peacefully.'" As I reflect on where this alternative space can be, I cannot help but wonder whether Yosemite would be a better home for the wild elephants of Jharkhand.[79] Yet I know that the regional border patrols that are central to curtailing the emergence of a liberatory politics, which may better serve the adivasis, would bar the elephants' departure. In this case, it is the elephants that are being confined to Jharkhand. In the next chapter, I turn to the eco-incarceration of the adivasis themselves, which also results from the idea of the eco-savage.

5. *Night Escape*

ECO-INCARCERATION, PURITY, AND SEX

8:00 P.M., 29 AUGUST 2001

The distant drumbeats from the village *akhra* (dancing circle) were drowned out by the loud patter of the monsoon rain on the roof tiles. I pulled my sari up a few extra inches to make sure that it wouldn't trail in the muddy tracks that had turned into little streams outside the house.

"Tuck that loose end into your waist. Otherwise you'll keep tripping and won't be able to dance," said Ambli, holding the bright red border of my sari. She had come to watch me get ready to join the dancing at the akhra for the rainy season festival of Karma. As I got ready to leave, Somra Munda, her man, came rushing in.

"He's gone. He's gone! I can't believe it. The old man has finally left! How can he do this to me? What shame he will bring to our family!"

"Where? Where has he gone?" asked Ambli.

"To join Mangra at the brick kilns in Uttar Pradesh. I just bumped into Yogesh, the labor contractor from the next village. He told me that he had put Father on the bus two nights ago." I put a few sacks on the floor to sit on. Somra held his head in his hands as he crouched down.

The past year had been very frustrating. Somra had spent most of it trying to convince Burababa to come and live with him, at home. Like any decent son, he wanted to feed and clothe his father. But Burababa, well over sixty years old, had chosen to work as a *dhangar* (a live-in, year-round, general manual laborer)[1] for one of the sadans, the descendants of the old village landlords, earning a mere Rs 1,200 for the year, and sleeping wherever he liked. With the beginning of the rains and the rice-transplanting season, Somra had finally convinced Burababa to leave the sadan and come home.

But I knew from Burababa that the last few weeks had been a great strain. For Burababa and many other villagers, the rice-transplanting season is the great annual festival period, a time for merriment and bonding. The village is a hive of activity. All the seasonal migrants have returned. Day in and day out, the mornings involve hard work. The men plow and prepare each other's water-logged fields. The women, with their legs coated in oil and their saris hitched up to their knees, sing and joke as they sow rice in the fields. The children have mud baths and catch crabs and snails to eat. In the afternoons, the high spirits of the fields are carried back into the village. There is no payment for this labor, and no accounts are kept—the idea is that everyone helps everyone else, and the owners of the fields that are sown on a particular day host a lunch for the men and serve them rice and wine from the mahua flower. The women are given nibbles of fried lentils and wild mushrooms with the wine. The party begins at noon and continues into the evening. Those with energy to spare (especially the youngsters) then move their singing and drumming to the akhra, where they dance the night away. The new day begins at four in the morning, with new fields to be plowed and sown, and a new party to be hosted. However, when Burababa returned to his son's house, he also returned to Somra's regulations—strictly vegetarian food, no alcohol, no dancing, and in bed well before 9:00 p.m. This was far too restrictive a lifestyle for the old man.

Several years ago, Somra had joined a group of Mundas who call themselves bhagats and who consider themselves to be a class above the impure and decadent Munda households of their birth. Somra's bitter memories of his childhood are dominated by those of moving from house to house as a dhangar, Burababa's lack of interest in providing his children with an education, and his increasing fondness for the local brew. At some point, Somra ended up working as a dhangar in a nearby village, where he fell in love with Ambli, the beautiful daughter of his Munda employer. To Somra's dismay, after he had lived in Ambli's house for ten years, her father married her off to a man from a neighboring village. However, Ambli was soon back

Dancing in the village *akhra* in the rainy season. *Photo by author.*

with Somra. Somra now felt the need to prove his worth to Ambli's parents, who had given their other daughters in marriage far up the social scale—to men in the army and police force. He decided to emulate Ambli's father and become a bhagat, training intensively for several months. He joined a group of Mundas living under strict rituals of secret prayers, refraining from food cooked by others and nonvegetarian food (all but sacrificial meat), and giving up liquor (except the foreign varieties, called "English" and beautifully sealed and packed in bottles labeled "Old Monk" or "Royal Challenge"). Through this cleansing and ritual training, Somra gained secret powers to cure minor illnesses and appease angry spirits. Apart from the whiskey and rum, Somra's lifestyle became closer to that of some Brahman families that I knew in neighboring villages than to that of his father, or even that of his brother Mangra, or his sister, Jitia.

By the time I moved to Tapu, Somra thoroughly disapproved of his former lifestyle and that of his siblings and his father. By night, I had seen and heard Somra's disapproval when Burababa stole away to enjoy the company of his friends. By day, in the confines of our courtyard, I had seen Burababa grow quieter. Eventually, at a time when few people remain at the brick kilns, the old man had made a secret arrangement with a labor contractor and one night escaped to the kilns.

Women sowing rice in Tapu. *Painting by author.*

Children helping to sow rice in Tapu. *Photo by author.*

Somra is not the only one to find the migration of people like Burababa a problem.[2] Migration has been a norm of human history. However, people often think that it is natural for people's identity to be rooted in the particular place where they were born, are citizens, or have ancestral roots. Such arguments are influenced by the static nature of nationalist discourse and its central image of the nation-state as people "living in the same place."[3] In this "national order of things,"[4] as Liisa Malkki has called it, migration appears as a disruption. An obsession with controlling migration is therefore a symptom of the quest to maintain this illusion.

The supposed problem is most acute in the case of migrating indigenous people because they are assumed to embody the essence of the human desire and need to be rooted in the land. They are often called the "sons of the soil."[5] In this image, as Arjun Appadurai notes in his critical discussion of anthropology and the concept of the native,[6] places become prisons containing natives. With the global rise of indigenous rights in recent years, migration and displacement have been represented as violent because they threaten the authenticity of the image of indigenous people as being rooted in their land. Indigenous people have become eco-incarcerated.

The rooting of indigenous peoples in land is not only considered normal, but it is also perceived as a moral and spiritual need.[7] For instance, the Indigenous Land Rights Fund, whose work is representative of international efforts by many NGOs concerned to protect indigenous peoples' connections with their land, proclaims:

> Indigenous communities are intrinsically linked to the land through their survival strategies, economies, ceremonies, language and spiritual traditions . . . Indigenous people have often used the phrase "of the place" to describe not merely the physical location from which an indigenous community originates, but to convey how deeply their homeland is invested in all aspects of their culture.[8]

Threats to one indigenous group's ties to the land and hence its lifestyle are understood as endangering the "fate of indigenous peoples the world over."[9] In May 2007, José Antonio Ocampo, then U.N. Under-Secretary-General for Economic and Social Affairs, opened the sixth session of the Permanent Forum for Indigenous Issues by saying that the United Nations had long recognized the profound cultural, spiritual, and material relations that indigenous people had with their land; and that indigenous sacred sites, traditional knowledge, religions, and ways of life were all tied to the land.[10] Today, when displacement and migration are constructed as profound spiritual and cultural problems by advocates of indigenous people's rights around the world, are we hearing the varied experiences and views of the indigenous people themselves? What if they do not agree with the advocates' views? Commenting on a Rainforest Action Network's candlelit vigil for indigenous people that took place on a North American university campus, Liisa Malkki rightly wonders, "If an 'Indigenous Person' wanted to move away, to a city, would his or her candle be extinguished?"[11] As Francesca Merlan comments on the case of aboriginals in Australia, stressing indigenous links with their land makes those who live in cities "inauthentic" and not "real" indigenous people, and thus relegates their concerns for social welfare and economic opportunity to the back burner.[12]

Although, as argued in chapter 1, India has very different trajectories of migration than Australia and the New World, where claims to autochthony rest on a history of much sharper native-alien distinction, claims to land rights and attachment to the land have become crucial in adivasi struggles.[13] The imagery of India's indigenous people as spiritually and culturally rooted in the soil had an emotional impact around the world when activists used the hill tribes of western India as the icon of the fight against the building of the Narmada Dam, funded by the World Bank. The fight became seen as, among other things, a struggle against the violent displacement of the poor, ecologically noble primitives who would be lost without their land.[14] But the narrative of indigenous people's rootedness in their land may be nowhere more evident than in the various autonomy movements which have fought specifically for the territorial sovereignty of indigenous populations.

The Jharkhand Movement, which sought regional autonomy in nationalist discourse, is exemplary for its imagery of adivasi embeddedness in the land. "The rise and fall of *adivasis* depends on their land," said a tribal member of the Bihar Legislative Assembly—who was a lawyer by training—to Myron Weiner in 1978. "If you take away their land they are like fish out of water."[15] This statement is now a motto for indigenous rights activists in Jharkhand, who use it to stand for the dispossession, exploitation, and oppression of Jharkhand's indigenous populations in at least two ways. First, it indicates the violence of the displacement of adivasis from their land via the foreigners who are flooding into the state to make use of its rich mineral and forest resources. And second, it suggests the impoverishment of adivasis, which is allegedly forcing them to migrate from Jharkhand in search of work. Jharkhandi activists vehemently argue against the emigration of adivasis from Jharkhand, and for development policies that will discourage displacement in order to preserve the idea of Jharkhand. If the current trend in migration continues, warns one activist, "the real Jharkhandis will be all gone from the region before it is too long."[16]

There are in fact significant parallels between the discourse of today's indigenous rights activists and that of the Christian missionaries in Jharkhand, for whom migrants were also a problem. One of the first attempts to stop the flow of migrants from the Chotanagpur area, in this case to the tea plantations of Assam, began at the end of the eighteenth century and was led by Father Hoffman, a Roman Catholic missionary who thought that obtaining the trust of tribals was dependent on their living in insecurity. He said, "Christianity can grow and thrive only on abject poverty and that in reality is rooted in, and rests on pauperism."[17] Migration to Assam made the work of missionaries in Jharkhand superfluous and in some cases impossible, as it created new domains of security for the tribals in geographic areas that were out of bounds of the Chotanagpur Mission, so that the missionaries' contact with and influence on the adivasis was considerably reduced. Father Hoffman appealed to his fellow missionaries not to lose the converts to Christianity whom they had gained with so much labor and sacrifice.[18]

Today adivasis who migrate seasonally are inconvenient for the activists, not only because their physical absence threatens the idea of Jharkhand as a state full of adivasis, but also because continued migration undermines the imagery of adivasis as rooted in their land. In this rhetoric, migration results in the real adivasis, the true sons of the soil, being wrenched from their land by stealing, rapacious outsiders, or dikus, who transport them to faraway places. Alienation from their land is represented as leading to the slow death of the adivasis. "The tribals can only be agriculturalists. They can not work in industry. Agriculture is in their blood . . . They must have their land. If they do not, then they will become extinct like the American Indians," said one tribal representative in the State Assembly.[19] Such parallels with indigenous peoples across the world are constantly made. For example, another Jharkhandi activist writes:

> Indigenous people have a special relationship with the land they hold. To them land is not simply a factor of production as for other people, but a source of spirituality as well . . . As an aboriginal leader from Australia said, "My land is my backbone . . . Without land we will be the lowest people in the world, because you have broken down our backbone, taken away [our] arts, history and foundation."[20]

Even the best scholarly accounts of Jharkhand's adivasis do not question the representational politics of the moral connection of adivasis to their land. For instance, in Kaushik Ghosh's neat analysis of the activism against the building of the Koel Karo Dam, there is a surprising reproduction of the romantic imagery of adivasi rootedness in the land, which is made possible by Ghosh's overdependence on one rural elite informant, a village headman, who argues that nobody in the region would dare to sell his or her land.[21] Or take another example, that of Kumar Suresh Singh, who, in his account of the Birsa Movement, writes:

> The land was not an arithmetic of a few acres, it was a part of their sociocultural heritage: it contained the burial ground of their ancestors with whom they would be united after their death and the sacrificial grave where they propitiated their spirits. The emotional ties with their lands having gone, they were, to quote an anonymous Munda folk poet, "adrift," "afloat like a tortoise."[22]

With the formation of Jharkhand and its takeover by what they consider to be an outside government (one led by the BJP), Jharkhandi activists are more than ever driven to produce a regionalist cultural politics that will protect adivasi livelihoods and cultures. This cultural politics necessarily functions to simultaneously exclude outsiders and to primordialize insiders.[23] In Jharkhand, the other side of this cultural politics of campaigning to protect adivasi forest, land, and water, along with the promotion of a nature-worshiping indigenous religion discussed in the last chapter, is the production of an eco-incarceration. Adivasi cultures are presented as locked in their land. But perhaps, as Amita Baviskar points out is the case in western India, the activists' attention to ecological sustainability and cultural dignity are far-fetched concerns for the masses of the rural poor, who are struggling to make ends meet by tilling their fields and migrating in search of work as manual laborers.[24] Migration to other states in India threatens the image of the rich and glorious ecological tradition of adivasi life as being rooted in the villages of Jharkhand, and undermines the rationale of the new state.

In an article entitled, "Immigration of Adivasi Women Hasn't Stopped," one prominent indigenous rights activist wrote in the Jharkhand daily newspaper, the *Prabhat Khabar*:

> For whom has Jharkhand been formed? The recognition of its language, culture, water, forests, land and preservation of self is an important question . . . The image of tribal womenfolk is associated with the glorious history of the land. To re-establish this historical past, it is necessary to eradicate "migration" from their lives. It is sad that even after the formation of Jharkhand state the migration continues. As long as this migration continues to be a part of their life, the new foundation of Jharkhand state is worthless.[25]

Jharkhand's adivasis are therefore the subjects of policies and strategies aimed at keeping them incarcerated.

ESCAPE

Ironically, the imagery of adivasis as being rooted in their land, and the resulting desire to control their migration, seems to ignore both the local origin myths of the Hos, Mundas, and Oraons of Jharkhand and well-known historical accounts which stress that all of these groups were in fact migrants to the Chotanagpur Plateau.[26] Historical accounts concur that the Mundas were the earliest settlers to arrive from northern India, and that they were subsequently joined by the Ho, with the Oraons coming later from the south.[27] Moreover, as we know from the local history of villages like Tapu (see chapter 3), most of today's villagers are the descendants of people brought by landlords from other villages in the nineteenth century.[28] In Tapu, there are even Munda rituals to move the spirits of the ancestors, which lie in the stone burial grounds of the village, to new stones that will be erected in new lands.

As is the case in other regions, contemporary patterns of migration in Jharkhand are not, as is often claimed today, merely a result of modernization but have long been a central, perhaps permanent, feature of life in the subcontinent.[29] In the late 1800s, West Bengal, Andaman and Nicobar Islands, Assam, Bhutan, and even Burma

Munda burial stones in Tapu. *Photo by author.*

attracted migrants from Jharkhand.[30] The people of the Chotanagpur Plateau were preferred by the British for colonial railway and road building projects, and especially for work on tea plantations, as they were considered to be "more industrious and tractable than other classes."[31] By 1895, at least 50 percent of workers in the Assamese tea plantations came from the Chotanagpur Plateau.[32] Some estimate that by 1921, nearly a million tribals, a third of Chotanagpur's tribal population, had emigrated.[33] In Tapu, I heard many tales of the adventures of the villagers' forebears, and some personal recollections of those who went to build roads and pick tea near the border of China, where the "rain" fell in little white flakes, and one's feet turned to ice.

With the labor needs of the tea plantations met, many of the offspring of those who used to migrate to Assam and Bhutan instead went to the new brick kilns of West Bengal, Uttar Pradesh, and North Bihar. At least 47 percent of the adult residents of Tapu have traveled at some point to the brick kilns in those states. The sadans rarely migrate; it is mainly the Mundas who do. In 2000–2001, 36 percent of Tapu's Munda population over the age of sixteen migrated—a total of 73 people, 47 percent of whom were male. They joined a stream of seasonal migrants across the Indian landscape traveling in search of work. Although it is difficult to estimate the magnitude of Jharkhand's annual migration, most experts agree that there are at least several hundred thousand migrants.[34]

Jharkhandi indigenous rights activists reflect the concerns of much scholarly work in presenting the seasonal, casual labor migration of people like Burababa as part of a broader system of exploitation and oppression characteristic of capitalist production.[35] Migrants are often considered ecological refugees,[36] forced to move due to the effects of deforestation, water scarcity, insufficient agricultural production, and demographic pressures. In this analysis, the migrant's point of view is often subsumed in the larger part that migration plays within the broader social system. The migrant is rarely depicted as opting for departure and is assumed to be a victim of poverty, dispossession, and oppression, with little alternative but to leave the home area for the dry six months of the year in order to survive.[37]

In Jharkhand, it is easy to conceive of this migration as merely a survival strategy, or as Jan Breman puts it, as a defensive coping strategy.[38] For instance, Tapu initially appears to the outside observer to be an economically depressed place in an underdeveloped region. Although every household owns some land, limited irrigation means that many are able to harvest only one main crop per year. After the November harvest, livestock rearing and manual labor in the village stone-chipping industry and in nearby government projects are the main sources of livelihood. It would therefore be reasonable to assume, as the U.K. Department for International Development and those responsible for the Indian government's development projects in the area did, that people from the lower classes of the village, especially Scheduled Tribe and Caste families, have little option but to migrate. But the situation in Tapu is more complex. Economic motives may be significant, but they are not incompatible with others on which I wish to concentrate here. Indeed, it is the latter that the migrants stress most as being their motives for migration.

Toward the end of November 2001, I read in the Jharkhand daily newspaper, the *Prabhat Khabar*, the views of a Jharkhandi rights activist who was vehemently arguing for an antimigration bill to be passed in Jharkhand. The activist wrote:

> Why should adivasi girls . . . be oppressed by the brick-kiln owners, contractors and middlemen? Why should they be forced to work as bonded and low-waged workers? These questions are about protecting the reputation of the glorious history of this land and are about living

freely in a democracy with equality of rights, the protection of human rights and the right to freedom.[39]

On the day this article was published, I had spent several hours chatting with Sonamani, a woman from a village about 40 kilometers away from Tapu, who had taken up labor contracting with her brother after her failed marriage and she had been gang-raped in her husband's village. For the previous thirteen years, she had spent half the year at the kilns and half in her natal village. In 2000, however, a long-running dispute culminated in the theft of some cement and bricks recently purchased by her family. Sonamani suspected an act of revenge by a rival contractor, whom she feared had the backing of the Naxalites. Seeing this as a dangerous threat, Sonamani wanted to avoid staying in her natal village and was desperate to return to the kilns. When I asked her about all the commonly reported atrocities women suffer at the kilns, she insisted that I had got it wrong.

I was stunned by the stark contrast between the two viewpoints, coincidentally revealed to me on the same day. I think that we should not undermine the fact that laborers are exploited in the kilns, and that female laborers, in particular, are susceptible to being sexually exploited by kiln owners and managers. However, as in the last chapter, I am struck by the disjuncture between activists' views and the stories I heard in the countryside—for instance, what leaving the village may have meant for Burababa. Although Burababa's story might seem exceptional because of his son's puritanism, in fact Burababa's escape that rainy season was in part only a repetition of what had happened in that courtyard several times before.

Somra had, for instance, arranged the marriage of his brother Mangra to a suitable girl, only to find that Mangra had brought home, from the brick kilns of Uttar Pradesh, a woman of the Ho tribe from southern Jharkhand. Mangra's Ho-speaking partner had difficulty with Nagpuria, the local language in Tapu, and felt ostracized by the other villagers. As a result of this, unlike most other people who migrate seasonally to the brick kilns, Mangra has since chosen to live at the brick factory almost year-round, bringing his family to Tapu only occasionally, for a few weeks in the rainy season. He thus chose not to farm the fields that are his share of the family land, and not to live under the eyes of his watchful older brother, Somra.

Jitia, Somra's sister, had been married to a man from a neighboring village, only to return to Tapu a year later, declaring her love and determination to live with Minktu, a married man there. After one night at the akhra, several years earlier, Minktu and Jitia had met secretly. On Jitia's return, Minktu left his first wife and child. The new couple ran away to the kilns to escape the accusations of dishonor and came back the following season, with Jitia expecting her first child.

As for Somra's remaining sibling, Budhwa: Ambli (Somra's partner) had a paternal cousin, Chotki, who spent all her days at Ambli and Somra's house and fell in love with Budhwa. Chotki and Budhwa eventually ran away to the brick kilns to consummate their love in peace. After having two children, the couple decided to stop migrating, look after their village fields, and follow in Somra's footsteps to become Bhagats. Although Budhwa's fate was slightly different from that of Mangra and Jitia, what is common in all the stories is that, at some point, migrating to work seasonally in the brick kilns of other states provided an escape for the siblings from the claustrophobic restrictions of their brother and others in the village.

From their point of view, migration to the kilns did not just represent a way to earn money, nor was it seen as the torture and drudgery that much of the scholarly and activist literature portrays. Moreover, taking their views seriously does not mean one has to contest the view that migrant labor at the kilns is part of an exploitative system of capitalist production. Indeed, many migrants acknowledge that they provide cheap labor for wealthy industrialists, and that they expect to be cheated at the kilns. As Paul Willis proposed some years ago, with regard to why working-class children in England want working-class jobs, "there really is at some level a rational and potentially developmental basis for outcomes which appear to be completely irrational and regressive."[40] It is not contradictory to view labor migration to the kilns as exploitative, while also appreciating that most migrants not only view their movement as a choice but also seeing the kilns as an important, if temporary, space away from the social constraints back home.

In a survey of the village that I carried out, I found that 57 percent of those who have migrated from Tapu described their first trip to the kilns as a temporary escape from a problem at home, an opportunity to explore a new country, a means of gaining independence from parents, or a way to have a prohibited amorous relationship. Regardless of the compulsion to earn money, the migrants themselves rarely stressed economic motivations. They saw the brick kilns as a space in which they could do certain things and be certain people away from home. These are important dimensions of seasonal, casual labor migration which are rarely considered as a primary impetus for migration in the scholarly literature and which have generally been ignored by the activists.

For many migrants, life at the kilns is seen as free. The desire for freedom is, as Saba Mahmood has so aptly noted, historically situated: its motivational force cannot be assumed to be self-evident.[41] I am not suggesting that the kilns give migrants from Tapu freedom, but I do see it as significant that these migrants often describe the kilns as a place where they can live freely. With the cases of migration I heard about and witnessed, I began to wonder if migration activists might have overlooked the possibility that, from the migrant's point of view, economic motivations may be less important than liberation from the constraints of village life.[42]

I also began to wonder what the costs of this oversight may be for the poorest people in villages like Tapu. Perhaps the activist position actually results in unintended detrimental consequences for such adivasis. This was certainly the case in the fight against the Narmada Dam. As we learn from Amita Baviskar,[43] when the dam was finally built, the main supporters of the antidam movement—the wealthy, middle-caste landowners and a group of educated adivasis who had the resources to look after their own relocation—were taken care of. However, there was nobody to support the poor members of the hill tribes who had been used as the face of the movement. While the struggle was going on, these poorest people had been denied access to knowledge about their entitlements by the activists—who feared that such knowledge might encourage adivasis to vote with their feet and move to the relocation sites, thus undermining the imagery of adivasis as being fundamentally tied to their land. But when the fight against the dam was lost, the activists moved on to other issues, leaving the hill tribes to their own devices, in effect marginalizing them once again. In order to further explore the issues that are central to the campaign against seasonal, casual labor migration, in February 2002, I joined laborers from Tapu at the Daisy Brick Factory at the side of the Ganges River in West Bengal.[44]

SEX AND THE KILNS

Getting off the train in Calcutta, I pulled out the scrap of paper on which Jeevan had scribbled the location of the brick kiln and a phone number. My thoughts flashed back to the moment he had given me these details. It was in the rainy season the year before, in 2001, just after Burababa had left for the kilns. Jeevan had come to Tapu and hosted a small party in the next courtyard. A pig had been roasted, and there was plenty of rice beer and mahua wine consumed. Jeevan was trying to get some of the Tapu adivasis to work with him rather than another sardar, or labor contractor. Jeevan did not quite fit the image of the evil labor contractor that I was so used to reading about in scholarly and activist accounts,[45] the malevolent enemy of migrants who often disguises his intentions in the language of patronage, while cheating, bribing, and luring migrants through exploitative routes to exploitative destinations.

Fighting my way onto the train to my next destination, I thought that the system of labor contracting seemed significantly transformed since the time of writers like Mahasweta Devi and Father Hoffman, who had stressed the force and violence employed by the few outside contractors who had arrived in Jharkhand and taken adivasi labor to the tea plantations and later the brick kilns. People in Tapu say that "these days there is a contractor in every house." Contractors are often known as somebody's *mama* (mother's brother), *chacha* (father's brother), or *sahia* (a friend with whom a kinship-like bond has been formed). Some become contractors for a few years, only to give up the work later. Although there are a few larger contractors—for every three villages, there is usually one contractor who takes 40 laborers; for every ten villages, there is often one contractor who takes 200—most contractors (some of whom are women) take only ten to twelve people. In Tapu, everyone who migrated in 2000–2001 went with one of thirteen smaller contractors, of which three were from Tapu, one (Jeevan) from the neighboring village, and the rest from the natal villages of women who had married into Tapu. This decentralization of the recruiting system has meant that contractors are, in some ways, in quite a vulnerable position. If there is a bad experience with one contractor, or with one kiln, the following year, laborers can go with another contractor or to a different kiln. There is stiff competition for labor, and the contractor has an incentive to form a bond of loyalty with his laborers, so that they will go with him in future years. This was one reason why Jeevan was hosting a party that rainy afternoon in Tapu.

My thoughts were soon brought to a halt as the train chugged to a stop at Bandel. I hired a cycle rickshaw, and the driver began to weave his way along the road that separated the palm-fringed Bengali middle-class housing and the brick factories that lined the Ganges. I knew that there were about 350 such factories in the Hooghly District alone. Would we ever find our way through the maze of factories? But the rickshaw driver pedaled hard, stopping a couple of times to ask for directions, and eventually we arrived at our destination, where I asked for Jeevan.

"Ah, so I did indeed give you 'photocopy' instructions," said Jeevan warmly, as he led me down the path which skirted a six-story mansion. This was one of the factory owner's houses that he had wanted to convert into a luxury tourist resort, with a swimming pool and golf course stretching to the banks of the Hooghly River. But in February 2002, the mansion overlooked what was locally known as the largest of the brick factories in Hooghly District, employing 800 laborers and producing 1,400,000 bricks in one baking in the kiln, totaling around 5,000,000 bricks a year.[46]

Jeevan took me into the furthest part of the housing camp for migrant laborers, past about 200 brick shacks, including the empty one frequented by local Bengali middle-class heroin addicts who wanted to shoot up in peace. Each shack was six by three meters in size and had a low tile roof. It housed about four people and contained a line to hang clothes on and a coal-fired stove. Some shacks had a single rope bed. At one end of the compound, three taps supplied water to the whole camp. There was no sanitation, bathing facility, or electricity in the camp, although the kiln a few meters away was floodlit at night.

Most laborers worked in blistering heat six days a week, eight and a half hours a day in three shifts: 5:30 to 8:00 a.m., 10:00 a.m. to noon, and 2:00 to 6:00 p.m. While low-caste Bihari laborers specialized in molding bricks and Bengali workers extracted clay, Jharkhandi laborers loaded and unloaded bricks to and from the furnace, trucks, and stores. In the Daisy Brick Factory, Jharkhandis accounted for almost half of the labor force. Local factory owners say that, unlike Jharkhandis, Bengalis cannot endure carrying bricks and consider it a menial task.

Jharkhandi women balanced up to eight unbaked bricks on their heads. The men either received these bricks from the women to place in the furnace, or carried a load of up to sixteen baked bricks on a bamboo sling across their shoulders. Payment was at piece rates — Rs 22 for carrying 1,000 unbaked bricks, and Rs 32 for 1,000 baked

The Daisy Brick Factory and labor camp in West Bengal. *Photo by author.*

Women from Jharkhand carrying bricks in West Bengal. *Painting by Kundan Shah.*

bricks. Plastic counters, tallied every Sunday, were collected for the loads of bricks moved. Payment took place at the end of the season. A monthly sum of money was given to each worker to cover living expenses, and subtracted from the final pay. Laborers expected that, after paying their living costs, hard-working couples could take home Rs 8,000–9,000 for the six-month season. Such couples were rare, however. It is far more common to hear of individuals who manage to save only Rs 2,000. Although it is likely that the major reason for this shortfall is cheating on the part of employers and contractors, the explanation that laborers often give for this low amount, as I will show shortly, is that the individuals were too busy having fun.

It is difficult to imagine that the motivation to endure such hard work and living conditions could be anything other than the migrants' extreme poverty. But what did migration really mean for those who moved? The answer often seems so straightforward and accepted that the question itself is rarely seen as worth posing. Were the stories about the fun to be had at the kilns that I had heard back in Tapu simply a consequence of the migrants' reluctance to admit that the kilns are actually awful, and that the only reason for moving is the economic difficulties in staying at home?

Although carrying bricks is tough, and although I was at the Daisy Brick Factory for only a week, it would in fact be a distortion of my experience in the labor camp to portray life there as unremittingly bleak. I was living in one of five shacks of migrants from Tapu, with four unmarried and unrelated girls who had all migrated despite their parents' pleas. The oldest, twenty-year-old Shila, had left the village one night without her parents' consent. In the winter months, children disappearing at night were a common phenomenon in Tapu. Although parents were usually upset, they rarely worried. It was assumed that the children had gone to some brick kiln, and that the parents would hear from them in due course.

By the time I arrived at the migrant camp, Shila had been there three months, and I was struck by how she had transformed herself from a shabby girl wearing a blue school skirt into an elegant woman dressed in a sari. Excited to see me, she stressed how she had decided to be on her own and explore a new part of the country. I later heard many young people describe the migratory process as an individual, exploratory one, and I realized that of course there is often a contradiction between the actor's description of individual autonomy in the migration decision and what actually happened.[47] Although kin did not necessarily form the most important social network in the kiln,[48] the young people from Tapu usually migrated with people from surrounding villages and socialized with other Jharkhandis in the kiln, repeating an established pattern of migration.

Shila was proud to show that she had learned to cook at the kiln. This, however, was the least of her surprises. It transpired that the relationship between Jeevan and Shila was more than platonic.[49] In fact, as is common of relationships between younger brothers and their older sisters-in-law in Tapu, I often found Jeevan's younger brother flirting, teasing, and joking with Shila. However, in the week I was there, some complications developed in Jeevan and Shila's romance.

Jeevan had been married for twelve years but, though his wife and child were in the village, the other girls did not think him a suitable match for Shila. They had found Shila a quiet young boy from Ranchi whom they referred to as *bhatu* (brother-in-law). The Saturday before my arrival, there had been a night of drinking and dancing to celebrate Saraswati Puja. That night, Shila had served rice beer to the bhatu, and Jeevan had danced beside a female labor contractor. A jealous tension thus developed between Shila and Jeevan. On my second evening, Jeevan went off to the market for a few hours in his shiny new jacket. About the same time, the female labor contractor, in lipstick and high heels, left the camp. After his return from the market, Shila sarcastically taunted Jeevan, saying he ought to leave his door open that night so that his *mal* (property) could slip in.

The next night, Shila invited the bhatu back to our shack, where he sat quietly while the other girls giggled and joked. Jeevan became increasingly infuriated. When the bhatu left, Jeevan shouted at the girls to shut up, bellowing that the shack had turned into a "free zone," and that they were ruining their reputations. He threatened to send Shila's father a message telling him what she was up to. This outburst produced an uncomfortable silence. Shila stopped eating, trying to make the point that Jeevan had hurt her.

On Sunday, a holiday, everyone dressed in their best. While some went to explore the Hooghly Bridge and the planetarium in Calcutta, I went with Jeevan, Shila, and a few others to visit the Roman Catholic church in the nearby town of Bandel. After we gazed in awe at the statues and pictures and climbed to the roof for an aerial view of the brick factories lining the banks of the Ganges, Jeevan bought Shila a necklace. In the evening, Shila made chicken curry for Jeevan, his brother, the other girls, and me. After a few cups of rice beer, relations between Shila and Jeevan seemed to be sunny again.

Shila and Jeevan's affair was only one of the flirtatious relationships between young men and women that I saw that week. Joking and flirting, as a type of joking with sexual possibilities,[50] between men and women was common as they worked,[51] but it was in the confines of the labor camp that amorous relationships were expressed more fully. Indeed, I was surprised to find that unmarried men and women openly flirted with each other there, sat on each other's laps, held hands, and lay next to each other on the floor or in rope beds—behavior I never saw in Tapu. Sleeping arrangements were quite flexible, and while food was always cooked and consumed in the shack in which one was supposed to live, some nights some of the girls slept in the shack of Jeevan's parent's in-laws, while some of the young men slept in one of the girls' shacks.

Back in Tapu, my survey of every house and its migration patterns had focused on those who had migrated to the brick kilns the year before, in 2000–2001. In that period, 40 percent of the 79 migrants were unmarried youth who said that they went to the kilns for the fun of visiting new places, being away from parents, and especially in the hope of pursuing amorous relationships. Villagers said that amorous relationships are pursued with ease at the kilns because most young people choose to go to different kilns from the ones their siblings or other close relatives go to. In many cases, having family around is indeed likely to cramp one's style.[52] To some of the young Mundas from Tapu, the brick kilns provide a convenient temporary space away from the authority of, and responsibility to, immediate family.

PROHIBITIONS IN THE VILLAGE

7:30 P.M., 20 FEBRUARY 2007

I was in Etwa's house, where I had lived from November 2000 until June 2002, and into which he had moved after my departure. We were just licking the last of the dal and rice off our brass plates when there was a faint knock on the door. Fagu Munda and his wife, Mangri, walked in gingerly, barely greeted us, and sat on the floor in a solemn silence. Etwa and I washed our hands and mouths outside and came back in.

"What's up?" I asked. "I've never seen you look so upset."

"I'd like to borrow your cellphone," said Fagu.

"Sure. We'll have to walk down into the valley, as I can't get reception here. But what's the urgency?"

"We've found out where our son, Budhwa, and the young Sanicharwa have run off to. They're at a brick kiln in Uttar Pradesh. We have the mobile number of the labor contractor," Mangri said, as she pulled a scrap of paper out from under her blouse.

We went down into the valley. My life in the village had changed dramatically on this last trip to Tapu because of the mobile phone network that now covered most of India. Although Tapu still had no electricity, running water, or landline phones, my cellphone (the only one in the village) was definitely being put to good use. I saw some bars of reception, stopped, and dialed the number. I knew the contractor who answered, and he said he'd find Budhwa. After Budhwa got on the phone, I passed it to Mangri.

"How dare you! How dare you treat us like this! What did we spend all that money on your education for? So that you can leave your books on the shelf to stare back at us? You passed your matriculation exams with first-class grades. You only had a few more months left before your intermediate exams. And you chose to shame us in this way instead! Your father has taken to drink. I can't sleep at night. How could you!" Mangri broke down and started sobbing.

Fagu gently took the phone from her hand. He said to Budhwa, "Come back immediately. Come back and we will promise to allow you to get married to each other. I want you to take your exams. I promise it won't be like before. You can be together. Sanicharwa's parents have also agreed. Look how you have upset your mother. Is this the way to do things?"

Although I left that cellphone with Etwa, I don't yet know if Sanicharwa and Budhwa got married. However, their case revealed to me that the brick kilns were still an important space for lovers to escape to when their affairs might be prohibited back in the village.

To understand why people felt unable to explore amorous relationships in the village, it is necessary to know something of Munda sexual norms in Tapu. Despite the fact that Mangri and Fagu were upset, premarital sexual relations are common in the village. The restriction on such relations, however, is that they must not become permanent. Marital partners should not be chosen by the boy or girl, but by their parents. While it was not necessary for a bride to be a virgin, marital partners should not have previously engaged in sexual relations with each other. In fact, some of my more skeptical informants even suggested that this is the main reason why parents prefer brides for their boys from outside the village—to ensure that the potential partners had not had sex. As was the case with Budhwa—

and with Somra and his two brothers, as noted earlier in this chapter —premarital lovers who want a more permanent relationship commonly use the tactic of leaving for the kilns. Frequently, they return after the woman is several months pregnant. In the village, pregnancies resulting from illicit affairs are aborted early. After childbirth, however, such affairs are legitimized.

Another restriction on premarital sexual relations is that the older generation must not know about them. This is why parents have contradictory reactions when their children run away to the brick kilns. On the one hand, they are upset, not just because a child's departure means one fewer worker in the fields, but also because they know that the kilns provide a space for developing love affairs. On the other hand, many parents understand the youngsters' desires—they have been in the same situation themselves, and many of them met their own marital partners at the kilns. Thus when parents express displeasure and hurt when their children take off to the kilns, it is often because—as parents—they ought not to endorse the sexual freedom that everyone knows migration there entails. This is not to say, however, that every young person who goes to the kilns engages in amorous relationships. The important point is that the ability to explore amorous relationships more fully at the kilns than in the village makes migration attractive to some.

Migration also provides the space to explore unions within a clan or between tribes and castes that are prohibited in the village,[53] as well as postmarital affairs. Divorce and postmarital affairs in Tapu are now, if they ever were, not readily accepted. Nevertheless, they do occur and often end in people leaving their first partner to live with a new lover. I calculated that of the 83 married Munda men in Tapu, approximately 30 percent were not living with their first spouse. Affairs after marriage—or the continuation of premarital relationships after marriage, as in Somra's sister's case—are pursued with greater ease at the kilns. In at least 50 percent of the subsequent unions of Munda men in Tapu, migration to the kilns had allowed the second relationship to develop.[54]

MORE REASONS FOR MIGRATING

Not all Tapu migrants at the Daisy Brick Factory in 2001–2 had come to explore prohibited sexual relations, or for the fun and games of the kilns, and not all of them were as young as Shila, the other girls

I stayed with, or Budhwa and Sanicharwa. Let me turn to the residents of the other four Tapu shacks to highlight additional reasons for migration. In the shack neighboring that of the four girls was an old man who had run away from his son under circumstances like those of Burababa. He hoped that his escape would make his son regret his behavior, and that when the father went back, he would be better treated.

Pera Munda, in his mid-thirties, was in the third shack with his Oraon wife, Budhni, and their son. Pera had been coming to the kilns for seven years, for various reasons. Initially, migration had been a way for him to escape from his father. Between the age of six and his late teens, Pera had been a dhangar in a village near Tapu. When he returned to live in Tapu, he argued with his father constantly. Migrating to the kilns provided some relief from the tensions at home. When his father died, Pera inherited land and livestock and considered staying in Tapu throughout the year. Soon afterward, however, Pera's older brother was accused of a murder and put in jail. Pera and his brothers mortgaged their land to pay a sadan who claimed he could get the older brother released. Pera thus continued going to the kilns to pay off the debt. At the kilns, he fell in love with Budhni. In Tapu, their intertribe union was stigmatized, which provided another incentive to continue migrating to the kilns. By 2001, circumstances had changed. Pera had not only recovered enough of his family's land to stay in Tapu all year long, but Budhni had also given birth to a child. As a result, the couple's union became more legitimate. Pera now wanted to settle in Tapu, where they had a bigger house, livestock to look after, and fields to cultivate. But while Budhni recognized the difficulties of looking after a baby in the hot camp, she was convinced that life at the kilns would be liberating in comparison to the claustrophobic atmosphere of the village, where she would be looked down on for her lower-caste status. At the kilns "all people are equal," she said, and people forget the rules of "purity and pollution." This is clearly not always the case (for example, Jharkhandis rarely mixed with low-caste Biharis), but it is also true that at most kilns, there would be only a few people from home for whom the hierarchy of the village and its rules of purity were relevant.

Next to Pera's shack lived his father's brother's son, Samu, then forty-five, with his second wife, Anita, and their son. Anita said that she would continue to migrate as long as she could do the work. Another exceptional family that had been going to the kilns for more than ten years, their reasons also had changed over time. Before her first marriage, Anita had gone to the kilns with her sister's husband and other young people, "for fun." She subsequently eloped with her first husband to the tea plantations, staying there for four years until her partner was caught having an affair with another Jharkhandi woman. When she returned to her natal village, she felt ostracized as a single woman. This stigma and the fact that she had a daughter to marry off led her to continue migrating to the kilns, where she eventually became an assistant labor contractor. One Karma festival, Samu, a widower, visited her village. Anita seemed to be his perfect partner, and he took her back to Tapu. Each season, they migrated to be "alone" at the kilns, until Samu was finally able to build a house in Tapu for them to live in, thus permitting their separation from his extended family. I was puzzled as to why they should continue to migrate after that, and Anita finally told me that in Tapu she was accused of witchcraft, and the brick kilns provided a welcome space of escape from the malicious village gossip.

Fatra, a middle-aged Munda man, and his fourteen-year-old daughter lived in the fifth shack, while his wife and four other children were back in the village looking after the fields and livestock. He told me that he and his wife had first left for the kilns when they were newly married and wanted to be independent from his joint-family household. Unfortunately, his paternal land had not yet been divided, precluding their setting up their own household. Moreover, his parents had wanted the newlyweds to stay in the village and help in the fields. Fatra and his wife, who were not getting on with his parents, had rebelled and left for the kilns to earn enough money to set up their own household.

In 2001, Fatra had returned to the kilns for a different reason. He had mortgaged some of his fields, as his family in Tapu had suffered recurrent bad luck with malaria, and he had had to spend a lot of money on sacrificial chickens and remedies given by the healers. Fatra said he was at the brick factory that year for the sole purpose of earning money to redeem his land. In some years he went to the kilns, while in others he stayed in Tapu. He explained that it was not always necessary to migrate, as he could get by with tilling his fields and working as a contract laborer. However, in years when his family's financial situation was precarious, as in 2001, it was safer to go to the kilns, where he was sure to save money. Like many others, he explained that in the village, money rapidly flows away in drink and celebrations with relatives and friends. At the kilns one saves more, not necessarily because one earns more but because one spends less, since wages are paid only at the end of the season. For Fatra, the kilns provided a space away from home where he could concentrate on hard labor without the distraction of kinsfolk.

It is clear that the migrants from Tapu had a variety of reasons to come to the Daisy Brick Factory that year. However, the most striking feature of all the stories is how rarely migration was seen as solely an economic necessity. Instead, it was often also perceived as meeting an emotional need—to be away from the village and the constraints and obligations of kinship, domestic disputes, and a narrow-minded and oppressive environment. For six months of the year at the kilns, migrants could lead what they saw as a more autonomous life without disrupting kinship and friendship networks in the village, or a long-term connection with their house and fields. Migration to the kilns, after all, was always seen as a temporary phase in a person's life.

Let's turn to the year before, 2000–2001, when there were 79 migrants, to get a broader picture of migration from Tapu. Seventy percent of these migrants felt that there were sufficient resources in the village (from cultivable land, livestock, forests, and casual labor), and that they did not need to supplement their lifestyle with money from the kilns. I have already indicated that nearly 40 percent of total migrants (or more than half of the people who said they did not migrate for money) were unmarried youth, who said they went for the fun and adventure of amorous relationships, life away from parents, and to visit new places. It is clear that seasonal casual labor migration must be seen in terms of the migrant's stage of life, and that it is the youth, in particular, who are attracted by the freedoms offered by migrating to the brick kilns. What of the other migrants?

More than 20 percent who said that there were enough resources at home for them not to have to migrate—that is, 16 percent of the total migrants that year—were people with young families who wanted to be independent from joint households. In these cases, paternal land had not yet been divided so they could not set up their own households, and the young families did not get on with their parents. While the parents wanted newly married sons to stay in the village and help in the fields, these young couples rebelled by leaving for the kilns to be free of family constraints and to earn enough money to return and set up their own households.[55] They were not migrating just for fun.

Three of the Tapu migrants in 2000–2001 had quarreled with their relatives and left the village abruptly in protest. One woman, who left the village after a fight with her husband, was followed by him to the kilns.[56]

Just over 10 percent of the 2000–2001 migrants wanted to get away from relatives for a different reason, and that was to ensure that they saved a certain amount of cash. The money was usually needed to pay off a loan (as in the case of Fatra Munda) or to buy some cattle. Although they could earn this money in the village, they said it was easier to save at the kilns.

Twenty-three migrants, just under 30 percent of the total in 2000–2001, said they would find it difficult to make ends meet in the village. Of these, four were women whose husbands had left them and who, as a result, felt vulnerable and ostracized in Tapu. They had no land, and because of their marginalization, they had been unable to develop survival strategies to cope with village life year-round. Three were older men, now single, who could not live with their siblings, sons, or daughters. They had no desire to cultivate their share of land, especially because they could not rely on kin for help. Sixteen were individuals who felt ostracized in the village because they had either had intertribe marriages or had been accused of witchcraft. They felt more comfortable at the kilns and had therefore neither made their land productive, nor developed alternative livelihood strategies to enable them to stay in the village year-round.

It is perhaps possible that, at a practical level, economic imperatives may be more salient than many Tapu migrants admit. Indeed, it may well be that without seasonal migration, Tapu people would not have the same standard of living. And of course, in a different part of Jharkhand or at an earlier time, when there were fewer alternatives at home, migration might have been expressed as being more economically driven. However, I should note that, even in earlier periods, there is evidence that migrants in many cases had actually run away from home.[57] Nevertheless, these figures, and the complex stories that lie behind them, suggest that from the migrant's point of view, economic motivations are eclipsed by the space that migration to the brick kilns provides for both social and cultural autonomy from the village.

PURIFICATION AND MIGRATION

In this chapter, I have focused on the eco-incarceration of adivasis that results from the depiction of indigenous cultures as rooted in their land. Migration of adivasis out of Jharkhand is a threat to this representation by indigenous rights activists. I have shown how, in fact, seasonal migration as casual laborers to brick factories in other states gives the poorest adivasis not only the ability to cope with everyday livelihood struggles but also a space from social constraints at home. The brick kilns can serve as a temporary space of freedom to escape domestic problems, explore a new country, and live out prohibited amorous relationships. Perhaps the activists' construction of such migration as a problem has as much to do with their ethnic and regionalist vision of what the new tribal state ought to be like as with exploitation and poverty. Activists see migration to the kilns as a threat both to the idea of the connection with the land that adivasis allegedly have, and to the purity and regulation of the social and sexual tribal citizen. In concluding this chapter, I want to suggest that this perspective is actually dangerously close to creating a climate that paradoxically helps reproduce the conditions of capitalist exploitation and the extraction of surplus value, while leaving aside the crucial issues of improving the conditions of labor migration for the poorest migrants.

In recent years, scholarly work has been concerned to examine the processes through which national representations are constructed by states and national elites to appear unquestionably natural.[58] In this endeavor, an obsessive concern with the establishment and control of boundaries and borders, as Mary Douglas has shown, is central to the maintenance of purity.[59] Yet in Tapu, many Mundas, especially members of the older generations, did not think of India as a nation-state within which Jharkhand was a state, or of England as a different country. Despite my attempts to explain otherwise, they said that they knew that England was a village very far away, and in fact that some of them had been there when they went to work in the tea plantations, where it was also very cold and the rain fell in the form of ice. When I asked Chotki whether she'd like to come to London with me, she said, "No, man! I do want to see your parents again, but the only reason I don't want to come is it's just too far away, I'd be afraid of getting lost."

The older generation of Mundas continues to imagine the world as a continuous landscape of villages — some so large that they are cities — separated by land, forests, or sea. Meanwhile, for many of the rest of us, the boundaries between and within nation-states solidify so that they naturally appear to be separating places and people which are thought to be essentially different. In this construction of a "national order of things," anthropologists and geographers have argued that the question of controlling migration is one of how separate and culturally distinct places can be produced.[60] The antimigration campaign of Jharkhandi activists reflects a desire to redefine Jharkhand as a state of indigenous people rooted in their land, where adivasis become eco-incarcerated, and to reimagine a purer adivasi, the indigenous citizen of the new state.

Did those who railed against migration to the brick kilns not know of its noneconomic significance for the majority of the migrants, or that many workers find a silver lining in the romantic possibilities of such spaces? In Tapu, everyone was aware of them. This was true even of the higher-caste landlord descendants, who do not migrate to the kilns—despite the fact that some engaged in hard manual labor in the village and are now often less well off than some of the migrant families. For the landlord descendants, such migration signifies a jangli, impure life of low bodily self-control regarding food, drink, and sex—something that is demeaning for higher castes, but natural to those lower in the social hierarchy.

People like the Bhagat, Somra Munda, with whom I began this chapter, were eager to distance themselves from this jangli representation of tribal people. One of the main ways in which they did this was by emulating certain higher-caste values (in attitudes toward food, drink, and sex), together with stigmatizing the life at the kilns. Most of the older generation of Mundas in Tapu, however, had more ambivalent views on migration to the kilns. Although they respected Somra, they also quietly appreciated the fact that they and the higher castes had different views of the Jungle Raj.

The most vehement protestors against brick kiln migration were the same middle-class tribal activists based in Ranchi City who were celebrating indigenous festivals as nature worship. They say that seasonal migration is compulsory because of extreme poverty, and that migrants not only leave behind the rich glory of their home traditions, but are also exploited and oppressed at every stage, starting from the labor contractor at home through the managers and bosses at the kilns. Although I would agree that the kilns mark an exploitation of manual labor, I want to suggest that these opponents of migration are also, at some level, aware of the complex motivations for migrating that I have been discussing, and seek to draw a veil over them. There is at play in Jharkhand a performance of indigenous rights activism.

Given the fact of historical mobility, the antimigration campaign serves to recreate and reinforce the image of Jharkhand as an indigenous state. The control of migration provides both an opportunity for a better and clearer display of the ideal vision of the state,[61] and a space for the manipulation and recreation of that image.[62] The anti-migration campaign allows the Jharkhandi activist elites to massage and produce the image of the ideal adivasi indigenous citizen of the state—an embodied image of a socially and sexually transformed Jharkhandi. The campaign contests the upper-caste representations of tribals as morally impure, drunken, and sexually promiscuous, producing an alternative image of purer adivasi bodies—the aboriginal citizen not only of Jharkhand, but also of the Indian state.

This purifying project to create the ideal indigenous citizen, away from the idea of the jangli adivasi, as argued in the last chapter, is uncomfortably similar to that of the extreme right-wing Hindu nationalist BJP, which argues that Jharkhand's tribals should be made into proper Hindus by emulating higher Hindu castes. Jharkhandi activists are outwardly hostile both to the upper castes, who they claim have exploited adivasis and whom they identify as BJP supporters, and to Sanskritization as a way of improving social status. Instead, the activists aim to raise tribal status on the grounds that they are the authentic sons of the soil and the original Indians.

In seeking to recreate Jharkhand's authentic adivasi tradition, institutions like the *dhumkuria* (better known in areas of the Muria tribe in Chhattisgarh as *ghotul*), a village dormitory where unmarried young men would sleep and engage in erotic singing and dancing, are being revived as learning institutions, rather than as spaces which also permit premarital sexual relations.[63] In similar fashion, the akhra is being revived as a village meeting place, emphasizing the so-called communitarian nature of adivasi villages, rather than as a village dancing circle where girls and boys dance together to sexually charged songs and rhythms. In Tapu, I was often told that it was actually increasing Brahminical and Christian influence that led to the disappearance of the dhumkuria and the decline of the akhra in some areas.

Divorcing the image of sexual promiscuity from the notion of the authentic indigenous communities has also been conspicuous in the Tapu area in campaigns to strengthen the so-called traditional tribal system of governance, the parha, begun by one MLA in the late 1960s and intensified by another in the 1990s—as discussed in chapter 2. Of the twenty-nine disputes I recorded which had been resolved by the parha, the most common were postmarital love affairs or elopements, locally called *dhuku-dhara*. One of the most famous dhuku-dhara cases, in which Vishwanath Bhagat, the MLA from JMM, was involved in the 1990s, was that of Tela Munda's daughter and Sukra Oraon's son, who were engaged in a passionate affair. When Tela began to arrange his daughter's wedding to a suitable boy, the girl ran away with her boyfriend to the brick kilns. A JMM member of the village decided to involve the parha and went with party members, representing the parha, to the brick kiln to put an end to the affair. In this case, the interventions were unsuccessful, as the couple resolutely refused to separate. The girl was pregnant and, when they finally returned, they were allowed to marry.

As this case illustrates, notions of sexual propriety are crucial to the dislike for migration to the brick kilns that middle-class Jharkhandi indigenous rights activists share with the rural elites (many of whom are local parha and JMM members). The problem is significantly gendered, for at its heart is a concern with the sexual purity of migrant women. While many JMM and parha members (exclusively men) privately admitted to having had premarital or extramarital affairs, their rhetoric is exclusively focused on the chastity and modesty of women, never on men: "We have to protect the honor of our *ma*, beti, and *bahin* (mothers, daughters, and sisters)."[64] It is this honor that they—and probably many Ranchi-based Jharkhandi activists also—feel is threatened in the brick kilns.

This situation has significant parallels in the history of early European industrialization, when middle-class constructions of female sexuality were important in forming public attitudes about the female industrial labor force. It has, for instance, been argued that in the outcry that led to the first sex-specific protective legislation in Britain, the 1842 Mines Regulation Act, the most significant pressure for reform was the affront to bourgeois notions of sexual propriety and proper femininity that the supposed promiscuity of the mines represented.[65] In Jharkhand, perhaps an additional dimension to the middle-class discourse is that it lays blame not just on the women themselves, but above all on immoral or outside men who seduce and steal mothers, daughters, and sisters away, thus corrupting the moral core of Jharkhand. The likely effect of this double-standard, moralizing discourse is to limit the freedom of poor women in an area in which they have been relatively autonomous.[66]

Perhaps stories from the Tapu area suggest that the brick kilns have become a functional surrogate for the spaces of freedom of the Jungle Raj that were once provided by the akhra or the dhumkuria. As a space of freedom, the brick kilns represent an obvious threat to the image of indigenous society, and more specifically that of tribal womanhood, that the elites would like to have accepted. Toward the end of my stay in Jharkhand, I tried to test my findings about reasons why people migrated from Tapu, with Ranchi-based activists and academics. While I uncovered several stories of people who had nieces in the rural villages who had run away to the kilns, the most interesting revelation came from a university professor who had conducted a survey of why people in four districts of Jharkhand migrate. Its results confirmed my own and, since they were strikingly at odds with the arguments of his colleagues and friends who protested against migration to the kilns, the professor decided to shelve the survey.

Whereas Jharkhandi activists are able to talk about migration to the kilns in terms of a human-rights discourse — as a movement to be stopped on the ground that it furthers adivasi exploitation — the migration enables many migrants to reject the Jharkhandi tribal elites' notions of an authentic, morally pure adivasi citizen of the state. Ironically, the spaces of freedom provided by the brick kilns may serve to maintain older notions of the self. Thus, rather than being a phenomenon dictated by mere economic necessity, migration to the brick kilns may also be seen as part of a distinctive Tapu politics of challenging the purifying discourse of the adivasi state.

However, Lila Abu Lughod is correct to be wary of romanticizing resistance and points out that such acts of resistance should be treated as indicative of historically changing relations of power.[67] Opponents of migration, who see the kilns as a threat to ideas of purity and the regulation of the social and sexual tribal body, create a moral climate that paradoxically encourages many young people to flee to the brick kilns where they think people can be free of these regulations. Jharkhandi activists are inadvertently encouraging the continued exodus of adivasi peasants into the arms of the exploitative forces of capitalist labor markets. Munda conceptions of the brick kilns as a space of freedom may point to broader structures of power, in which the new puritanism of indigenous rights at home unwittingly encourages the possibilities for the capitalist exploitation of, and the extraction of surplus value from, the rural poor. Moreover, in the indigenous activists' anti-migration stance, the material issues which really should be at stake in improving the lives of poor adivasi migrants get lost. Mosse, Rogaly, and their coauthors importantly point out that there is a pressing need to pay attention to improved wages; better living conditions for workers, with clean water, proper sanitation, and health facilities and better housing; and better representation through labor unions for adivasi seasonal labor migrants.[68] But in Jharkhand, the current performance of indigenous rights activism does not allow for sustained discussions, let alone policies and practices, on these subjects to emerge. It is the poorest adivasis who ultimately suffer the cost of the purificatory middle-class performance of indigenous rights activism. Perhaps there is greater hope for the poorest in a class-based struggle, than in one focused on identity politics. It is to this potential that I turn in chapter 6.

6. The Terror Within

REVOLUTION AGAINST THE STATE?

5:00 P.M., 3 JUNE 2001

Rattle, rattle, rattle. I heard the familiar sound of a bicycle coming up the track and being leaned up against my house, and the tinkling of milk cans as they swung against the bicycle frame. Shiv, looking a bit sheepish, poked his head around the wooden door as I lit a match to make some tea. I smiled and asked, "So, why are you late today? What mischief have you been up to roaming the streets of Bero?"

Shiv was a relative of the landlord descendants of Tapu. To the slight disquiet of my Munda family, he and I had become great friends. Every morning, as I fumbled around for my milk pot, I'd wait for Shiv to tease, "I haven't got all the time in the world—haven't you got your pot ready?" He would give me half a pint of his buffalo milk before proceeding to sell the rest to Bero roadside restaurants, locally called line-hotels. When he got back to Tapu at noon, he would bring me a copy of the *Prabhat Khabar*, the only copy of a newspaper to arrive in the village. I'd eagerly await his return to hear stories from Bero and discuss the headlines.

As I put extra sugar in his tea, Shiv asked if I would look at something in the possession of one of his friends, a man named Khand Oraon, who owned a line-hotel just outside Bero. From his tone, I could tell that Shiv was requesting my involvement in something he could not openly talk about. Khand was strikingly tall, slim, smiling, and eager to discuss life in England. I had met him on various occasions when I had stopped at his line-hotel with Shiv for a cup of tea, en route to Bero. I recalled that Khand was not from the Bero area: he had pursued postgraduate studies elsewhere and had moved to Bero in 1987, to live near his cousin. The customers at Khand's line-hotel were mainly truck drivers traveling on the Great Eastern Road, but Khand also used the restaurant as the headquarters of the Bero branch of the All Jharkhand Students Union (AJSU), which he led. AJSU had been set up in Ranchi in 1987 to work toward an independent Jharkhand State and as a more militant wing of the Jharkhand Mukti Morcha (the Jharkhand Liberation Front, known as the JMM). Curious to know more about Khand and his political activities, I agreed to accompany Shiv to the restaurant.

Soon after this, Khand led us through various dark curtains at the back of his line-hotel to a small bedroom. From an envelope wrapped in plastic, he withdrew a million-dollar bill with a certificate of authenticity printed by something called the "American Bank Note Company" in 1988 for an "International Association of Millionaires." "Is it genuine?" he asked. Feeling out of my depth, I replied that I could try to find out if such notes had ever been printed. A Google search later revealed that the bill was the marketing idea of someone named Tari Steward, who had produced it as a collectible priced at $18.50. I gathered that the note had been passed around among a few men I had previously met at Khand's restaurant, who were all curious about its value. The men were from neighboring areas and were all involved in the extreme left-wing guerrilla Maoist Communist Centre (MCC), widely believed to be leading a revolution for an alternative state supported by the poorest rural Indians.

In 1967, in Naxalbari, West Bengal, a violent revolution broke out against landlords. It was supported by tribal peasants, who forcibly occupied land, burned records, and canceled peasants' debts. This left-wing extremism caught the imagination of many people around the world and came to be known as the Naxalite movement—an armed uprising of peasants and workers against landlords and capitalists, inspired by Marx, Lenin, and Mao.[1] Since 1967, as official histories show, the Naxalites have declined and split into factions along ideological, organizational, and geographical lines.[2] However, the movement gained new strength in 1984 when the Yadav caste supporters of one of its most violent branches, the MCC, brutally killed forty-two Rajputs in the Aurangabad and Gaya districts of Bihar.[3] The women had been beheaded with axes, and the men had either been shot or had their throats slit. The Bihar government's response to its "flaming fields"[4] included the banning of the Naxalites

Shiv's bike outside my house in Tapu. *Painting by author.*

under Section 16 of the Criminal Law Amendment Act, 1908.[5] The Naxalites increasingly became identified as an extremist or terrorist group. Their goal was seen to be the creation of a liberated territory from Nepal to Andra Pradesh, and, in the late 1990s, Jharkhand became a crucial region in their struggle.

The MCC declared that their protest in Jharkhand was against bourgeois state oppression and on behalf of the neglected indigenous poor, with an overall goal of forming a parallel administration in a Liberated zone. In this region, the MCC would prevent interference from the state.[6] In 2001, within a few months of gaining power in Jharkhand, the right-wing Hindu Nationalist BJP declared extremism or terrorism to be the major problem it had inherited from the previous state government. While newspapers reported the violent acts of the MCC, the new government launched a major operation against it. It proclaimed ten of its twenty-two districts as terrorist infested "red" zones and allocated a large sum for police modernization, the acquisition of paramilitary forces and in particular the Border Security forces and the Central Reserve Police force and the creation of armed camps in the red areas. The agenda appeared to be in line with that of the BJP-led national government in New Delhi—which, in

December 2001, feeding off the global anxiety after September 11, had sharpened its crackdown against terrorism by introducing the controversial Prevention of Terrorism Ordinance, which soon became an act of Parliament.

Under the act, the MCC and the other main Naxalite factions in Jharkhand, Party Unity and the People's War Group, were identified as terrorists. By March 2004, according to the Union Home Ministry, Jharkhand had seen the largest number of arrests under the act. Since the formation of the new state, 234 people had been arrested, more than 650 people had cases pending against them, and more than 3,200 people had been named as being involved in terrorist activities. Naxalism was increasingly defined not only as a major law-and-order problem but also as a national security issue, as it was creating red terror in the country. And in 2006, the Prime Minister of India, Manmohan Singh, described the Maoists as the biggest internal security threat that India has ever faced.

But in rural Jharkhand—where the poorest people have time and again been neglected, and where the claims of indigenous rights activists, as I have argued in previous chapters, do not necessarily represent the views of those poorest people—the expansion of the class-based struggle through the revolutionary Naxalites may be a cause for celebration. Indeed, sociologists and geographers have argued that with the spread of the Naxalites, for the first time in years, the poorest have somebody to support them against the oppressive and exploitative forces of the state or the upper castes and classes.[7] For the first time, the most marginalized people may have a chance of moving from their consistent betrayal by the dominant political establishment to genuine "people's power."[8] In Jharkhand, in particular, it is hardly surprising that the poorest are turning to the Naxalites, given the failure of the new BJP government to pay attention to Jharkhand's indigenous communities.[9] Indeed, from the BBC to *The New York Times*, international media reports now argue that most of the supporters of India's Maoist guerrilla war are India's tribal poor.[10] This line of thinking has an international resonance as economic inequality, underdevelopment, and poor governance are increasingly seen as the causes of armed conflict, crime, and terrorism, in what some commentators have called a "security-development nexus."[11] Development ventures in these zones are seen to have to co-opt another civilizing mission and integrate agendas of conflict resolution, postconflict reconstruction, demobilization, and good governance into their programs. Given these seemingly obvious conjectures that in Jharkhand the MCC's main supporters are the poorest indigenous populations, and that its main target is the state and alliances of politicians and contractors, I was struck by the fact that the stories my friends and informants told me seemed to suggest almost the opposite.

In this chapter, I will question the received wisdom that the MCC is necessarily a movement of the poorest indigenous people against the state when it first spreads into an area. Rather than supporting the poorest, or being supported by them, I will show not only that the MCC's early spread in rural Jharkhand is dependent on rural elites intimately connected with the state, but also that the MCC is sometimes used by and in collaboration with state officials. Moreover, people are not the only basis for focusing on the similarities between the MCC and the local government. As the representatives of the state have done previously, in return for support from rural elites, the MCC sells protection—both for access to the informal economy of the state, and from the possibilities of MCC's own activities. This protection is, as the political scientist Charles Tilly has famously argued, a double-edged commodity, evoking both the sense of a comforting presence that provides shelter from enemies and the image of criminal rackets, in which the locally powerful demand tribute in order to stave off their own violence.[12] Showing state makers as entrepreneurs who sell protection, Tilly crucially points out that "if protection rackets represent organized crime at its smoothest, then war making and state making—quintessential protection rackets with the advantage of legitimacy—qualify as our largest examples of organized crime."[13] Terrorism, banditry, piracy, gangland rivalry, and state making all belong on the same continuum of selling protection.

The commodity with which the MCC has been most closely associated is violence, not protection. But violence is a means, not an end—the commodity really at stake is protection.[14] The MCC's grassroots support is based not on a shared ideology or on violence alone, but on having greater control over what can be termed a market of protection,[15] in which violence is used to sell protection for bargaining for power and material benefits. The MCC operates in a market previously controlled by parts of the local state. In this chapter, I unveil this market of protection in order both to question this alternative claim for the development and liberation of the poorest people and to contest the boundaries between the state and its alleged enemies, the terrorists, in rural Jharkhand.

I never found out how the million-dollar bill came into Khand's possession, but the incident led me to begin reconstructing the history of Shiv's involvement with the MCC. Reflecting on the issues of researching what many have called a terrorist organization, I am reminded by the million-dollar bill that I did not in fact set out to study the MCC. As a result of my existing relationships with a few men who had become targets of MCC expansion, information on the movement began to fall into my lap, and I slowly became interested in exploring specific questions and identifying emerging patterns.

Among the accounts of my informants, I have put most faith in what I learned from Shiv and Bhavesh Chatterjee, my longest, closest, and most trusted friends in the Bero area. As the story of how I came to know about the million-dollar bill suggests, secrecy and caution regarding information is a central concern for those who have links with the underground movement. Thus, unless one is a member of the MCC or a state official who has access to classified information about the operation of the movement in a particular area,[16] it is very difficult to openly and systematically research the movement in depth. The available material generally reconstructs the social and political history of the movement through its leaders; written sources such as diaries, propaganda, and poetry; or newspaper and government reports.[17] Commentators on participant observation in other violent social contexts suggest that it is more beneficial to start at the top, since access guaranteed by leaders will generally be respected all the way down through the ranks.[18] Conducting research as a Naxalite sympathizer[19] or analyzing state-level activities, however, have their disadvantages. Most notably, they are susceptible to bias toward either the movement's or the state's point of view. Moreover, they tend to focus on the Naxalites exclusively, so that it is difficult to see the organization in its context of local social processes and understandings. In comparison, my long-standing relationship with my informants, which began before I learned of their involvement with the MCC, allowed me to see the organization in a rather different light. This chapter is an attempt to give voice to my informants' experiences of the MCC, and to illuminate the emerging patterns and practices about which they speak.

Just before I arrived to live in Tapu, on 14 September 2000, nine

Muslims were shot dead and four more were injured in a village about twelve kilometers west of Bero by a group of uniformed and armed men, who then disappeared into the surrounding countryside shouting, "Long live MCC!" The areas to the immediate west of Bero Block were said to be Naxalite strongholds, where regular MCC meetings took place to resolve village disputes, and from where some young men had been sent to join underground military groups. The organization wanted to expand further east, and it did not take much imagination to see that the forest around Tapu, greater and denser than that of surrounding villages, was attractive not only to wild elephants.

In the midst of some wedding celebrations in February 2001, Khand had arrived at Shiv's house with three strangers, some fried chickpeas, and a few bottles of rum. After several shots of rum, away from the excitement of the wedding, the men revealed their identity. Their cause, they explained to Shiv, was noble. Despite more than fifty years of Indian independence, despite the separation of Jharkhand from Bihar, there was still no real freedom for the poorest, most exploited, people of Jharkhand. The government was corrupt, and political parties did not have ideologies appropriate for the poor and were interested only in winning votes. There was neither justice nor equality. The poor were becoming more and more exploited. The only solution, the men said, was a revolution. Gandhi had ruined India with his nonviolent policies. Now Indians needed to take up arms to overturn the status quo. The problem, the men explained, was the difficulty of mobilizing poor people to participate in this revolution. The people of this area, they said, were unaware of their situation: they did not know the nature and extent of their exploitation; they had no idea of their rights, let alone how to activate them. Therefore, these poor people needed to be enlightened by the MCC. And the MCC needed to reach them by gaining access to villages like Tapu. To this end, the men said, they needed a good worker like Shiv to build a base in Tapu, introducing the MCC and eventually holding meetings and settling village disputes.

Later, two of the three men were identified as Chandra and Anil Ganjhu—a surname given by the maharajah to families who became landlords. Shiv learned that the MCC grew in the following way. Men like Khand, who knew the local terrain, became MCC informers. They introduced the MCC to strategically selected people, like Shiv, who would teach them about the geographical and social structure of a village, and provide shelter in their houses when required, while an

MCC base was established in the forest. If the police came, the villagers would disguise the MCC members as their guests.

Then the MCC men would introduce themselves to the villagers, gaining support among them by practicing classic vigilante activities such as the "resolution" of village disputes in "people's courts." Such disputes often drew on preexisting village tensions that might not otherwise have become disputes. If dispute resolution did not enable the MCC to achieve greater dominance, the organization could resort to more coercive means to bring the village under its control.

When all the villagers had come within the fold of the MCC, a few youth would be recruited for MCC bases in other places, to be trained and armed as members of squads that form the group's underground guerrilla army. Those who had helped the MCC gain access to the village could be sent to neighboring regions as area commanders, to spread the organization further. In this network fashion, the organization was able to expand.

Thus, people became involved with the MCC to different degrees and were promised different types of reward. Whether it was the case or not, men like Shiv speculated that only the squad members, and those above the status of area commander, received monthly salaries for their services—of between Rs 1,000 and Rs 5,000 a month. Others, like Khand, were spoken of as "getting involved," and the degree of their involvement was often described in percentages. Indeed, toward the end of my stay, Khand would talk about himself as being 80 percent involved; Akshay, 70 percent; and so on.

As Shiv recounted these plans, it became evident to me that this type of expansion challenged at least one conventional notion of the MCC's grass-roots support. Bela Bhatia, one of the few scholars to have done serious, grounded work on the Naxalites, has argued that in central Bihar, "for the first time, on a sustained basis, after 1947, the poor can turn to their [Naxalite comrades] in the time of injustice and know that there is somebody who will stand up for them against oppressive and exploitative forces, whether it be upper castes/classes or the state."[20] More recently, other scholars have described the failure of Jharkhand to pay attention to its tribal communities as accompanying a "rising tide of Naxalism" and argue that this is no coincidence—that turning to the Naxalites represents a reasonable choice for poor, tribal people, given their opposition to the state.[21] These scholars also argue that, in this Hobbesian world, the MCC's success in empowering the poorest is often in defiance of the state and its officers, and is dependent on its ability to contest the power of established alliances between politicians and contractors.[22] Indeed, local newspapers and international magazines report politician-contractor groups to be the MCC's first target for elimination.[23] The new BJP government in Jharkhand also attributes the rise of the Naxalites to the predominance of a poor, rural population who know no better than to join the movement, thus implying that such people are the undeveloped masses it inherited from the failed modernizing mission of the previous government. The Jharkhand State, the MCC, the media, and academics all express the conventional rhetoric: that the MCC's main support comes from the rural poor, and that the movement is fighting against the local elites, who are intimately connected with the state.

While this received wisdom may ring true for central Bihar or for the later spread of the MCC, the evidence from the Bero area shows that the MCC's initial grass-roots support in Jharkhand was not the poorest population, but already established rural elites. Shiv, Khand, and their friends were educated men from the more wealthy village families that included both the older elite of landlord descendants and a newer, educated (and often Scheduled Tribe) elite. The majority of villagers, such as the families I lived with, in Tapu were descendants of former tenants; today, they are the poorest villagers. Most of these people had not heard about the MCC, and those few who had believed that it existed only in other areas. Indeed, when I pushed my Munda family and their relatives about who the MCC might be, most had only the vague idea that it was a group that moved around, committing violence. Just as the Mundas want to keep away from what they consider a dangerous and alien state, as shown in chapter 2, they want no involvement with this foreign group and had no idea that it had come to their village.[24]

The "problems" that are "resolved" by the MCC in neighboring villages further reflect the movement's bias toward rural elites. This is evident in the MCC's reprimanding people involved in premarital and postmarital sexual affairs—of the five MCC dispute-solving cases in nearby captured villages, three concerned such affairs, each of which resulted in the accused lover's being beaten. Although such affairs are common among both the rural elites and the poorer peasants, as I suggested in the last chapter, their moral policing among the poor is often of concern to elites, who seek to reproduce the image of a purer, less sexually promiscuous tribal population.

A bias toward rural elites is also evident in an MCC antidrinking campaign. Following the pasting of antidrinking posters on buildings in Bero in 2000, uniformed men from the MCC broke the pots of tribal peasants who were selling village-brewed rice beer and alcohol distilled from the mahua flower in several markets west of Tapu.[25] There are a few interesting points to note about this campaign. The first is that it does not threaten the sellers who belong to the elite of their village, the landlord descendants, who in their line-hotels or shops illegally sell the "English" variety of alcohol—usually whiskey, rum, gin, and beer, but not the local brews. The second is that, as I argued in chapter 4, while village elites Sanskritize and Brahminicize themselves, claiming that it is morally wrong and ritually impure to consume alcohol, drinking mahua wine and rice beer is very much a part of Munda market and ritual culture. Munda men and women of different generations openly drink together, and the first drops of drink are always given to the spirits. In practice, of course, although the MCC banned the consumption of alcohol, a central part of their networking with the village elites is drinking and meat-eating sessions, which take place behind closed doors. On these occasions, "English" alcohol is preferred, as local brews are considered distasteful. The third point is that, like the reprimanding of people involved in premarital and postmarital sexual affairs, this antidrinking campaign is one promoted by a political party, the JMM, in earlier years—a point to which I will return.

With the recent resurgence of the Naxalites, commentators have recognized that it is unusual for its grass-roots supporters to understand their mobilization in terms of a Marxist-Leninist vision of armed struggle by peasants and laborers against landlords and capitalists.[26] However, they maintain that not only are the Naxalites a people's movement of the poor and exploited, but that the grass-roots struggle focuses on issues such as land redistribution, better terms for sharecroppers, minimum wages, access to common property resources, basic social rights and respect for lower castes, and effective policing of criminal gangs.[27] It is clear that, at least in the Tapu area, the initial stages of MCC operations reveal little commitment to such ideological reasoning among grass-roots supporters. As for ideology's influencing the actions of elite groups in villages, the Jharkhand evidence suggests that the MCC is seen to embrace an alternative vision of modernity and morality, in which a more disciplined rural poor will better control their drinking and sex lives. This vision promotes higher-caste notions of better citizens, not only reflecting a morality that is not always practiced by the elites themselves and that is repressive for tribal peasants.

Beyond their own elevation within the social hierarchy, however, there are other, more pressing motives for the village elites to support the MCC. As shown in chapter 3, the abolition of zamindari in the early 1950s meant that these elites, who faced gradual impoverishment, increasingly attempted to sustain their lifestyles through state-related resources—whether directly (as in through government jobs) or indirectly (for instance, through government contracts). The landlord descendants reproduced and the newer elites created their position through extensive links with the state. They were entrepreneurs who maintained their financial position relative to the tenant descendants, such as the Mundas, in large part because of their participation in the informal economy of state programs. As a result of their intimate connections to state officials, they were particularly effective in siphoning off money from the state.

The expansion of the MCC is intimately linked to the politics of access to this economy of state patronage. In return for their cooperation in harboring and fostering the movement, recruits in areas under MCC control are offered privileged and protected access to state resources. Hence, when the MCC arrived in Tapu, they promised Shiv contracts from, in particular, the block development office programs of the Ministry of Rural Development. Most of the block office programs involve construction projects for common use (e.g., roads, dams, and community buildings) and require that the contractor be a villager. The funds for the project come in the form of checks made out directly to the contractor who, as explained in chapter 3, is expected to siphon off up to 10 percent of the block-level money for himself. For individuals attempting to diversify their incomes, becoming a contractor is very appealing.

There are not many block office contracts, however, and they attract much competition. To obtain a contract, one needs a patron, a powerful person with leverage over the state officials who award the contracts. One also needs supporters who will both threaten competitors and also offer protection from their supporters. In effect, the MCC guaranteed Shiv a contractorship and the subsequent protection to siphon off illicit money from state programs. Thus the MCC entered a preexisting market to sell protection, engaging in activities that were already established in the area.[28] Indeed, the Bero scenario shows that the MCC's expansion pattern reflects a preexisting history of people connected not necessarily by caste, but by their participation in the earlier campaigns of a political party, the JMM.

These continuities are illustrated by Shiv's experiences. Shiv met Khand in the early 1990s, when Khand led the Bero branch of the AJSU. Then, Shiv was frustrated that, despite his college education, he seemed to have little prospect of a better life than that offered by Tapu's mud huts. For several years, Shiv had delivered some of his buffalo milk to Akshay Roy's line-hotel in Bero. Akshay, a descendant of the landlord of a neighboring village, was also known as the right-hand man of Vishwanath Bhagat (one of the two men from the Oraon tribe at the center of the parha battle described in chapter 2), who was the Bero Block JMM president and a candidate for the state legislature in the 1995 election. Through Akshay, Shiv became involved in Vishwanath's election campaign. While, as I have shown in chapter 3, there were other reasons for his involvement, Shiv—like many others—was primarily attracted by the promise that if Vishwanath was elected, his workers would receive contracts for block office projects.

Vishwanath held considerable leverage over the distribution of resources by the head of the office, the block development officer (BDO), because as an MLA, he could influence the BDO's transfer to a new post every three years. To advance his own career, a BDO would therefore want to maintain a good relationship with the local MLA—by, for example, awarding construction projects to the MLA's workers. Knowing that not every MLA candidate's promises would be kept, and despite competition from other landlord descendants in Tapu, Shiv felt that he would get a contract because of his long-standing relationship with Akshay.

In 1996, following Vishwanath's election, Shiv did attain Tapu's first contract from the block office, to build the first dirt road to the village. In order to acquire the contract, Shiv had received support from Akshay, Khand, and Vishwanath, who protected him in various ways from the attentions of other landlord descendants. One night, for instance, a group of men from one landlord descendant lineage, armed with axes, knives, and sticks, woke Shiv when they threw a clay pot full of their urine and feces at his door, but Shiv scared them away by waving a gun that Khand had given him. It became generally known that Shiv was supported by Vishwanath and his workers, who—backed by state officials—had the reputation of beating up those who got in their way, and who were feared by the landlord descendants in Tapu. As MLA, Vishwanath was considered by the rural elites to be a part of the state, and in collaboration with certain state officers, he basically offered protection to his supporters, entrepreneurs like Shiv, to illicitly glean resources from the local government. While this was protection from competing entrepreneurs, it was also protection from the state itself. By having leverage over, and working in collaboration with, local state officials — who also took an unofficial cut from the funds for development projects — Vishwanath offered his supporters protection from competitors and from being scrutinized and punished by the government.

When the MCC came to the area, its members marketed a very similar kind of protection to what Vishwanath had offered his workers in the past. To Shiv, the MCC became one more group that, like the MLAs and certain state officials, protected entrepreneurs' illicit access to state resources. In fact, as the MCC gained greater support in the area, the boundaries between the local government and the MCC became ever more porous, as certain officials themselves sought MCC protection. By cultivating a web of associations with each other, the MCC and the state enjoy a degree of interdependency, as demonstrated by the following story.

As Shiv was being introduced to the MCC, about five years after he had built the dirt road to Tapu, Vishwanath had proposed to the Ministry of Rural Development a project to build a dirt road between two villages neighboring Tapu. As a large project, this road would have involved substantial commissions. When the project was approved, the Ranchi District Commissioner ordered a block officer, not a villager, to be the project's contractor. Not telling Vishwanath that the project had been approved, the BDO selected an officer named Khasi as the contractor. The BDO feared that if Vishwanath knew about this decision, he would choose a different block officer, and the money from the project would go into Vishwanath's pockets, rather than the BDO's. The BDO appointed Khasi because he had a reputation for being feeble and could easily be manipulated. In order to ensure that the work was completed, the BDO also asked that a man named Bhavesh be involved.

The main source of my story is Bhavesh, another good friend who was a neighbor when I lived in Bero in 1999. Although he could easily have been mistaken for one, Bhavesh was not a state official. He was reputed to be an excellent engineer and knew the local terrain so well that, in exchange for an illicit cut, block officers relied on him to complete large projects: Bhavesh was the unofficial engineer for almost all large block office projects.

One day a block office clerk leaked the news to Vishwanath that the contractor for the road had been appointed. No longer having powers over the BDO as his MLA days were over, Vishwanath called Khasi to his house and told him to take his fixed percentage but said he, Vishwanath, would construct the road. Khasi and the BDO turned to Bhavesh for assistance, as the BDO had MCC contacts in Bharno, a town west of Bero. Bhavesh asked the MCC to protect Khasi in exchange for 5 percent of the total cost of the road. Wanting to expand in the area, the MCC agreed. A few days later, Vishwanath and Akshay were called to Bharno and threatened. Scared of the MCC, they backed off, and Khasi began the construction of the road.

I left Bero soon afterward and did not hear the end of the story. However, the proceedings until then reveal a number of points of connection and interdependence between the state and the MCC. First, the state officers bought protection from the MCC to exploit state resources.[29] Khasi and the BDO called on the MCC for protection from a rival claim made by a former elected representative (Vishwanath), to ensure that they would make illicit profits from the construction of a state project. Second, the threat of violence toward competing contract bidders was a strategy that Vishwanath himself had employed when he was an MLA. Thus, by guaranteeing contract awards through violence and intimidation, the MCC used a strategy that was familiar to state officials. Let us return to Shiv's story and, in particular, to what happened after the MCC's visit.

FEAR

After he was approached by the MCC in 2001, Shiv neither agreed nor refused to help the movement. Building the dirt road to the village in the mid-1990s had been life-threatening, and Shiv decided to stick to income from his cattle and fields. However, he realized that evading the MCC would not be easy, and he decided to maintain a marginal position as a silent observer, hoping to acquire enough information to be able to avoid them.

As the months passed, Shiv kept a close watch on the proceedings. Although Khand had initially encouraged him to support the movement, in quieter and more sober moments, he gave Shiv conflicting advice and stressed that it was important to maintain a certain distance and not trust anyone. However, as time passed and more men, like Akshay Roy, were meeting secretly with Chandra Ganjhu (one of the men whom Khand had first brought to meet Shiv), Khand began to pressure Shiv to cooperate.

The increased police crackdown on the MCC by the BJP-led government in other parts of Jharkhand led to an incident that reinforced Shiv's conviction that he ought to stay away from the MCC.[30] One day in August 2001, when he brought the *Prabhat Khabar* for me from Bero, we read that Chandra and six associates had been arrested by the police in Mandar, a neighboring administrative block.[31] According to the police reports, Chandra had confessed his involvement in at least twenty heinous crimes that included eight incidents of mass killings, one of which had resulted in six deaths; attacks on police pickets; looting weapons; and planting land mines. The reports also stated that Anil Ganjhu, whom Shiv had also met in that initial contact, had been with Chandra when he was arrested, but had managed to escape.[32] While Chandra was identified as a commander, the identity of the six others was not confirmed. The incident convinced Shiv that, despite the MCC's rhetoric of protection for its workers, the most likely to be arrested were its grass-roots workers, not its commanders.

For a few months after the incident, things were quiet in Bero, and Shiv continued his daily visits to town to sell milk. However, starting around November, Anil returned to the Bero area, and the networking and planning sessions at Khand's line-hotel resumed. The pressure on Shiv to set a day for the MCC to come to Tapu increased, and Shiv became preoccupied with how to evade them. He began spending days at the houses of his in-laws and sisters in other villages; when in Tapu, he pretended to be sick and asked his father to deliver the milk to Bero instead. Away from Bero, he could avoid Khand and Anil.

However, in early February 2002, they finally caught up with him and told him that in ten days, eight men would come to Tapu for a picnic at night by the forest. By this time, Shiv no longer wished to push for details, for fear of starting a conversation that would move the date forward. On 13 February, when I was in Ranchi preparing to leave for the brick kilns in West Bengal, Shiv came to tell me he could no longer evade the MCC. He wanted urgently to accept an acquaintance's offer of a job in Maharashtra (two and a half days away) at a grease-making factory. Fortunately, the acquaintance was to leave for Maharashtra the next day. Shiv returned to Tapu that night to inform his shocked and upset family that he would come back to Tapu in five months, for the rainy season.

When Shiv left, Khand was eager to take me to the MCC hide-out in Mandar. Although it was always portrayed as a very secret place, the fact that I knew about this hide-out suggests it might have been a place where selected non-MCC members were taken, in order to publicize the MCC. Nevertheless, I was reluctant to go for several reasons. First, the trip was always described as an opportunity to go fishing and have a picnic, and I knew this meant extensive drinking. Second, most of the time I felt like an object of curiosity to the men who hung around Khand's line-hotel. Not knowing the men well, I was reluctant to be the only woman on the trip. Third, I felt that although it would have been interesting to learn more about the men and their relationships with each other, I was not sure I would learn anything particularly insightful about the MCC, other than what they wanted to tell journalists and the outside media. In fact, I had learned from Shiv that the men had been considering taking me to the hide-out for several weeks, as they thought that it would be fun for them and that it would be approved of by the higher leaders as a good advertisement for the MCC. In the end, I decided not to go. However, Khand continued to insist. Like Shiv, I found myself trying to avoid him, thus cutting off this source of information on the spread of the MCC in the area.

Two years later, I returned to Tapu. In Bero, Akshay and Khand's brother both said that Shiv had recently visited his family but had returned to Maharashtra. I was therefore surprised when I spotted Shiv behind his father in the Bero market. His grandmother's death and his brother's separation from the joint family meant that he now had to stay in Tapu. He had been there for two months but was keeping a low profile, trying not to be seen. He was still afraid that Khand and Akshay would pressure him to support the MCC. As for Khand, his line-hotel was locked and empty. I was told that occasionally he would go there after dark. There were rumors that Vishwanath and the current MLA were also competing for the protection of the Naxalites for votes in the next election. Although the tenant descendants still thought that the MCC had not come to their area, the movement was slowly increasing its influence among the rural elites.

The MCC's success appeared to be based on its increasingly coercive control of the area, so that the village elites not only felt that cooperation would give them protection to continue their involvement in the informal economy of the state, but they also had come to fear not cooperating. In fact, one striking aspect of Shiv's story is the fear that the MCC induces among its grass-roots targets. Shiv took the drastic decision to leave Jharkhand because he feared not cooperating with the MCC. His actions exemplify how, within this dominant frame of fear, it is not easy to find individuals who actively resist involvement in the movement's violence (or threat of violence).[33] Members of the rural elites in Jharkhand repeatedly told me that they had to support the MCC for their *suraksha* (safety and protection). It was clear that what they meant by suraksha was not simply protection from competing factions, but also protection from the MCC's threats of those who were not its supporters.

Anthropologists have recently pointed out that violence defies easy categorization,[34] and visible forms of violence are often intimately linked to less visible ones. Intricate combinations of visible and invisible means are also deployed in selling protection. For instance, the sense of the need to comply, at least to some degree, with the agenda of the MCC in return for protection from the movement itself was underpinned by the production of fear of the organization through both visible and less visible means. This fear of the MCC is linked not only to its massacres and to the knowledge of those individuals who are involved in its grass-roots operations, but also to a fear of not cooperating exacerbated by the less visible qualities of the MCC as a very powerful, almost mythical and mystical organization. Fear is often stronger in the absence than in the presence of whatever causes the fear.[35]

The idea of the immense power of the MCC is perpetuated in several invisible ways. First, it is created through an idea of a highly centralized, hierarchical, and organized movement—the notions that each region is divided into zones, subzones, areas, and villages; that all these divisions have hierarchically connected leaders; and that the overall purpose is to create a Maoist territory from Nepal to Andhra.

Second, the image of immense power is perpetuated through the clandestine nature of its operations, and the circulation of secrets and hidden resources. False names are used,[36] for instance, and people recruited at the local level have only vague ideas about who else is involved in the hierarchy above their area commander, or in geographically adjoining MCC units. The rural elites understand that this structure is strategically constructed so that if they are caught by the police, they will be able to reveal only a very limited amount about the organization. This cloud of secrecy generates uncertainty about the size and spread of the organization. The belief arises that the MCC is, or could be, anywhere and everywhere—a kind of folklore about its spread. Although this idea is dependent on secrecy, it is also perpetuated by the apparent breach of secrecy[37]—the leak here and there that the MCC has arrived in X village or is planning Y attack, or even by taking a journalist or foreign anthropologist to a supposed MCC hide-out. Such tactical breaches of secrecy enhance the idea of the MCC as a powerful organization, making people fear the consequences of not supporting it and thus accelerating its spread. In areas of new expansion, it is easy for someone to suspect that anyone else could be involved, for this to create the impression that everyone is involved, for the original someone to then become involved, and for this to result in everyone's feeling like the original someone, thus leading to everyone's being involved.[38]

Third, rumors add to the myth of the MCC—I was constantly told by people in Bero that the MCC has its members and supporters everywhere, even in the government. Block officers, forest officers, and police have a double identity: beneath their uniforms are actually MCC men. In fact, when I returned to Bero in January 2004, one of the main rumors circulating was that when the Bero police were about to arrest an MCC collaborator, the speaker of the Jharkhand Legislative Assembly intervened, and the young man was released. The point being made was that like all politicians, the speaker profited from the protection of the MCC. And in Ranchi circles, the gossip was that the MCC was in bed with many government functionaries and political party leaders, and even that Jharkhand's Land Reforms and Revenue Minister was a former Naxalite squad commander.[39] Such rumors created the idea that the MCC is so powerful that it is increasingly infiltrating the government.[40]

These invisible qualities of the MCC combine with stories of its capacity for violence to reproduce the myth of its power. Media reports spread chilling news of the MCC's notorious violence nearby (such as when the nine Muslims were killed)[41] and elsewhere. The threat of violence is perpetuated by the MCC strategy of disarming an area it aims to expand in. In April through June 1999, when I was hanging around the Bero block office, the MCC demanded and collected all registered civilian rifles and guns in Bero, most of which had been in the possession of the landlord descendants. The most common way for the MCC to take weapons was to first send a threatening letter, demanding them. This would be followed by an unannounced visit in the middle of the night by a group of armed MCC men, who took the weapons away.[42] The weapons are no doubt used by the MCC underground armies, which is one benefit of disarming people. At the local level, however, there is another important result: the establishment of fear through the idea of the power of an armed organization in a disarmed area. The MCC sold protection to its supporters by spreading the idea of its increasing coercive control of the area and therefore creating fear of itself.

STATE OR TERRORIST?

Through the analysis of various representations of indigenous rights activists, the previous chapters have suggested that there is an important class dimension to the indigenous rights movement, which is smoothed over in the identity politics it produces. The movement's urban, educated, middle-class proponents may unintentionally be further marginalizing the poorest adivasis, on whose behalf they claim to speak. In this chapter, I have explored an alternative movement that may hold greater hope for the indigenous poor, the expansion of a class-based struggle through the revolutionary guerrilla Naxalite movement, the MCC. However, this chapter has shown that the initial spread of the radical left-wing movement is in fact supported by and moves through the rural elites, and not the poorer adivasis. Movement through the rural elites may in fact be a strategy of the Maoists to get a foothold in the area. As this book goes to press, I am once again in rural Jharkhand, although this time in a different area where the Maoists have had a strong presence over the last twenty years and where the sociology and the function of the movement are transformed from the early spread I explore in this chapter. At the time of the fieldwork conducted for this book, however, rural elites were supporting the MCC not because of a shared ideology, but because it offered better protection for them to access the informal economy of state resources.

Exploring the MCC's grass-roots expansion in Jharkhand unveils that the operations of the MCC and those of parts of the local government are a struggle for control over a market of protection. In this market of protection, parts of the government are the MCC's competitors and collaborators. This protection is a double-edged commodity: protection both against competitors for access to the informal economy of the local government, and from its own activities. The market of protection works by creating both an enchantment with power, and a fear of the protector.[43] In rural Jharkhand, the MCC is successfully competing with networks of politicians and lower-level bureaucrats in this market of protection, fragmenting the local coercive control and thus winning over the support of the village elites. This is made possible by the MCC's success in presenting itself as a dual structure: a visible and an invisible one.[44] The visible powers of the MCC include its involvement in local politics, its embodiment through local people, and its everyday activities, while its invisible powers involve its secrets, its vast hidden resources and higher authorities, and its capacity for violence.

Establishing the Naxalites as terrorists, the Jharkhand State juxtaposed the alleged rationality and legitimacy of its government to the irrationality and violence of the extremists. The government claimed to be combating the threat that a dark age of chaotic, Hobbesian violence would take over its vulnerable rural tribal heartlands. It called for an increase in state security, in the name of protection for its citizens. Philip Abrams suggests that the state is a triumph of concealment, to be approached as the reification of an idea that masks real power relations by legitimizing them under the guise of public interest.[45] In light of the recent American and British war against terror, fought in the name of protecting the West from terrorist threats, Abrams's call to demystify the idea of the state, to understand how that idea works, seems especially pertinent. One way of exploring the idea of the state, in support of Taussig's suggestion of writing back against terror,[46] is to look behind the mask that protects a state by hiding its own violence, potentially contesting the boundary between the state and the terrorist.[47] Recent anthropological work on the relationships between those who speak in the name of the state and its citizens or subjects has explored the ways in which forms of rule are often produced through forceful and violent imposition, rather than straightforward consent.[48] Consent to govern is often given as much out of fear as through free choice.[49]

As the MCC expands in rural Jharkhand, one is left wondering about the nature of the Indian government. It appears that the monopoly of state protection in the Jharkhandi rural landscape is beginning to disintegrate. The MCC's visible and invisible qualities seem more pervasive than those of the government in producing the myth of its power and authority, and in creating fear among its grass-roots targets. There is indeed a great deal of continuity between the activities of the state and the MCC in rural Jharkhand—not only did the state remain the major source of resources, but both rural elites and state officials who once supported local politicians had come to support the MCC. The people who represented the MCC are the same as those who previously represented the state. Indeed, local politicians too are now seeking the protection of the MCC. Looking at these continuities raises the suspicion that, at the grass-roots level, the MCC and the state have begun to look very similar. In many ways in rural Jharkhand, what the state is, the MCC is too. While at one level, the state and the MCC work in tandem, at another, they are at war with each other.

What does this discrepancy tell us about the production and creation of both parties? Anthropologists have argued that states and illegal practices, be they terrorism, black marketeering, or illegal immigration, enjoy some variety of coexistence.[50] The point is not simply that this is a symbiosis of default, that the boundaries produced by one enable the definition of the other, but rather that states often tolerate or encourage forbidden activities. Perhaps a mutually beneficial relationship may develop from a rhetoric that sets the MCC against the state. In the case of the state, for example, the point is not simply that the presence of the MCC resulted in the physical expansion of the state apparatus into regions where it previously had a minimal presence,[51] it is also that the state can increase its power, for instance through demands for additional resources. The anti-extremist, antiterror campaign enabled the BJP-led Jharkhand government to demand more resources from the central government, and to perform its protective capacity by making arrests under the terrorism act. As Michael Taussig has fascinatingly suggested, the terrorist other can become a contemporary savage—subject to mimetic desire and fascination—against whom the state can indulge in an excess of terrifying violence.[52] The poor adivasi savage is turning into an adivasi terrorist, and the violence of the state against this alleged terrorism is legitimized in the name of civilizing the savage. Through action against terrorism at the margins of the state, the state not only enhances the terror and power of the MCC, it can also promote its own power.[53] One suggestion is that to some degree, in Jharkhand, the state and the terrorist (the antistate) may enjoy another kind of symbiotic relationship: a theatrical rhetoric of one against the other that actually promotes the idea of both. Perhaps to some extent, and at least for some time, in order to promote the idea of itself, it is in the interest of the new Jharkhand state to have a competing notion of an enemy state within.

Most worryingly, however, it is possible that the identification of terrorist and terrorized areas enables the state to make those regions a state of exception. Under these conditions, in the name of protection from insurgency and terrorism, the state is able to suspend normal legal procedures: it might then be able to evacuate entire village areas and move the inhabitants to refugee camps, as has happened in the neighboring state of Chhattisgarh.[54] Will it be surprising, then, if in the long run this displacement just happens to prove extremely useful, as swaths of India's mineral-rich lands on which adivasi land rights had been protected are emptied of inhabitants and their claims? Remember Walter Benjamin's insightful comment that documents of civilization are at the same time documents of barbarism.[55] Perhaps it is not only at the grass-roots level that there is a symbiotic interest over material resources between the state and the Maoists. Perhaps the stakes are actually much higher than my material has allowed me to show.

Whether made by the state or terrorists, claims to work for the poor in rural Jharkhand are reappropriated by nexuses of rural elites and officials at the expense of the poorest people. There is a disjuncture between the perception of MCC activity in the popular media and academic literature and the evidence for it at the village level. While some argue that the dominant influence within the Naxalites has been members of the upper castes and classes,[56] the movement's grass-roots supporters have always been considered to be the very poor. To this extent, there should be hope that this redistributive, class-based struggle will better represent those at the bottom of the social hierarchy. In Jharkhand, however, the MCC's initial grass-roots support comes from the rural elites, including entrepreneurs who have tried to maintain their dominance through their connections with an informal economy of the state. The actions of the rural elites reveal that their support of the MCC is not based on a shared ideology, but on the promise of protection that will allow them to continue to capture state resources. Revolutionary claims for the development and liberation of the poor, indigenous populations of rural Jharkhand appear through the class hierarchy of rural elites, blurring the boundary between the state and the terrorist, and reproducing the processes through which those at the bottom of the social hierarchy, the old descendants of the tenants, remain marginalized.

Epilogue

ARCADIAN SPACES BEYOND THE SHADOWS OF THE STATE

There is every reason to be sympathetic to indigenous rights activists, particularly when they seek to influence policy in contexts where state practices have treated marginalized populations as expendable. However, such sympathy needs to be combined with reflection and sensitivity to the violence that may result from well-intentioned but simplistic arguments and claims. Though the situation in Jharkhand is by no means uniform, either spatially and historically—and though the politics of indigeneity might play out differently there than elsewhere in the world—it does suggest that there is an important class dimension to indigenous rights movements that gets lost in the identity politics they produce. In Jharkhand, the indigenous rights activists come from urban, educated, middle-class backgrounds. Their visions and values are often very different from those of their poorer counterparts, such as the Mundas of Tapu, whom they claim to speak for, and whose lives and livelihoods they may unintentionally be further marginalizing. As John Gledhill suggests, the danger of indigenous rights propositions is that they create an identity-based politics which ultimately divides people and prevents the formation of a more significant, redistributive class struggle.[1]

While a class-based struggle that better represents adivasi people is clearly important for the Mundas, I have reservations about the promises of the revolutionary Naxalite movement—inspired by Marx, Lenin, and Mao—based on its initial expansion in this part of Jharkhand. The movement's tactics may change in the future, and of course may be different in other areas, but at the turn of the millennium in the Tapu area, it is the rural elites that the movement is recruiting, and there is a profound blurring of the boundary between it and the state. Moreover, there are striking similarities between the puritanical idioms articulated by the movement and those used by the indigenous rights activists.

Above all, however, I am concerned that such movements may be destroying the Munda spaces from which a radical politics might one day emerge. By way of an epilogue, rather than a conclusion, I would like to briefly speculate on what the ethnography presented in this book could mean in the search for alternative, more informed models of political life. This involves taking a distinctly different approach to what I hope has been a sensitive, nuanced, and robust analysis of the complex, contradictory, and differentiated realities of indigenous politics in Jharkhand. It involves using ethnographic holism and rigor to suggest normative possibilities that are beyond the narratives and academic debates of our texts.[2]

In this case, I would like to unveil those spaces of Munda life from which an alternative radical politics could emerge. I call these spaces "arcadian spaces" because they contain the elements of what the world could be for the Mundas. Walter Benjamin inspires me to think of arcadian spaces as holding the possibilities for better futures. In his *The Arcades Project*, Benjamin explores the residues of a dream world from which the working class could develop a class consciousness for itself that was true to its real-life conditions and that would enable it to break away from nineteenth-century hegemonic conceptions of history.[3] Benjamim emphasized that such residues of a dream world were important fields of struggle in revolutionary practice. Munda lives and perspectives today, as intertwined as they are with the broader political economy which dominates and exploits them, contain such arcadian spaces from which could emerge a politics that would better serve them. These are not simply spaces of utopia, or imagined projections of ideal models of society. Instead, they are based on elements of Munda society, of the Jungle Raj, which exist today. Furthermore, these are not spaces which oppose a modern world with a traditional one, but spaces where the distinctions between tradition and modernity do not exist, and where contemporary Munda lives and values form the revolutionary potential of possible futures.[4]

Are these arcadian spaces, then, spaces of resistance? Are they, in James Scott's words, the weapons of the weak that show that

In search of alternatives. *Photo by Rob Higham.*

the poorest people have not been ideologically dominated by elite norms? Does this study join the many accounts arguing that hegemony does not inevitably follow political and economic dominance, in the sense of a cultural dominance that is naturalized?[5] The answer is no. But before I explain further, let me take you back to the Tapu area, for the last time.

7:00 P.M., 16 JANUARY 2007, BERO

The sun had just set. Jitu Munda pulled his red baseball cap down on his head. He looked up and down the main road, and then at his watch. He knew he should be getting back home. His parents would be worried.

"One more bottle of whisky, Jitu," shouted Akshay Roy from inside the brick building. "This time it's your turn. You're getting married next week. Come on, get that photo out, and let's have a look at our sister-in-law to be."

Jitu slid back behind the dark curtain that split Akshay's line-hotel in two sections. One section was for customers stopping for a quick bite to eat while passing through Bero. The other section, the one behind the dark curtain, was for the local rural elites, who used it as a

meeting point to gossip and strike deals over bottles of whiskey and rum, labeled "Royal Challenge" and "Old Monk."

"There's no chance of getting home before 9:00 p.m. now," thought Jitu, as he tucked his shirt neatly into his trousers before sitting down. He couldn't possibly refuse Akshay's invitation to stay. All the educated young men in the surrounding area who wanted to join the rural elites admired Akshay. Not only was he a symbol of an alternative livelihood to doing hard work in the village fields, but he was also a symbol of what it meant to be a man in the rural area, what it meant to be both fearless and feared.

"Two more Royal Challenges," shouted Jitu to the young boy who worked in the restaurant. He might as well meet the other men's expectations. "Here she is," he said, as he nervously pulled out the photo of his future bride. He wondered if Akshay and the others would bring up the day when he had cried in front of them because his beloved Shila was married off to another man, and his father had brought back this photo.

7:00 P.M., 16 JANUARY 2007, TAPU

The birds were singing with a shrill intensity, and small bats were flitting between the bamboo and the papaya tree. Somra Munda was standing tall at the edge of our courtyard, looking out across the red sky and toward the horizon. He untied the knot at the end of his lungi, removed some tobacco, and gently crushed it with his thumb against his palm. He was worried.

The sun had set, and Jitu, his son, was nowhere in sight. Jitu had left at noon, despite Somra's pleas that he needed help to harvest the potatoes. Jitu had simply said he had to "work." Somra knew what that meant—roaming the streets of Bero, hanging out with men who were up to no good, and drinking alcohol and eating meat in roadside restaurants.

"Is this what I educated Jitu for? Where did Jitu get the money from?" Somra wondered. The taste of the tobacco and the eventual feeling of warmth it gave him did not relieve his anxiety. He felt trapped. How much should he scold Jitu? He had already ended his love affair with Shila. What would happen if Somra stopped Jitu from gallivanting off into Bero town? Perhaps Jitu would leave him entirely. But what if Jitu brought back his friends from Bero? What if he brought them to beat his poor father and mother up? Anything was possible these days, with the fear of the Naxalites in the air.

These experiences of my adopted brother, Somra Munda, and his son, Jitu, in 2007 show how relations between the Mundas and the rural elites are in flux. Over the eight years since I have been visiting Jharkhand, a small group of educated Munda youth has slowly emerged. Unlike their uneducated parents, some of these young men are no longer willing to till the soil and work as manual laborers. They are increasingly seeking to engage in state-related practices, do not see the state as something to keep away from, and want to join the rural elites and move up in the class hierarchy. Meanwhile, their parents strongly disapprove of their sons' involvement in state activities and now see the dangers of the state in many more forms—including the Naxalite movement.

I recall these events here to help explain why I cannot call my arcadian spaces "spaces of resistance." Rural Jharkhand is constantly changing, and these events represent just one example of its transformation. Moreover, with this emerging group of educated adivasi youth, in particular, new lines of conflict between generations are emerging from within the households of the poorest people. To call the arcadian spaces "resistance" would undermine these transformations and the resulting internal conflicts and tensions.[6]

Above all, however, we cannot see arcadian spaces simply as spaces of resistance because most Mundas do not see their continued practices and values as subordinate to those of the rural elites. Somra is worried because he does not want Jitu to become like Akshay. For many Mundas, their values of living in the Jungle Raj are simply different from those prescribed by the rural elites. And it is on the political potential of the values of the Jungle Raj—the arcadian spaces which emerge from an ethnographic analysis of the Mundas of Tapu—that I want to add some cursory—very cursory—reflections.

There is first the issue of the eco-incarceration that is produced by the dual representation of adivasis as being somehow morally and spiritually rooted in the land, and as living in harmony with nature. One result is that this commoditized representation of nature is threatening Munda livelihoods when it reappears in the form of the wild elephants that haunt the night in Tapu. The Mundas can neither kill the elephants that are destroying their livelihoods nor chop down the forests that they feel have brought the elephants to the area. The Mundas are trapped.

They are also trapped by the rhetorical power of their alleged ties to their land, a rhetoric that goes hand in hand with the idea of the eco-savage, which is at the heart of attempts to reclaim Jharkhand as an indigenous state. Migration for the Mundas, however, is a norm of human history, and in their imaginings of the world, there are no borders or nation-states, and nobody is incarcerated by such performances of the state. This is an arcadian imagining of a world landscape of freely moving people, which may strengthen the fight against the increasingly stringent patrol and control of borders—a control that eclipses the material issues of better conditions of work and living standards in distant places for migrant workers.[7]

Relatedly, there is the issue of reclaiming those values of the arcadian spaces of the Jungle Raj that have been called savage and backward, or jangli, by the dangerously despotic puritanism of the rural elites and indigenous rights activists. The activists clamp down on premarital and postmarital sexual relations; replace rice beer and mahua wine with water, and offer the spirits coconuts instead of animal sacrifices; and want to eliminate the belief in the spirits altogether. Yet it is precisely the importance of some of these practices, which the activists seek to eliminate or domesticate, that make the Mundas proud to belong to the Jungle Raj. They are proud to be able to propitiate the spirits with blood sacrifices and plenty of alcohol, and some Mundas, especially the younger ones, try to create some of the values of the arcadian spaces of the Jungle Raj in the brick kilns, to which they escape to experience the amorous relationships that are prohibited back home. As Ajay Skaria argues of western India, such "wildness" can stand not only for a way of life with a difference, but also for a different and desired ideal of both pleasure and power, which may give marginalized adivasis a certain edge in power politics.[8]

Finally, there is the issue of moving beyond the shadows of the state and toward the possibilities of an alternative political order. In the last two decades, we have seen the rise of what has been termed a "culturalist critique"[9] of the Indian government, which argues that the notion of the postcolonial state in India is an inherently alien ideology that some of its citizens will necessarily culturally misunderstand.[10] It might seem that the Munda's desire to keep the state away is evidence for this critique of the state.

However, the demonization of the state does not make the Mundas a society against the state or a stateless society. The Mundas are not evidence of a collective desire among so-called nonmodern ethnographic subjects to fight the emergence of the postcolonial state, and Munda imaginings are not evidence that the state is inevitably an alien cultural ideology. Rather, the Mundas are our contemporaries, and the state, as I have tried to show, has had a profound effect on their lives, ironically producing those arcadian spaces from which may be resurrected an alternative political order beyond its shadows. I have argued that the Mundas have sought to keep the state away partly because they have experienced it as exploitative and oppressive, and partly because of the activities of rural elites moving up in the class hierarchy who seek to colonize the state's resources and who, in order to maintain their material dominance, encourage Munda imaginings. While this is the case, it has also led to the Mundas' resurrection of an alternative order to the secular state.

Unlike the secular structures of indigenous governance that the activists are trying to reclaim for the new state, institutions such as the parha and authorities such as the pahan and paenbharra have legitimacy for the Mundas because they represent a cosmology in which the sacred and the secular are intimately connected, even identical. This sacral polity embodies a moral politics endorsed by the spirits that is neither self-interested nor divisive, and that is underpinned by the values of egalitarianism, consensus in decision making, and mutual aid. This is a final aspect of the arcadian space of the Jungle Raj, which should not be reduced to a superstitious belief in ghosts but which might inspire a new kind of concept of democracy emerging from a sacral polity.

Talal Asad argued long ago that writing ethnography is a political act.[11] From our ethnographic analysis can emerge ideas of how life could be lived, or imaginings of the world, which may show the potential for a radical politics that can better serve the poorest people. I suggest that well-meaning indigenous rights activists and their middle-class ideals may be shrinking the spaces from which a truly radical politics may emerge. As scholars, we should not hesitate to show that this is the case, and I believe we should consider tracing the emerging contours of visions of alternative moralities, which we can compare, debate, and explore as the beginnings of new arcadian spaces. In that light, this book marks the beginning of the search, and not the end.

Glossary of Terms

adivasi: popular term for a member of one of India's indigenous groups, officially classified as Scheduled Tribes by the Indian government
akhra: dancing circle
baiga: religio-political village authority, more commonly called a *pahan* in my research area
bhagat: medium for spirits
bhuinhar: original settler
bhut: spirit
bhutkhetta: land allocated for those responsible for appeasing the spirits; literally, "land of the spirits"
dalal: mediator
dalit: popular term for a member of one of India's Scheduled Castes
daru: alcohol; usually used to refer to distilled alcohol
dhangar: used in my research area to refer to a live-in, year-round, general manual laborer, although often used in other areas to refer to bonded laborers
dhumkuria: village dormitory for youth, called *ghotul* in some areas
diku: outsider
Fagua: adivasi festival that takes place in the spring
ghairmazrua land: land with no right of occupancy
ghotul: village dormitory, more commonly known in my research area as dhumkuria
gram sabha: body of people who are registered on the electoral roll of a village or group of villages, who elect a *panchayat*, or village council
hadia: rice beer
jangli: literally meaning people of the jungle, a derogatory term used to describe people as wild, dirty, savage, or backward
Karma: adivasi festival that takes place during or at the end of the rainy season

kurta-pyjama: outfit consisting of a long, baggy top and pants
line-hotel: roadside restaurant
lungi: wrap-around loincloth
maheto: village functionary of adivasi areas who is appointed to deal with outside authorities, such as tax collectors
mahua: flower, and alcohol distilled from the flower
mela: festival
paenbharra: helper of the *pahan*
pahan: religio-political village authority
panchayati raj: decentralized system of governance in India divided into village, block, and district levels
parha: a tribal intervillage authority consisting of a number of villages
parha-likha: educated
raj: kingdom
raja: king
sadans: nonindigenous residents of Jharkhand who nevertheless had a long ancestry in the region that dates back to the colonial period
sal: a tree (*Shorea robusta*) which has been made into a symbol of Jharkhand
sardar: labor contractor
Sarhul: adivasi festival that takes place in the spring
sarkar: the state
thekkidar: contractor
zamindar: landlord

Notes

PROLOGUE

1. The conversations explored in this book are based on actual conversations which, though not audiotaped, have been reconstructed from detailed field notes as well as from memory. The conversations were carried out in either Hindi or Nagpuria. In Tapu, the main language spoken in every household is Nagpuria, a Sanskrit-based dialect promoted by Jharkhandi activists as the adivasi language of the Chotanagpur Plateau. Only some of the villagers—mainly the educated rural elite—spoke Hindi, and only when necessary. Kurukh, the Oraon language, is spoken by a few of the older generation of Oraons. Mundari is generally not known in Tapu, except by women who have come from Munda areas in other parts of Jharkhand.

2. I have changed the names of all my friends and informants in Jharkhand, apart from a few well-known people, to protect their identity. In any case, most people have several names. Many Mundas were known by the name of the day on which they were born—for instance, Somra for Monday, Mangra for Tuesday, and Budhwa for Wednesday. However, those who had caste certificates had often been registered with a more Hinduized name. The higher-caste Hindu landlords who did not consider the names of days "proper" names for people carried out most of these registrations for the Mundas. So in some contexts, some Mundas were also known by these more Hinduized names. In this book, I use their non-Hinduized names as pseudonyms for the Mundas and use alternative Hindu names for the Hinduized descendants of zamindars. Where material is particularly sensitive, I have also changed a few other identifying features of the lives of my friends and informants, to prevent them from being identifiable. Tapu is also a pseudonym.

1. THE DARK SIDE OF INDIGENEITY

1. The first international legal mechanism for the protection of indigenous peoples came into being in 1989, when the International Labour Organisation adopted its Indigenous and Tribal Peoples Convention, also known as Convention 169.

2. See especially the recent collection by de la Cadena and Starn (2007).

3. See Conklin and Graham (1995).

4. See Turner and Fajans-Turner (2006), who use Scott's (1985) analysis in *Weapons of the Weak*.

5. See Fox and Starn (1997).

6. See, especially, Escobar and Alvarez (1992).

7. K. Ghosh (2006, 505).

8. See Karlsson (2003, 407).

9. The shift in term from "tribe" to "adivasi" has a long history which I do not want to dwell on at length here. The contested history of the term "tribe" goes back to colonial times, when race and racial ideology were the norms of a broader political order, and anthropological constructions categorized the country's aboriginals as so-called primitive tribes. Colonial policies of subordination, domination, and protection helped unite a wide variety of communities living in India's forests and hills. In the late 1920s, this shared history became the ground for a political movement, with its center in what is now Jharkhand, to better protect the rights of the people involved by demanding a separate state in the Jharkhand region. In this struggle, the term "adivasi," as a more positive political identity, replaced the more pejorative "tribal" or "primitive." For more details, see Shah (2007a) and Hardiman (1987).

10. Bosu Mullick (2003, viii).

11. Weiner ([1978] 1988); see also Jha (1990).

12. "Tribes of Mind," the title of this section, was also the title of a panel organized by Erik de Maaker and Ellen Bal at the 2006 meeting in Leiden, the Netherlands, of the European Association of South Asian Studies. They were inspired by van Schendel's "The Invention of the 'Jummas'" (1992), and there are obvious parallels with the classic text by Dirks on "Castes of Mind" (2001).

13. See Kuper (1988).

14. As described by Pinney in his essay on "Colonial Anthropology in the 'Laboratory of Mankind'" (1990).

15. As described by Bates (1995).

16. Space making, as shown by K. Sivaramakrishnan, was also an important dimension of this colonial state making—certain areas were to have a distinctive regime of administration because they were, for instance, seen as impenetrable hilly jungle with a cultural geography of extraordinarily primitive people different from those of the river valleys and the plains

(1999). Some scholars, such as Skaria (1997), have also argued that India's tribes were seen as the living remnants of Europe's evolutionary past.

17. In particular, this is the argument of S. Guha (1999, 16).

18. For instance, see Damodaran (2006).

19. See Hardiman's study of *The Coming of the Devi* (1987) in western India in the 1920s, where several thousand people followed the commands of a new goddess who spoke through mediums, asking people to give up liquor, in this case a palm wine called toddy; fish; and meat, and to bathe twice a day. As will be further explored in chapters 4 and 5, Hardiman importantly points out that such movements should not be equated with Srinivas's (1956) description of Sanskritization because one of their necessary features was a challenge to the upper castes.

20. These rebellions mark what Ranajit Guha ([1983] 1999) in a benchmark work of subaltern studies has called "elementary aspects of a peasant insurgency." Some such insurgencies were also concerned with a reformist, purificatory project. For instance, in K. Singh's (1966) account of Birsa Munda and his movement, we learn that the famous revolutionary hero of Jharkhand, most often depicted with a bow and arrow, also tried to free Munda society of vices and practices such as drinking, spirit worship, and witchcraft. However, it is likely that other insurgencies invoked the positive conceptions of wildness that Skaria (1999) outlines in his fascinating account of western India. Here in the eighteenth and nineteenth centuries, wildness was associated with pleasure—for example, the freedom to hunt, migrate, or drink. This is a theme that I will develop further at the end of the book.

21. Thus, as Vinita Damodaran argues in her critique of Sumit Guha's work, colonial rulers were not just defining tribes as isolated, difficult, and different; a set of humanitarian concerns to protect people in the area were also in play (Damodaran 2000). Damodaran's argument is in line with a broader project that seeks to break away from an essentialist Saidian Orientalist prejudice, and that argues instead for a variety of imperial agents, interests, and aims which were often sympathetic to local populations (Grove 1995). This relationship between adivasi rebellion and the production of tribal autonomy through colonial state policy was not confined to the Chotanagpur Plateau but also played out in other forested and hilly areas of India. Nandini Sundar, for example, provides an account of the way in which the material struggles and ritual events of popular rebellions in Bastar, central India, served a dual purpose. The rebellions were not only forms of resistance to colonial policies, but also the means through which the British (and later the Indian) government reframed the politics of tradition and custom (Sundar 1997).

22. In his much-quoted introduction, Hardiman (1987, 13) speculates that the term "adivasi" appears to have originated in the Chotanagpur region of Bihar in the 1930s.

23. Devalle calls this a "reformist ethnicist" project (1992, 136).

24. See the analysis of Tete (1990).

25. See Devalle (1992) and K. Singh (1982).

26. The late 1930s were a time of heightening nationalist struggle in India. However, the Indian Nationalist Movement had little support from the Chotanagpur Adivasi Mahasabha. The Congress Party had swept the 1937 elections, and the Adivasi Mahasabha felt that Congress did not represent the interests of the adivasis. Interesting short-term alliances were formed—for instance, in the 1940s, between the Adivasi Mahasabha and the Muslim League, which wanted to secure a corridor to connect East and West Pakistan through the tribal areas of south Bihar (see, for example, K. Singh 1982; Sinha-Kerkhoff 2004). In 1939, Munda Jaipal Singh, the Oxford-educated field-hockey star, became the chairman of the Adivasi Mahasabha; he supported the British in the Second World War and recruited adivasis for the army. Uninvolved in the Indian Nationalist Movement, the Adivasi Mahasabha launched a struggle not against the British raj, but against the diku raj.

27. Ghurye ([1943] 1963).

28. Ibid., 19.

29. See the critique by Prasad (2003).

30. Some of the best works are Elwin (1936, 1939, 1943, 1946, 1955).

31. In his sensitive and beautifully written biography, Ramachandra Guha (1999) shows the many faces of Verrier Elwin.

32. See Galanter (1984).

33. These include the cultural wing of the Rashtriya Swayam Sevak Sangh, the political party called the Bharatya Janata Party, and a more international body of the Vishwa Hindu Parishad.

34. For an analysis of the rise of this "Saffron Wave" in the democratic process of India, see Hansen (1999) and Bhatt (2001).

35. Research into how adivasis are being recruited to the Sangh Parivar that moves beyond the classic arguments of attributing adivasi participation to false consciousness or because of their poverty is slowly emerging. Some work, such as Froerer (2006, 2007), following Brass (1974), outlines the deployment of instrumentalist strategies in Chhattisgarh, central India, whereby powerful outsiders—proponents of the Sangh Parivar—use their positions to communalize social identities and relations by actively promoting the idea of a threatening Christian other. The success of the Sangh Parivar is also allegedly based on the provision of health and education in areas where medical and educational facilities are poor. Sundar (2005b) has analyzed the pedagogy of such schools in adivasi-dominated areas of southern Chhattisgarh. Education also plays an important role in the spread of the Hindu right in other, perhaps more subtle, ways. For instance, Baviskar (2005) shows how Hinduization coincides with the rise of a new generation of educated adivasi youth. In contrast to their parents, these youth are fluent in Hindi, dress in shirts and trousers (instead of loincloths), hang out in the market towns or bazaars, and are fluent in the market culture that was previously dominated by a Hindu majority elite. To this new genera-

tion of adivasi youth, seeking government jobs and entering the bazaaria lifestyle, the Sangh Parivar offers to incorporate adivasis, on the basis not of their cultural difference, but of their cultural and religious similarity with a hegemonic Hindu majority in a Hindu nation.

36. See Devalle (1992, 56).

37. See Corbridge (1988).

38. It is, however, important to note two points. First, census figures are reputed to be unreliable. The early ones relied largely on guesswork, and the later ones (before independence) undercounted Scheduled Tribes (Bates and Carter 1992, 215). Second, the distribution of Scheduled Tribes in Chotanagpur is uneven, so that in some districts, such as Ranchi and Singhbhum, the Scheduled Tribe population was much higher than it is today.

39. Kaviraj (1993, 15) argues this more generally for nationalism.

40. See Bosu Mullick (2003).

41. See Corbridge (2002) and Mawdsley (2002).

42. See Hocking (1994).

43. As Mawdsley (2006) argues, neotraditional discourses of the environment can be actively mobilized by the Sangh Parivar.

44. See Areeparampil (2003).

45. See also the work of academic activists, such as Padel (1995), supporting such arguments.

46. To cite the title of Ranajit Guha ([1983] 1999).

47. In some countries, protectionist policies take the form of multiculturalism, which itself has many critiques. De la Cadena and Starn (2007) engage in a brief discussion of multiculturalism and indigeneity, but see also the work of C. Taylor ([1931] 1992) as well as Bauman's (1999) excellent critique, which warns against the reifying of cultural difference in Taylor's arguments for a politics of recognition.

48. See Brown (2007, 187).

49. See especially Freid (1975).

50. One of the best examples of this line of argument is the work of Willmsen (1989) on the San in southern Africa. But see also the critique of Solway and Lee (1990).

51. See the thought-provoking work of Brown (1998, 2003) on indigenous cultures and intellectual property rights.

52. See Kuper (2003).

53. Béteille (1974).

54. Béteille (1983, 1991).

55. See Parry (1999) for an empirically grounded critique.

56. Béteille (1998).

57. See Bates (1994a).

58. Béteille (1998, 190).

59. This is a line of thought reiterated in Sumit Guha's environmental history of forest communities that impressively goes as far back as 1200. Guha shows that in the past, identities and ethnicities were more fluid than

has been supposed and that the primitivization of people—still a powerful identity in India in the late twentieth century—is a recent consequence of the breakdown of the political systems and strategies of differentiation, dominance, and exploitation (S. Guha 1999). Guha warns that today's attempts to organize public life around claims to authentic indigeneity and to protect equality as ratio, according to the length of your genealogy, rather than equality of right can only lead to explosive consequences of ethnic conflict.

60. Béteille (1998).

61. Kuper (2003).

62. Ibid., 389.

63. For example, Kenrick and Lewis (2004) responded to Kuper.

64. Kenrick and Lewis (2004).

65. This has recently been proposed by Barnard (2006).

66. See the well-argued Sieder and Witchell (2001), but also Harris (1996), which draws attention to the law and its effect on reifying particular practices and demands of minority groups.

67. See especially Clifford's (1988) chapter on "Identity in Mashpee."

68. A term that Warren (1998) uses for pan-Mayan activism in Guatemala.

69. See Li (2000).

70. Chakrabarty (2006, 231).

71. See, for example, Xaxa (1999).

72. See Baviskar (2005) and Karlsson (2003).

73. As Karlsson (2003) argues.

74. This is indeed the approach that Karlsson (2003) usefully pursues in exploring the transnational politics of the participation of indigenous delegates from India in the annual UNWGIP sessions in Geneva.

75. See Damodaran (2000).

76. See Tsing (2005).

77. See Scheper-Hughes (1995).

78. See Hale (2006).

79. Gayatri Spivak (1988a, 1988b).

80. The original manifesto of the subaltern studies project was presented by Ranajit Guha as one of recovering the "small voices of history" which are drowned in the noise of statist commands (1982, 1). A range of very interesting scholars was involved. The early participants especially were united, as Guha puts it, by the attempt to make an extra effort and develop the special skills, and above all cultivate the disposition to hear these voices. A comprehensive collection of the key debates in the field is found in Chaturvedi (2000).

81. Spivak (1988a, 171).

82. Menchú (1984).

83. Stoll (1993).

84. Stoll (1999).

85. See the review essay by Smith (1999), and also Lofving (2005) and Hale (1997) on the implications for the analysis of the war.

86. See Sylvain (2002).

87. See Dombrowski (2001, 2002). One perhaps ironic result of this corporate-sponsored cultural revitalization is that many native people who are marginalized out of the process have sought refuge in joining Pentecostal churches.

88. See Baviskar (2004).

89. Brown (2007, 187).

90. See Skaria (1997).

91. Jean-Klein and Riles (2005, 175).

92. Ibid., 190.

93. In 2001, the Indian census showed that national literacy was 54 percent. However, the figures given here are based on my own survey of Tapu and show literacy rates in the same year to be much lower. The sadans in Tapu have much higher literacy rates than the Mundas. Only one Munda young man had passed the intermediate exams, and two had passed the matriculation exams.

94. The area receives an annual rainfall of around 1,250 millimeters, which is concentrated mainly in the monsoon from June to October. Rice constitutes more than 80 percent of the *kharif* (monsoon) crop; it is grown especially on medium and low land (*doin*). Other common kharif crops are ragi, black gram, maize, pigeon pea, and groundnut. The main crops grown in the *rabi* season (November to March) are mustard, horse gram, linseed, and groundnut in the upland, and horse gram, gram, and wheat in the lowland. Vegetables are grown all year in fields with good irrigation facilities.

95. Hiding upper-caste surnames among tribal activists is also reported by Baviskar (1997, 212) for western India.

96. See especially Sarat Chandra Roy (1912, 1915).

97. Indeed, this may be one reason why Karlsson reports that the representatives of the Indian Council of Indigenous and Tribal People (led by Jharkhandis) appear to lack a grass-roots base and have become quite alienated from people's everyday struggles (2003, 408).

98. Li (2000, 172).

99. Cowan, Dembour, and Wilson (2001, 11).

2. NOT JUST GHOSTS

1. The *pahan* is also known in some areas as the *baiga* or *naegas* (in the Kurukh language).

2. The *paenbharra* is also known in some areas, and sometimes in Tapu as well, as the *pujar*.

3. There is a huge literature on the importance of commensality, or who eats with whom, and how this signifies social boundaries and hierarchy (see, for example, Parry 1979). Marriott (1968) has even developed a matrix of transactions of different types of food to show who gives food to

whom and who receives it from whom, and how this can signify the relative position of a caste in the hierarchy.

4. As the Mundas are rarely able to quantify the land they cultivate, and I was never able to get more official figures from the landlord descendant family who holds the current land records for the village, I was not able to quantify the exact amount of land given to the pahan and the paenbharra. In theory it should be the same as that which is noted in the 1932 land records, which indicate that 1.73 acres of lowland are reserved for the pahan (of which 1.5 acres is the best lowland, and 0.23 acres is second-quality lowland), and 0.4 acres of upland. The records also suggest that 2.55 acres are reserved for the paenbharra, of which 2.4 acres are second-quality lowland and 0.15 acres are third-quality lowland. The seven *bhut-khetta* beneficiaries (discussed later in this chapter) had between them 4.56 acres of land. A more useful quantification of the land is how much rice it produces. This is of course locally interpreted as dependent on how happy the spirits are with the pahan and paenbharra. In 1999, the paenbharra harvested 25 *oriyas* (there are 40 kilograms in one oriya) of *dhan* (husked rice), the year before 40 oriyas, and the year before that 50 oriyas. Onga Munda told me that no one had ever harvested more than 75 oriyas a year.

5. The importance of alcohol in Munda life is like what Hardiman found among the people in western India: "Their deities were extremely fond of *daru* and toddy and . . . they could be appeased by such offerings. It was common to pour a libation before starting to drink. Alcohol was considered a 'food of the gods' and drunkenness incurred during the act of worship was seen as a form of intoxication by the divine spirit. In local legend liquor was believed to have been given originally to the people by the gods . . . Such beliefs ensured that drinking was considered a respectable act in *adivasi* culture, and *daru* and toddy accordingly consumed without any feeling of guilt . . . A person who did not drink could hardly, in such light, be a part of *adivasi* society" (1987, 99–101).

6. Fuller (1992) has noted that winnowing baskets or fans used to separate grain from chaff are symbols of separation in general, and in particular of the separating out of polluting and inauspicious elements that can be cast away.

7. *Arwa* rice (which is raw and husked) is used at these ceremonial occasions. It is different from the more commonly eaten *usna* rice, which is first boiled, then husked, and reboiled before eating.

8. The University of Victoria, in Canada, even offers an M.A. in indigenous governance.

9. As represented by the World Bank (1992). For a good comparative discussion of the key issues in democracy and decentralization, see Crook and Manor (1998).

10. See Nicholas (1996), Stavenhagen (1996), and especially Brown (2007) and Alfred (2001) for critiques on indigeneity and sovereignty.

11. Indigenous systems of governance are being revived in other areas as well (Karlsson 2005).

12. See Sundar (2005a).

13. See A. Ghosh (2006).

14. For example, Participatory Research in India (PRIA).

15. For example, Sharan, Singh, and Sahu (1999) and Sundar (2005a).

16. This is in Oraon and Munda areas. In Ho areas, the head of the village was called a *munda* and a group of villages a *pir*, whose head was a *manki*. In Santhal areas, the village-level authority was a *manjhi*, a group of villages was called a *pargana*, and it was headed by a *parganait*.

17. The survey is sometimes also called the Haldar survey, as it was carried out by Babu Rakhar Das Haldar.

18. Reid (1912), F. Taylor (1940), and Webster (1875).

19. Webster (1875, 15–16).

20. See Dasgupta's (2004) work on Roy.

21. Roy (1915, 68–69).

22. Ibid., 69.

23. Ibid., 68–69.

24. Ibid., 70.

25. In the first state assembly elections, in 1952, the Jharkhand Party was the main opposition to Congress in the Bihar Legislative Council. The Jharkhand Party won over 70 percent of the thirty-four assembly seats reserved for Scheduled Tribes in Bihar. In the Bero constituency, the Jharkhand Party candidate secured 62 percent of the vote, with Congress's candidate coming in second with only 29.2 percent. This pattern continued for the next two elections (V. Singh and Bose 1988).

26. The information on Kartik Oraon comes from oral histories of some of his friends in Ratu and is corroborated by a short biography written by Dr. Shivaji Gautam.

27. In the fourth general election of 1967, the Jharkhand Party won only 24 percent of the reserved seats. By then, Congress had become the leading party in the area. Many factors are thought to have contributed to the loss of influence of the Jharkhand Party. In the 1957 elections, it had accepted financial support from the Janata Party in Bihar (which, unlike the central Janata Party, represented the interests of landed classes; Prakash 2001). Internal factionalism was apparent in 1963, when Jaipal Singh and his faction, supported by the Roman Catholic Church, left the Jharkhand Party and joined Congress. The secessionists portrayed this split as a tactical move and claimed that they would better be able to fight for the tribal cause of a separate state from within the government (as had been the case with the creation of Andhra Pradesh in 1953, Maharashtra in 1960, and Nagaland in 1963). Jaipal Singh's opponents, however, speculated that Congress had bribed him with a place in the government ministry (Vidyarthi and Sahay 1976, 100). The Jharkhand Party further lost favor as it was criticized as being controlled by Christian urban professionals and for

not having an agrarian program, accepting landlords and moneylenders whom it had been formed to fight, and failing to address the growing labor unrest and trade-union activities in TISCO and other industrial projects in the area (Devalle 1992, 140–41).

28. Victor Das (1992) has further information on Kartik Oraon and the parha. At a national level, Kartik Oraon, as member of Parliament for Ranchi District, made the momentous move of introducing a bill in the Lok Sabha (the lower house of Parliament) that sought to deny Christians and Muslims the right to be granted tribal status. Weiner has a fascinating interview with Kartik Oraon on why he introduced such a bill at the time ([1978] 1988, 185–86).

29. The activists are in some ways reproducing a long history of attempts to drive away what they see as the belief in ghosts, demons, and spirits. This was part of the project of the Christian missionaries who came to the area, but it was also a central theme of other movements. For instance, in 1914–15, the Tana Bhagat movement spread in Oraon areas with the divine command to give up superstitious practices, animal sacrifices, and drinking liquor (Roy 1915). It was also a feature of other adivasi areas in the country, as is explored in Hardiman (1987).

30. The introduction of panchayats in the 1990s has a long history, going back to the debate between Nehru and Gandhi about the shaping of the world's largest democracy. Gandhi proposed *panchayati raj* as the foundation of India's political system—a decentralized form of government where each village would be responsible for its own affairs. Although some states adopted panchayat institutions at independence, the Nehruvian vision of a centralized parliamentary constitution, with a directly elected assembly, shaped the modern Indian state. However, with the global moves to democratic decentralization, a more Gandhian view of directly elected village councils formed the basis of granting constitutional status to Panchayati Raj institutions. These are a democratically elected, three-tier structure of the *gram panchayat* at the village level, the *panchayat samiti* at the block level, and the *zila parishad* at the district level. They have a range of responsibilities, including the design and implementation of development plans at the village level.

31. Jharkhand remains the only state in India not to have held elections at the panchayat or municipal level. The reasons for this are obviously complex and highly contested. When Jharkhand was part of Bihar, the prominent argument was that the ruling parties in Patna did not want to decentralize democracy in Jharkhand for fear of losing their local dominance. Of course, this line of argument is similar to that made by Mamdani (1976) to explain why there is a deafening silence on the question of democratizing the local and quotidian forms of state power: broad democratic demands and bottom-up methods would weaken the rule of political elites and increase the autonomy of popular forces. Since the formation of Jharkhand and the passage of the Panchayat Extension to the Scheduled Areas Act, the progress of panchayat elections has been impeded by a

controversy over the extent to which customary laws should be protected and seats should be reserved for Scheduled Tribes and Castes. As Sundar (2005a) argues, on one side are those organizations that feel that the Jharkhand Panchayati Raj Act (2001) does not recognize customary structures that have been historically protected. On the other side are those who argue against the reservation of seats for adivasis in Scheduled Areas.

32. Sharma retired from the post of Commissioner for Scheduled Tribes and Castes in 1981 to work as an activist for tribal affairs. One of his books opens with the following sentence: "Let it not be said by future generations that the Indian Republic has been built on the destruction of the green earth and the innocent tribals who have been living there for centuries" (2001, 3). At the meeting, he was wearing a dhoti and a hand-woven cotton kurta, and he was eager to tell me that what I should really be studying was the economic expropriation of tribal people at the village level—how tribals were being robbed by the state and outsiders.

33. Though not important for the argument here, as in Bero everyone believed that it was 3 June, in fact the first Thursday of June in 1990 was 7 June. I have not discovered the basis of the discrepancy.

34. In recent years, a more worm's eye view of democracy has shown the fascinating ways in which democratic procedures are locally appropriated. In other parts of the world, the importance of religion and ritual has been seen as important in reshaping the local understanding of democratic procedures. For instance, West (1999) shows how official democratic procedures, such as elections, are reshaped in the idioms of sorcery in rural Mozambique, while among the Yoruba in Nigeria, Apter (1987) demonstrates how democratic procedures are transformed in ritual practice. Elsewhere, Goldman (2001) argues that democratic processes in Brazil need to be understood in the context of how people at the local level differentiate the domain of politics from the realm of culture. And Comaroff and Comaroff (1997) show how local arguments for a one-party state in Botswana are not a dismissal of democracy per se, but rather a rejection of procedural democracy in favor of a substantive democracy that draws on older notions of political authority, entailing both deliberation over policy matters and accountability by those who govern.

35. Though the Jharkhand case is no doubt extreme, the situation described is not unique to it. There are echoes here of Gell's (1997) analysis of the Dusshera ritual and rebellions in Bastar, central India, where tribal people asserted control over the king's person and used him to resist the extension of the power of the state. There are, of course, many examples from other parts of the world of people having sought to keep the state at bay—one exemplary account being that of the post-1960s Chachapoyas, in Peru, where the "local populace came to regard the modern nation-state as a 'foreign body': an entity wholly separate from, alien to, and dangerous for a way of life depicted as simple, natural and harmonious" (Nugent 2001, 273).

36. Jonathan Parry, personal communication.

37. Hardiman quotes B. C. Mehta: "The sight of a police-officer was enough to strike terror into the hearts of the aborigines. Whenever they caught sight of him, they hid themselves behind trunks of trees or behind tall grasses" (1987, 76). Mosse also cites Bhil villagers in eastern India who remembered a "time of fear of patrolling guards on horseback, constant surveillance [when] all households had to cut fodder and give it to officials as a form of tax, [when] British officers would search [their] bags, and punish them if they were caught drinking, [when] guests that came to the village had to be registered" (2005, 51).

38. Ranajit Guha ([1983] 1999).

39. See ibid. and K. Singh (1982).

40. See Weiner ([1978] 1988, 160–61).

41. See also Baviskar (2004) for comparative material on state oppression of adivasis in western India.

42. In 1999, in the most local office of the Ministry of Rural Development, the Bero Block Development Office, for example, all the supervisory staff were from Bihar—this included the head of the office, the agricultural officer, the health officer, the cooperative extension officer, the gram panchayat *sevak* (worker), the ladies extension officer, four junior engineers, the head clerk, and the cashier. Except for one who was Muslim, these officers were all high castes. When I returned for fieldwork in 2000, although many of the officers had changed and there were now two Muslims, all these positions were still filled by people from Bihar.

43. See also Hardiman's (1987) discussion of alcohol and the implications of regulation on alcohol production by the colonial government in the late 1800s, when adivasis replaced the more visible toddy (palm wine) tapping by distilling mahua, in order to keep out of the clutches of the Parsis. However, the adivasis were constantly fearful because firewood had to be procured, smoke from this fire was visible and carried the smell of alcohol far, and, moreover, there were other dangers in the villages in the form of high-caste peasants who might connive with local authorities.

44. I am grateful to Roger Begrich for discussions on the legality of alcohol consumption and production in Jharkhand.

45. Hardiman (1987, 129–30) describes how adivasis in western India found it safest to make alcohol in gullies along the riverbanks or in the forest, so that if the police came, the adivasis could easily run away, abandoning their cheap equipment.

46. Skaria (1999, 154) also reports that certain Bhil stories equate the coming of the British with the coming of sarkar.

47. See Sivaramakrishnan (1998) for accounts from forest officers in neighboring districts of West Bengal that show their sustained violent conflict with villagers in the 1960s and 1970s. Raids on village markets to curb illegal extraction and destroy wood carried by people on their heads for their homes were common in this period, and understandably they led to deep suspicion and hostility on the part of the villagers toward the forest department.

48. See also Elwin (1943, 8). The Munda attitude was in stark contrast to that observed by Pigg (1992) in Nepal, where the development discourse has been so widely adopted that it has altered the meaning of the village in social imagination.

49. See also Gell (1986, 127).

50. Linz, Stepan, and Yadav (2007) have argued that India's underprivileged classes are some of the strongest supporters of the democratic system. Drawing on research in West Bengal, M. Banerjee (2007) has even argued that Indian elections have come to be regarded as sacrosanct, as ceremonies in and of themselves that represent an expression of citizenship and an understanding of duties and rights involved in living in a democracy. In short, the overriding argument is that participation in elections represents a commitment to the norms of citizenship of the modern Indian state. Clearly, the situation in rural Jharkhand is significantly different, and the interesting comparative question for further research, which is beyond the scope of this book, would be why this is the case.

51. Feuchtwang (2003, 114).

52. Ibid., 98.

53. There are a few points to note here. First, within the household it is usually the oldest man who will assume the position, but it is not uncommon for both father and son to take on the responsibility jointly. I have not heard of a woman doing so, though in a reworking of the pahan and paenbharra system, this disparity should be redressed. Second, there are incidents where other adivasis or dalits have been chosen through this method of selection. In one case, when a Badaik was chosen, he was honored as the new pahan. However, in other cases, the non-Munda people chosen have declared that they would not know how to appease the spirits and have passed their duty to a Munda person of their choice. And third, there have been cases where chosen Mundas have decided against assuming the responsibility of being a pahan or a paenbharra and have given it to another Munda of their choice.

54. Such fines are not necessarily in cash but can involve the giving of, say, a chicken or, for more serious offences, a goat.

55. The most detailed contemporary ethnographic insights into the functions of officials approximating the pahan and the paenbharra are that of Froerer (2005, 2007), who worked in Korba District in Chhattisgarh. Froerer equates the role of the baiga (traditionally called pahan in other areas) to that of a priest and the role of the *patel* (traditionally called the maheto in other areas) to that of a king. Froerer's interest in the authorities is derived from her exploration of the spread of the RSS (Rashtriya Swayamsevak Sangh) in the area; though by no means central to her analysis, extensive personal discussion with her reveals that the equation of the baiga to a priest and the patel to a traditional Hindu king is far from clear. Unlike the separate castes from which the traditional Hindu priest (as Brahmin) and the king (as Kshatriya) derive, the patel and the baiga in Korba are in fact the same type of people. While their posts are hereditary,

they come not only from the same clan but from the same adivasi family, Ratiya Kanwars, who in general all have divine legitimacy that they have derived from the local deities who gave them the land to live on, in return for looking after them. Froerer has not yet traced the historical possibility, suggested by Roy (1915, 69), that the patel was introduced into the village only more recently as a medium to collect taxes. Yet her material arguably shows that in its uncorrupted form, the patel is no more than a vessel for the spirit of the deities, and that the baiga is in fact a chief priest who sacrifices to the deities, can speak to them, and can interpret their wishes and desires for proceeding with good life in the village. I am extremely grateful to Peggy Froerer for sharing her material with me and helping me think through these issues.

56. See Fuller (1992) for a brief analysis of divine kingship.

57. See especially Dumont (1970b) and Mauss ([1925] 1990).

58. See Parry (1998).

59. Louis Dumont is one of the most famous and most controversial commentators on Indian society. Among his many critics is Nicholas Dirks (1987, 1989), who argues that in precolonial India there was no fundamental ontological separation of the religious domain from the political, that kings were the most powerful and derived much of their power from worship, that temples represented the preeminent position of the king, and that therefore Dumont's arguments are a product of an uncritical view of the role of colonialism in inventing caste. See Parry (1998) and Peabody (1991, 2003) for a critique of these views. The most significant point for the importance of Dumont to the analysis of the sacral polities of rural Jharkhand is that most of his critics seem to forget that Dumont's interests were in pursuing a broader comparative enquiry into the way in which religion, politics, and economics have come to be seen as separate domains (Parry, 1998, 168).

60. Parry (1998, 159) is reworking Dumont, who speaks of the "original sacral sovereignty" (1986, 47) and "the archetypal model of sacral kingship" (1986, 50).

61. See Dumont (1959, 29; 1970, 67–68).

62. See Dumont (1970a, 72, 76; 1959, 29; 1986, 47).

63. Hardiman (1987).

64. Achille Mbembe, cited in Geschiere (1997, 7).

65. See Geschiere (1997), Bayart (1993), Rowlands and Warnier (1988), and West (2005).

66. Spencer (1997, 13).

67. Hansen and Stepputat (2001, 6).

68. Madan (1987, 754). But see also Nandy (1998).

69. Partha Chatterjee (1993), Ranajit Guha (1998), and Nandy (1998).

70. Hansen (2000, 257).

71. Clastres (1974).

72. What are we to study when we study the state? This important question for the anthropology of the state has arisen in the last two decades.

My approach has been most strongly influenced by Abrams (1988, 82), which calls attention to the fictional character of the state, arguing that the state—as a unified political subject or structure—does not exist; it is a collective illusion, the reification of an idea that masks power relations under the guise of public interest. For Abrams, the state is not the reality which stands behind the mask of political practice—it is itself the mask which prevents our seeing political practice as it is. He thus concludes that the mystifying illusion of a center of power called the state must be unmasked for the reality of disparate relations of power to emerge. Relatedly, Mitchell (1991, 85) has usefully elaborated that where a distinction between the state and society exists, it "must be taken not as the boundary between two discrete entities, but as a line drawn internally *within* the social processes through which a social and political order is maintained." This analysis has been important for the Jharkhand situation, where Munda imaginings of the state as separate to the parha were a product of their relationship with the rural elite (as I will show in the next chapter), their historical experiences of state officers, and their vision of an alternative form of politics indivisible from a spiritual realm. In illuminating this case, I suggest here that one way to demystify the state would be the study of everyday social relations, through which constructions of the state might emerge that lead to a more sophisticated understanding of the way in which the state-society relationship comes to exist on the ground.

73. As Mosse (2001) suggests in his study of tank irrigation in Tamil Nadu, a stronger idea of the state can promote a stronger idea of the community.

3. SHADOWY PRACTICES

1. At that time, the Indian rupee was worth roughly $45.00.

2. Despite containing some of the country's richest mineral and forest resources, as well as agricultural land, Jharkhand is one of the poorest states in India. As I have indicated, government calculations of the "below the poverty line" figures are by no means accurate at the village level. Moreover, at the national level, they are also extremely controversial within and between states as higher state-level poverty figures mean more benefits from the central state, including aid. This is well pointed out by Sanjay Kumar, an Indian Forestry Service Officer: "as per BPL Census of 1997 the percentage of BPL families to total population of undivided Bihar was c56%, increasing from 52% in 1992. After bifurcation of the state, the Planning Commission advised on the basis of NSSO data that BPL percentage for the new states should be 44% (+/-10%) for Jharkhand, and 56% (+/-10%) for Bihar. In this scheme of things, Jharkhand was to receive less central aid than before, and . . . Jharkhand officials contested these *low* poverty figures. It was agreed thereafter that Jharkhand may continue with the 2002 BPL Survey within an overall ceiling of 54 (+/-10%) (*per. com.*

Additional Secretary to Government of Jharkhand, Rural Development Ministry)" (Kumar 2004, 2, n. 5). Leaving aside the controversy over figures, there is general agreement that Jharkhand houses some of the poorest people in India. According to the Ministry of Rural Areas and Employment, Jharkhand contains more than 10 percent of the poorest hundred districts in the entire country, a ratio surpassed only by Bihar, from which Jharkhand separated in 2001. The 2001 Census puts the literacy rate in Jharkhand at 54 percent, but in Tapu, my own survey in 2001 shows that of those people not in school at the time, only 15 percent have finished primary school.

3. These figures are from the state government's *Vision 2010*, discussed by Rao (2003).

4. See Mosse (2005) for an insightful ethnography on an equivalent project in western India.

5. In 2001–2, rural development expenditure accounted for 34 percent of the planned budget for Jharkhand. Several rural development schemes were specifically targeted for those below the poverty line—including the Indira Aawas program—Swaranjayanti Gram Swarojgar, and Sampoorna Gramin Rojgar Yoajana programs—and the funding for these came from the central and state governments at a ratio of 75:25. When I first began research in the block office in 1999, block development officers said that the most important schemes were the Indira Aawas program (to provide housing for the poor), the Employment Assurance Scheme (to provide employment in the lean agricultural period of the year, specifically targeting tribal areas), and the Jawahar Rojgar program (to alleviate poverty by creating employment opportunities and later called the Jawahar Gram Samridhi program). In 2001, the latter two were combined to form the Sampoorna Gramin Rojgar program. At the time, I was interested in a little-noticed development program aimed at women and children in rural areas, and the block officers I met with did not know that the program had been merged a couple of months before with the Integrated Rural Development Programme to form the Swaranjayanti Gram Swarojgar program. Other major schemes for the rural poor were launched in subsequent years—the National Food for Work Programme in 2004 and the National Employment Guarantee Programme in 2005, as a result of the passage of the Rural Employment Guarantee Act in September 2005.

6. In 1999–2000, for example, the central government spent RS 342 billion in this sector. And in 2003–4, the allocation of the Ministry of Rural Development alone was RS 190 billion (see Kumar 2004).

7. My intention is not to argue that everybody from such a background (landlord, revenue-collecting, or educated) became the brokers of state development resources, but to say that in general it was people from this background who did. In a study of local elites in Orissa and Gujarat, Mitra (1991) draws attention to the social heterogeneity of local elites, arguing that adivasis and *harijans* were a significant proportion of these elites, and a fifth of the elites were illiterate. However, Mitra does note a significant

difference between the two states, arguing that in Orissa, adivasis and harijans were not dominant among the local elites. In the part of rural Jharkhand where I worked, the older analysis of Frankel (1978) still applies, and the state has been colonized by and extended itself through existing local elites, which has been the means of their continued domination.

8. The concept of the informal economy was popularized when the anthropologist Keith Hart's arguments about African cities got picked up by the International Labour Organisation in the 1970s. Hart (1973) argues that, contrary to the way many development economists would read the situation, the people in African slums were not unemployed but were busy generating all sorts of income opportunities for themselves that would be ignored in the formal economy. There are lessons to learn in the Indian situation, where young men like Dharmesh and Neel, roaming the streets of Bero, will too readily classify themselves as unemployed or *berozgar* to the outsider (see Heuze 1996; Jeffrey, Jeffery, and Jeffery 2008) but in fact this is part of a way of speaking a language that they feel will be understood by the outsider—despite being educated, they do not have formal employment. Generally networking in Bero is in itself considered by them to be a form of work.

9. In this regard, I concur with Olivier de Sardan (1999; 2005, 168), who argues that we should treat corruption not as a theme of moral denunciation, but like any other research subject, and understand that so-called corrupt practices are embedded in wider social logics that give them legitimacy and anchor them in everyday practice.

10. The Ministry of Rural Development launched DWCRA in 1982 (it was partially funded by UNICEF until 1996) in response to the criticism that programs of economic and social development for the poor reproduced a structural male bias. DWCRA aimed at improving the economic condition of poor women and supporting their control over family incomes. To do this, DWCRA promoted the collective participation of women in income-generating activities, to enable groups of women to generate self-help savings and ultimately enhance their status.

11. See A. Gupta (2005) for an ethnographic account of the implementation of this scheme by a block development office in Uttar Pradesh.

12. The percentages are fixed slightly differently for different projects. The two main construction programs in 1999 were the Employment Assurance Scheme and the Jawahar Rojgar program.

13. Corbridge et al. (2005, 166) estimate that fund leakage from the Employment Assurance Scheme in Bihar is between 30 percent and 35 percent of the total funds.

14. In other Indian states, this participatory development structure is more formalized through the three-tier structure of the gram panchayat at the village level, the panchayat samiti at the block level, and the zila parishad at the district level.

15. I do not have exact information on the way this works in Bero, but Wade's (1982; 1985) model of the corruption-transfer mechanism in

Andhra Pradesh provides relevant pointers: Indian government bureaucrats are eligible for transfer to a new post every three years. Different posts have different degrees of desirability, usually linked to the amount of money going into the region; thus, the price offered for the post typically equals to the amount expected to be earned in the post. Depending on the strength of the governing party and the influence of the local MLA, politicians can be actively involved in the transfer system and usually participate in auctioning off posts. This is one of the main ways for officers to influence their assignments, and for villagers to exert influence on officers. The politicians, in turn, will be able to bear the cost of maintaining themselves as the dominant party as they will get a certain number of contracts from the officers, and a certain percentage of benefits from the villagers. The circuit of transactions is therefore that the bureaucracy acquires the control of funds that are channeled upward to higher ranks and politicians by paying for transfers, and the politicians use the funds for short-term material inducements in exchange for electoral support.

16. The amount varied over the time. It was Rs 50 in 1999, and Rs 60 in 2002.

17. Some recent discussions on the anthropology of corruption, particularly A. Gupta (2005) and Parry (2000), have stressed in their ethnography the narrative aspect of corruption through the use of stories or rumors of corruption which are neither eyewitness accounts nor someone's statements of his or her activities. I would like to note that I *am* talking here about people's own statements of their activities, and I think the fact that people often openly talk about these issues is evidence of the disparity between their moral reasoning and what is expected of them in the Weberian model of the state.

18. See Bayart (1993).

19. See Bayart, Ellis, and Hibou (1999).

20. S. Handelman, quoted by Humphrey (2002, 217).

21. See Gill (1998) and Vishvanathan and Sethi (1998).

22. In another report from Transparency International (2005), Jharkhand was not far behind.

23. See Parry (2000).

24. See Haller and Shore (2005).

25. This is still the Bank's guiding perspective (World Bank 2007).

26. In the case of the Indian state, some authors have argued that the state is rent-seeking and predatory, and that poor government performance is a result of the activities of state officials who act in their own self-interest and gain support by distributing public resources to their supporters. Indeed, they are seen to maximize their income by raising rents on the allocation of resources for which they are responsible, and taking bribes, smuggling, and doing business in the black market (Bhagwati 1993; Kreuger 1974). The obvious policy pitfall of the concept of rent seeking is the recommendations it can foster, either explicitly or by default. For instance, state-minimalist policies of liberalization and deregulation have been pro-

moted as antidotes to inefficiency and corruption. Indeed, in the 1980s and 1990s, development policy in India was dominated by the neoliberal paradigm of rolling back the functions of the state (Toye 1987). In many developing countries, state intervention can be understood as a necessary enabler of economic growth and social development. The market, championed by neoliberalism as the successor to the state, is not as free-standing as the notion of a free market might imply (Harriss-White 1996; Platteau 1994).

27. Lund (2006) looks at twilight institutions operating between state and society.

28. History and anthropology have shown that the economic actions of poor people are defined by a moral economy of rights and expectations which, though they may be rooted in economic practices and social exchanges, are not determined just by financial utility. Thompson (1971) argues that popular protests in eighteenth-century England were not just actions of mobs reacting to soaring prices, malpractice among dealers, or hunger, but operated within a normative framework of what constituted legitimate and illegitimate practices in marketing, milling, baking, etc. that had some support in the paternalist traditions of the authorities. That is, popular protests against changes resulting from the market practices of laissez-faire capitalism were grounded in a consistent view of social norms and obligations, "the moral economy" of the poor. Scott (1979) develops this concept, showing that the fear of food shortages and the desire to maintain long-term subsistence security, while minimizing risk, explain the peasant's resistance to innovation, become landowners, or maximize output and also underpinned their notion of justice. In other words, the desire for subsistence security grew out of peasant economics but was socially experienced as a pattern of moral rights and expectations.

29. See Das (2007) for a discussion of how the distinction between the legal and the illegal was very blurred in the everyday lives of the people who lived in Sultanpuri, in Delhi.

30. See Harris (1996) for a discussion on how laws often put people in different moral predicaments by the fact that they forbid or criminalize actions which the people concerned consider acceptable or even desirable within their own moral code.

31. Underlying the international discourse on corruption is the idea that for progressive economic development, people in modern society should allow the state to define and police the principles of morality, or good behavior, for the collective good through impersonal rules—such as the rule of law. As Robertson reminds us, "what in modern times we have been calling *corruption* is a by product of the formal rules that seek to separate persons from the offices they hold" (2006, 8). There is, as Hart (2005, 29) points out, a huge effort involved in separating the impersonal state from personal agency. When people step across this division, the word often used is "corruption," and that is one reason why some explain the origins of corruption as the extreme personalization of power relationships (Bayart

1993). Corruption violates the fundamental idea of the state as an impartial servant of the people, as the nonpersonal guarantor of a certain impersonal social order. This idea is a crucial one because the legitimacy of modern states, to a large extent, rests on this claim (Mooij 1992). Yet, as anthropology has recently shown us, the separation of the impersonal state from personal society is highly problematic: there is a complex relationship between personal agency and impersonal institutions, and personality or personal agency is intrinsic to bureaucracy (Brass 1997; Fuller and Harriss 2001; A. Gupta 1995, 2005).

32. For a fascinating analysis of sevaks which reflects the Jharkhandi situation, see Mayer: "true *seva* was that which was done in secret [and therefore] people who do selfless service were by definition not publicly known" (1981, 165–66). The blurring of the boundary between community workers and politicians has parallels elsewhere, and a case from the Cape Flats in South Africa is well analyzed in Jensen (2004).

33. Indeed, as Mosse (2001, 190 n. 47) also argues is the case in Tamil Nadu, it is now common to hear contractors complaining that "between the demands of state officials and those of [particular] villagers, there is no longer a livelihood from contracting."

34. Parry and Bloch (1989).

35. *Chai-pani* literally means tea water, but it usually indicates food and drink that are bought for the officers. These can range from tea or a box of mangoes to bottles of alcohol. Less commonly, and usually only in the case of higher officers, the gift can increase to material for a suit, or saris for officers' wives. In many cases, money itself changes hands for the purpose of buying the proposed items. However, the transaction is always depicted as one of things, rather than money. As Yan succinctly describes in the Xiajia case, the exchange is conditioned by existing power relations so that the recipient (the officer) gains prestige because the exchange shows that he or she possesses valued resources that attract gifts. Moreover, it indicates the donor's perception of the recipient as someone who can be bought off, and the recipient's acceptance of such an identity (Yan 1996, 171).

36. See Parry (2000).

37. See Goldman (2001) and Ruud (2001).

38. See A. Gupta (1998; 2005) and Neocleous (1996).

39. See Bailey (1969).

40. See Bierschenk, Chaveau, and de Sardan (2002) and Lewis and Mosse (2006).

41. In this sense, the sadans, as mediators to the state, living amid a poorer adivasi population who sought to keep the state at bay, have many parallels with Bailey's (1963) description of Bisipara in Orissa in the 1960s. A. Gupta (2005) is, of course, critical of Bailey's account of Bisipara, arguing that Bailey describes what he thinks is an ideal "traditional" village. Gupta juxtaposes Bailey's account with Shrilal Shukla's novel *Rag Darbari*, in which, in the village of Shivpalganj in Uttar Pradesh in the 1960s, government institutions are woven into all aspects of village life. However, I

feel Gupta fails to underscore that Shukla was an Indian Administrative Service officer, and that Shivpalganj was a roadside village in Uttar Pradesh —and hence very different from a village that was more difficult to reach, and in a region that was historically treated very differently by the state. Notwithstanding the literary qualities of the novel in depicting rural poverty in India (Lewis, Rodgers, and Woolcock 2008), I suggest that Shukla may inevitably have been more likely to stress the influence of the state in the nooks and crannies of village life in his village, and less likely to portray the way in which the whole discourse of the state can be mediated by a rural elite, as may have been the case in Orissa at the time of Bailey's field research.

42. de Sardan (2005, 174).

43. I use the term "patron-client" here to refer to the relations between two groups in which one is in some way in a superior or more powerful position than the other (Gellner and Watterbury 1977). However, I think that Gilsenan (1977) is correct that patron-client relations are often understood as a cause rather than a symptom, and this is certainly the case in the recent discussions of brokerage. I also think that the broader point of analysis should be to understand the deeper social and historical processes in which patron-client relations are embedded and produced.

44. Other common titles given by the maharajah include Pandey, Tewary, Devgharia, and Brittia.

45. As Hoffman notes, this was probably a controlling tactic by the maharajah and the Hindus he brought in, as it weakened the tribal village family ([1915] 1961, 336).

46. The Parn does not have descendants in Tapu today, and I was not able to acquire much information on this tribe. Hallett (1917) says that Risley's "Tribes and Castes of Bengal" refers to Chic Badaiks as a subcaste of Parns, who are a "degraded tribe" of Orissa. However, Hallett reports that apart from their profession, the connection between the two tribes is doubtful, and that in fact the Chic Badaiks claim to be Aryan and Hindus, while the Parns that were found in Munda villages spoke Mundari and followed many Munda customs (Hallett 1917, 69).

47. In fact, mistreatment of adivasis by zamindars is often given as an example of signs that the Roman Catholic Church would be likely to recruit converts in an area—such as Dighia, near Bero (De Sa 1975, 141). De Sa also notes that in Chota Nagpur, the Roman Catholic Church, especially under Father Lievens (1856–95), is reported to have gained mass support from tribals who wanted protection from the cruelty of landlords.

48. See Reid (1912).

49. See Patel (1954, 464–65).

50. Rudolph and Rudolph, for example, have argued that "abolition had a profound effect on Indian politics. A class that might have played historical roles comparable to those played by Britain's landed gentry and aristocracy, Prussia's Junkers, Japan's daimyos and samurai, or Latin America's latifundia masters was removed from the historical stage. As a result of

abolition, about twenty million tenants became owners and about fourteen million acres were acquired and distributed" (1987, 315).

51. This point was succinctly made by Cohn (1987), although he was writing about land reform in the late 1700s and early 1800s in what was then Banaras Province. He showed how the Bengal Regulations of 1795 made it possible to auction off to the highest bidder estates whose owners were declared to be in arrears with their taxes. In this way, there were many instances in which zamindar rights, as well as the obligations to pay the government revenue, were transferred from old Rajput lineages to urban residents. However, as Cohn notes, "with the sale of property, the legal position of the traditional *zamindars* changed; but in many cases their economic, social and political position within their villages and *taluks* [administrative divisions] was little affected, particularly from the perspective of those inside the village or *taluk*. It didn't seem important to low-caste cultivators or landless workers that the Rajput who for generations had dominated them was legally a *zamindar*, an ex-*zamindar* or a tenant" (1987, 410).

52. As Bailey notes, for Bisipara in Orissa during the 1950s, multiple inheritance and the low probability of siring a long line of only sons, prevented wealth from remaining within one lineage for more than two or three generations (1957, 85).

53. I calculated this figure from my observations on the work people do, and for whom they do it, while I was in Tapu between November 2000 and May 2002. Although I think that this estimate is accurate for the time period considered, I would like to point out that it is not always the same families that are dependent on the landlord descendants. In some years, for instance, some of these dependent families may decide to leave the village and migrate seasonally to the brick kilns.

54. Government rates in the early 2000s were then at least RS 15 more a day than village labor rates.

55. See Nuijten (2003).

56. This situation is very similar to that which Bailey describes in Orissa, where middlemen do everything in their power to foster misunderstanding between local community members and outside officials (1969, 169) or that which Collier (1976) describes in the political leadership in Zinacantan, Mexico. In other words, mediators are able to capture state development resources by taking every opportunity to stress the cultural differences between insiders (local people) and outsiders (the state and its agents).

57. See Roy (1915, 46), Russell and Lal (1916, 22–25), and Yorke (1976, 71–74). Yorke argues that in a Ho (Munda) village in Singhbhum, Jharkhand, the Ahirs (called Gopes or Gau) come in fact from a local Ho lineage, the members of which have taken up the profession of cattle herding as a hereditary occupation (ibid., 70). He even suggests that the lineage of a Ho man who took the job of cattle herder might, over time, become Gope rather than Ho. This points to the fact that the Mundas and the Ahirs

are closely related. Moreover, as Yorke suggests, as a service caste, the status of Ahirs was in fact lower than that of the Mundas (ibid., 74).

58. See Heesterman (1971).

59. This is the differentiation that Dumont and Pocock (1959) suggest in their analysis of possession and priesthood.

60. The situation in Tapu has some parallels with Schnepel's (1995) description of the jungle kings of South Orissa. Schnepel argued that an important means through which these jungle kings could pursue their legitimization was through their patronage of tribal goddesses. My argument, however, is slightly different from that of Schnepel. He suggests that tribal goddesses underwent various kinds and degrees of Hinduization as a result of royal patronage. For instance, he argues that the original aniconical representations were anthropomorphized, and the goddesses were housed in temples. In Tapu, however, the spirits are not called gods or goddesses, there were no anthropomorphized forms, and there are no temples for the spirits. Moreover, if the way in which spirits are propitiated appears at face value to have been Hinduized, my argument is that tribals do not see change to their spiritual practices as resulting from zamindar patronage. As such, the power of zamindar patronage was and remains in not being seen to interfere with the tribal spiritual world, but instead to support it. Schnepel does not make this case, although his own material supports such a conclusion. In some legends of Markama (a tribal goddess), the goddess kicks unconscious the Brahmin priest appointed by the king to do service at her temple and appears to the king in a dream demanding him to put the low ranking *paik*, the original temple priest, back in charge (Schnepel 1995, 149–50). Schnepel argues that this legend is evidence that at some point, local goddesses and indigenous worshippers resist further absorption. I suggest that the royal patronage is dependent on not absorbing the tribal goddess.

61. See also the importance given by K. Singh (1982) to the corpus of anthropological literature at the disposal of the Jharkhand Movement in order to create a new sense of history to legitimize adivasi search for identity. He points out Sarat Chandra Roy, in particular, as having given "eloquent expression to the tribals' demand for separation; his ideas and draftsmanship left their imprint on the memoranda submitted by tribal organisations before different government bodies. He was not a closet anthropologist but rather the first ideologue and active protagonist of the demand for tribal autonomy" (1982, 2).

62. Vitebsky (1993) shows how on the one hand the Soras of Orissa were intimidated by the state, but on the other hand, the spirit-endowed Sora shamans in the underworld had the power to marry even policemen or state clerks.

63. This reflects to some extent some of the findings of one of the few studies on the tribal voter, conducted by Sachidananda (1976)—who talks about the lack of importance given to voting by large numbers of voters. People went about the ordinary business of life on election day and were

not eager to vote unless one of the contending candidates' workers brought them to the polling booth. In the Bero area, rural elites who were political workers for particular MLAs had a significant role to play in convincing people to vote for their candidate. Neel Yadav and Shiv Gope of Tapu, two of Vishwanath's key workers in the 1995 campaign, explained that the work in elections was three-fold. First, they tried to capture the booth area, to prevent other parties from operating there—which was difficult, as it required enough supporters to physically prevent competitors from entering the area. Second, toward the end of election day, they attempted to cast bogus votes—that is, votes in the name of all the people on the electoral roll who did not turn up to vote. Both men took pride in telling me that when Vishwanath won the 1995 elections, they each cast at least thirty bogus votes. Third, and most crucial, they took Mundas to the polls to ensure that they voted for Vishwanath. To do so, they had to convince Mundas to make the effort to vote, and that their candidate was the best.

64. See Chambers (1983, 1997).

65. Ferguson's (1990) classic study uses the case of the Thaba Tseka development project in Lesotho to show how poverty can become reduced to a technical problem for which development needs to provide technical solutions, thereby depoliticizing poverty and enabling the subtle expansion of institutional state power.

66. Some of the best known critiques are those by Cooke and Kothari (2001), Stirrat (1996), Gujit and Shah (1998), Mosse (1994), and G. Williams (2004). For two excellent critiques of social capital, see Harriss (2002) and Fine (1999).

67. See, for example, Wood (2003) and Mosse (2007).

68. See Partha Chatterjee (2004).

69. As noted long ago by Thompson (1971) and Scott (1979).

70. See Hart (2005).

71. Hansen (2001b) fascinatingly charts the rise of the notorious Hindu Nationalist Shiv Sena in Mumbai, and questions the notion of ethics involved in Chatterjee's analysis of political society. Hansen's point is that when political society allows a party as lethal as the Shiv Sena to operate outside the rule of law, surely we have to have stronger ethical standards than are implied by Chatterjee's question, "How can we be sure that what we desire or approve is what is truly good?" (quoted in Hansen 2001b, 234).

4. DANGEROUS SILHOUETTES

1. Thornton and Currey (1991).

2. Anderson and Grove (1987).

3. Cronon (1995).

4. Mackenzie (1987).

5. Mawdsley (2004).

6. See R. Williams (1980, 77).

7. Especially for the Indira Gandhi period, see Rangarajan (2006; forthcoming).

8. See Peluso (1993).

9. Ibid.

10. See Fairhead and Leach (1996), but also see Nyerges and Green (2000) for a critique of their work.

11. Many of these arguments developed from the work of those who wanted outside development agencies to learn from indigenous knowledge systems. For example, Richards (1985) shows that African farmers develop skills to fit changing circumstances and needs, and argues that neither the environment nor culture are deterministic. In Latin America, Posey (1982) finds among the Gorotire Kayapo much to celebrate about practices of forest management in Brazil—indigenous people do not create deforestation.

12. Representative of this position is Douglas (1966).

13. See especially Descola and Palsson (1996). Recognizing that there is nothing natural about ideas of nature does not require accepting the extreme position that some postmodernist writing has proposed: that there is no nature (see Morris [1997] for a good critique of this view), that the existential world in which we find ourselves—the trees, the sky, the clouds—does not exist or is solely a human creation. Rather, it means acknowledging that nature is not always thought about everywhere in the same way.

14. See Latour (1993).

15. See de Castro (1998).

16. The idea that humans and the environment cannot exist apart from each other emerged most strongly in a collection of essays edited by Croll and Parkin (1992), especially through the work of Ingold (1992, 2000), who has shown how people know their physical world through action in it.

17. See Brody (1987).

18. Arnold and Guha (1995, 19) point out that, whereas modern environmentalism in Britain draws on rural romanticism and naturalism represented by the likes of Constable and Wordsworth, the patron of environmentalism in India is Gandhi, who was going not back to nature but to the village, peasantry, and rural asceticism at the heart of India. In the more ecologically idyllic colonial images, tribal inhabitants of India were attributed with a deep love of vegetation, often planting species for future generations—see von Furer Haimendorf (1948) and Elwin (1943).

19. For example, in his pioneering study of the relationship between colonialism and ecological decline in the western Himalayas, Ramachandra Guha notes that prior to intervention by the British forest department, "many wooded areas were not of spontaneous growth and bore the hill-folk's instinct for the plantation and preservation of the forest" (1989, 29). His important account of ecological change and peasant resistance argued that the Chipko Movement of Uttarakhand should be seen as peasant struggles against commercial forestry and a centralizing state that also af-

firms a "way of life more harmoniously adjusted with natural processes" (1989, 196). A particularly gendered version of this argument has been produced by those who argue that the environmental knowledge of women is greater than that of men (Banuri and Apffel Marglin 1993; Shiva 1988). That view is rightly criticized by others (Jewitt 2000; Kelkar and Nathan 1992).

20. See Rangan (1996).

21. See Shiva (1988).

22. The most influential of such writings was Gadgil and Guha (1993).

23. Greenough (2001).

24. Sinha, Gururani, and Greenberg (1997).

25. Since the late 1800s, in response to perceived deforestation, India has seen a diverse program of managed forest change widely known as scientific forestry. Gadgil and Guha (1993) have widely criticized these policies, claiming that the imperial greed for timber to build ships was the main motivation for forestry programs. This argument is challenged by Grove (1995), suggesting that colonial motivations were based on humanistic concerns about deforestation and drought. For an excellent history of the creation of "modern forests" by colonial and nationalist governments in Bengal, which moves beyond conventional oppositions between state and society, see Sivaramakrishnan (1999).

26. For critical analysis of JFM, see Jeffery and Sundar (1999), Arun Agrawal (2005), and Sivaramakrishnan (1999).

27. While some question the virtues of community-based approaches to conservation (Salafsky et al. 2001), others defend the participation of communities (Wilshusen et al. 2002), arguing it is essential for the long-term protection of biodiversity. See Saberwal, Rangarajan, and Kothari (2001) for a history and summary of the key issues driving a participatory approach to parks in India.

28. See Jharkhand Rural Livelihood and Natural Resource Management at www.worldbank.org/projects.

29. See Baviskar (1997, 213).

30. I draw here on Sivaramakrishnan's (2003) use of the term "ecological nationalism" to refer to a functionalist analysis of religiosity and conservation ethics. A later edited collection (Cederlof and Sivaramakrishnan 2005) uses the concept of ecological nationalism to link cultural and political aspirations with the program of nature conservation and environmental protection, so that ethnic movements based on ideas of the environment are seen not just as reaffirmations of cultural identity but also as claims to territory and resources.

31. Keshri (2003, 13).

32. This has been argued by a range of authors, including Kelkar and Nathan (1992), Keshri (2003), and R. Singh (1996).

33. See Froerer (2005), Sundar (2005b), and Baviskar (2005) on the spread of Hindu nationalism in Chhattisgarh and Madhya Pradesh. Mawdsley (2006, 2005) has shown the close relationship between Hindu

Nationalist readings of environmental history and environmental change, and the neotraditional accounts that are supported by such indigenous rights activists.

34. Bosu Mullick (1991), for example, argues for unity in the apparently diverse nature of the supreme being in the Sarna system of belief.

35. See Ramachandra Guha (1989) and Shiva (1988).

36. See Vartak and Gadgil (1981). Freeman (1999) has an excellent critique of this ideal of the sacred grove in Kerala, where most groves do not take this form.

37. Munda (2000a) and Dev Nathan (2003).

38. See Banuri and Apffel-Marglin (1993).

39. The 1878 Indian Forest Act gave the government a monopoly on India's forests. The act divided the country's forests into "Reserved Forests," "Protected Forests," "Private Forests," and "Village Forests." The control of Reserved Forests was removed from villagers, who could now only collect some minor produce such as fruit from them. In Protected Forests, villagers were allowed to graze cattle and collect wood for household purposes. Only Village Forests were now available for unrestricted use by the villagers. As a result, after having had customary use of all but private forests, many villagers became criminals overnight. With the exception of a small area of Reserved Forest in a neighboring village, most of the woodland around Tapu became Protected Forest.

40. See Conklin and Graham (1995). This criticism of what Redford (1990) calls the "ecologically noble savage" is widely shared by many anthropologists. For instance, Redford argues that indigenous people have the same capacity and desire to exploit their environment as Westerners. Goody (1996, 262) has also argued that protection as well as destruction of wildlife and forests is found in simple as well as complex societies.

41. See Baviskar (1997).

42. See Agrawal (1999); Agrawal and Sivaramakrishnan (2000, 9); Hardiman (1994, 92); Jeffery and Sundar (1999); and Saberwal and Rangarajan (2003).

43. See Mosse (2001), on the development of tank irrigation in southern India.

44. See Sukumar (1989).

45. For comparative material on man-animal conflict in other parts of India, see Sukumar (1989) for elephants, Saberwal et al. (1994) for lions in the Gir sanctuary, and Jalais (2005) for tigers in the Sunderbans.

46. The 1879 Elephant Preservation Act in India, prohibiting the killing of elephants, was extended to most parts of Bengal (including Jharkhand) by 1894. Rogue animals, whose killing has to be authorized by the district magistrate, are an exception.

47. This plaint echoes the idea that many people-wildlife conflicts can be understood in term of people-state conflicts. See Knight (2000).

48. Leach and Mearns (1996). This is not to say that there is no material history of forest increase or decrease in the Tapu area. Government records

show more and thicker forests at the end of the 1800s than in the 1990s. However, since the 1970s, the forests have increased. The point here is that people have different perceptions of whether the forests have increased or decreased over time, depending on their different temporal starting points —and moreover, that the forests are a lived experience for the Mundas.

49. Gold and Gujar (2002, 259) describe a similar case in Sawar, Rajasthan, where the past achievement of environmental well-being was evidently at the expense of poor farmers whose crops were threatened by wild animals. The Sawar King Vansh Pradip Singh forested his kingdom and proceeded to restrict the use of the forest products that his subjects needed, while importing and protecting wild pigs in the jungle that caused great hardship for the poor farmers and ate their crops.

50. Munda (2000a).

51. Damodaran (2006) has also noticed the recent rise of Sarhul *puja* in urban centers but, rather than question the contradictions and tensions this form of puja gives rise to in relation to the significance of the festival in many of the area's villages, she sees such inventions of traditions in Gramscian terms, as a struggle for hegemony in the political arena. In what follows, I want to show that the reinvention of Sarhul puja by elite urban, middle-class activists is far from a struggle over hegemony but actually represents a passive revolution that is little supported by many adivasis in the rural areas.

52. See Srinivas (1956).

53. Hardiman (1987) points this out in the context of the Devi movement in western India.

54. Von Furer Haimendorf (1948) describes a similar ritual that he calls the Durari rite (Durari is the name of the Hindu month that runs from February to March) among the Raj Gonds of Adilabad and explains the symbolism as representing the felling of the forest and then its burning before the new crop is sown. Unlike the Mundas of Tapu, the Gonds he worked with think that there is some connection with the death of Ravanna, although he comments that this is a recent explanation (1948, 311).

55. In fact, I did not see this part of the ritual as Neel, a landlord descendant, poured a bucket of colored water over my head. With some of the other sadan young men, he had wandered over to the Munda ritual to pull me toward the celebrations of the Hindu festival of Holi, which was taking place at exactly the same time in the part of the hamlet where the landlord descendants lived. I am grateful to the late Professor Vikram Pramar for inspiring me to pay close attention to the significance of Fagua in Tapu. His own suspicion, marking his teleological belief in the strong connections between Sanskritized Hindu rituals and adivasi practices, was that Fagua was what Holi had been in the past.

56. This is the only time in Tapu when a frog was used in rituals, and I am uncertain of its significance. Elwin (1955, 486) notes that among the Saoras, the frog may be used to bring rain, and there is a rite of burying a frog in a pit until the rain frees it.

57. Human sacrifice, although historically rumored to have been common in many of the surrounding areas (Campbell 1861; Elwin 1943; MacPherson 1865), is no longer openly talked about in Tapu. However, when questioned, some of my closest friends told me there were rumors that it had occurred in the past in Tapu, and more recently in surrounding villages. See Parry (2008) for comparative contemporary material in neighboring Chhattisgarh. There is, of course, a need to be critical of the role of rumors in spreading what might be myths, perhaps even created and carefully manipulated. See Bates (2006) for the way in which rumors of human sacrifice enforced the view of adivasis as savages and thus legitimized direct British control over Bastar, Chhattisgarh. See also the critique by Padel (1995) of British colonial rule and its allegedly civilizing practices surrounding human sacrifice.

58. A similar situation arises in reports of tribal and environmental activism in Madhya Pradesh, where the supposedly pure environmentalists of tribal movements are actually those from middle-class, upper-caste backgrounds, and where tribal peasants are in fact highly ambivalent about the tribal-nature relationship advocated by the activists as an ideal (Baviskar 1997).

59. Stopping the evils of drinking and the savage practices of sacrifice was a central part of the Christian zeal to civilize the adivasis; see, for example, K. Singh (1966).

60. See also the excellent analysis of sacrifice and reformist opposition to animal sacrifice in a pan-Indian context in Fuller (1992).

61. See Sundar (1997, 37) for comparative material on Chhattisgarh.

62. See Parry (2008).

63. Jackson and Chattopadhyay (2000, 153), who conducted research in a nearby village, also point out that indigenous rituals around nature did not necessarily affect people's actual resource management or make them more environmentally concerned or aware. See also Baviskar (1995, 149) and Ajay Skaria (1999, 51) on adivasi practices in western India as not being designed to be conservationist.

64. See Nathan (1988).

65. See Skaria (1999, 51) on the Dangis of western India.

66. See Sivaramakrishnan (1999) for a parallel argument, and Baviskar (1995, 41), who argues that for most rural communities (in contrast to upper-class environmentalists) there seems to be a continuity in the way in which land, forest, water, and other resources are regarded, primarily as sources of subsistence.

67. See Skaria (1999, 59).

68. There are striking parallels here with Jackson and Chattopadhyay (2000): on the one hand, "dalit and adivasi informants blamed construction activities and clearance for cultivation by Bhumihars (ex-landlords) as the main factor in deforestation; the loss of land and the loss of forests are consistently related to Bhumihar exploitation, and no mention of other possible factors, such as population increase, figured in their accounts." But

on the other hand, the Bhumihars say that "the trees have been removed 'due to population increase.' [They] do not accept responsibility for forest clearances for arable land but claim that poor people are the main cause of the problem because they are unable to buy timber or alternative material for making houses. They also blamed the adivasis for exploiting the forest and said that from 1977 tribal people had begun to cut large quantities of trees" (2000, 154).

69. In 2001, the Indian government's compensation rates for elephant damage were as follows: RS 100,000 for death or permanent disability; RS 33,000 for serious injury; RS 10,000 for the total destruction of a brick house; RS 6,000 for the total destruction of a mud house; RS 2,000 for heavy damage to a brick house; RS 1,000 for heavy damage to a mud house; RS 800 for general damage to property; RS 2,500 per hectare of crop damaged; RS 3,000 for the killing of a buffalo, cow, or ox; RS 500 for the killing of a calf; and RS 1,000 for the killing of a goat.

70. Lévi-Strauss (1966, 62).

71. In a critique of those who argued that women protected the environment because of their affinity with nature, the economist Bina Agarwal (1992, 149) aptly noted that women's interests in environmental protection are usually rooted in material reality.

72. Agrawal (2005) and Sivaramakrishnan (1999) explore the Foucauldian processes of this governmentality or environmentality through forest conservation policies in India. But this is, of course, a perspective that resonates with local perspectives on environment and development policy in other parts of the world as well. Ferguson (1990) famously concluded that the unintended consequences of the Canadian-funded Thaba-Tseka agricultural development project in Lesotho was to increase state power through the area. As I have noted, Peluso (1993) has shown more adversarial sides of state reach in Kenya and Indonesia. And Norman (2004) has shown that the creation of the so-called peace park in Mozambique, the Limpopo National Park, resulted in state coercion and violence not only against local hunters who become labelled as poachers, but also to stop a long history of migration of local people across the Mozambique–South Africa border.

73. See Damodaran (2006, 140).

74. I draw on the term "passive revolution" as it has been eloquently explained and outlined by Kaviraj (1984; 1991) in relation to Indian independence.

75. I am, of course, alluding to Douglas's conception of "dirt as matter out of place" (1966, 35).

76. As Agrawal and Sivaramakrishnan suggest, landscapes are malleable and, when seen that way, lead to "a consideration of the politics of identity and other similar processes through which social typologies are constructed, politicized, deployed and unravelled" (2000, 6).

77. The claims of indigenous rights activists must not be conflated with

those of the forest officers. While the activists were, at least in their rhetoric, advocates of the poor rural communities, generally the forest officers (though there are some rare exceptions) were for preserving biodiversity at the expense of rural communities.

78. I thank Dr. Tanveer Ahmed for sharing this film with me.

79. If, as I am arguing, indigenous people are in conflict with the elephants and not necessarily the repositories of local knowledge on effective conservation, some might ask what solutions I offer for conservation policies. I would still like to agree with Saberwal and Rangarajan that we need a middle ground between local knowledge and scientific "expertise," that there are biological problems "such as demographic bottlenecks associated with small populations of animals—that need to be addressed if we are to save Indian wildlife—[which] are unlikely to be part of local knowledge systems and dealing with them will require expertise that will mainly only be available among people formally trained to deal with these issues" (2003, 3). However, when faced in Tapu with the everyday violence of the elephants and their material consequences on the lives of poor people whom very few seem to care about, I felt compelled to ask the question in my Ranchi lecture, "Why are we interested in saving the elephant and not the rat?" There is, of course, really interesting literature on why we seek to save and protect those animals, such as the elephant or the whale, that we construct as being closest to humans (Einarsson 1993; Sahlins 1976). We must ask the question, "Who are we saving the elephant for?" Who else but the Western and middle-class Indian market ready to consume nature? If this is the case, perhaps we should advance the concept of ecological nationalism (Cederlof and Sivaramakrishnan 2005) through a critique of the stasis of the nation-state, the production of its ecological identity, and the violence of the patrol and promotion of the resulting boundaries. And perhaps we should consider more imaginative solutions that go beyond national boundaries and move the elephants to the United Kingdom or the United States.

5. NIGHT ESCAPE

1. In this part of India, a *dhangar* was someone who was available at any time for a multitude of tasks, ranging from farm work to general cleaning and building work, and who in return was given meals, clothes, housing, and a nominal annual wage by his employer. Most dhangars in Tapu and the surrounding village were children between the ages of five and thirteen.

2. As Spencer (2003) has pointed out, social theorists and policymakers tend to perceive migration as a problem, and policies and development strategies are often aimed at reducing pressures to migrate (De Haan 2002; De Haan and Rogaly 2002; Mosse et al. 2002).

3. Spencer (2003).

4. This is the term used by Malkki (1992; 1995) in her analysis of the rooting of peoples and the territorialization of national identity among scholars and refugees.

5. See Malkki (1992) for an analysis of the cartographic and biological metaphors that are used in nationalist discourse.

6. Appadurai (1988).

7. See Malkki (1992).

8. http://www.landrightsfund.org/intro.html (accessed 26 June 2007).

9. See Nicholas (1996) and also some of the writings of the U.N. Special Rapporteur on the situation of human rights and fundamental freedoms of indigenous people, Rodolfo Stavenhagen (1996).

10. http://www.un.org/News/Press/docs/2007/hr4917.doc.htm (accessed 26 June 2007).

11. See Malkki (1992, 29).

12. See Merlan (2007, 149).

13. James (2007, 16–17) has a thought-provoking discussion about why in some places — in the case she discusses, South Africa — the idea of "indigenous land rights" is so undeveloped. She links the South African trajectory not only to the history of migration but also to the history of the liberal legal principles within which challenges to the apartheid state were framed. These liberal principles, she argues, led to the development of a "rights" discourse that was forward looking and hence incompatible with the more primordial ideals of autochthony and belonging that are embedded in concepts of indigeneity. The analysis of the development of the narratives of indigenous land rights in particular states vis-à-vis the legal frameworks of those states is an important issue for further research.

14. See Baviskar (2004).

15. See Weiner ([1978] 1988, 157).

16. This is from an evaluation of the Jharkhand Movement in 2000 by Ram Dayal Munda, then a professor in the Department of Tribal and Regional Languages at Ranchi University, and also a member of UNWGIP (Munda 2000b, 22).

17. Hoffman (1909, 10).

18. See also Tete (1990, 103).

19. Quoted in Weiner ([1978] 1988, 167).

20. Areeparampil (1995, 17).

21. There is much to commend in K. Ghosh's (2006) broader argument that the new transnational discourse of indigeneity has generated a set of political leaders who are removed from a grass-roots base and grass-roots concerns. However, Ghosh's own ethnography is curiously lacking the voices of the poorest adivasis, the ordinary poor people, who will be affected by the proposed dam. The one informant he draws on in this article, Soma Munda, after all remains a local leader — a village headman who has spent fifteen years in the Indian army, even serving with U.N. troops in the Congo for two years. It is true that he is not part of the international elite,

but he is part of a rural elite. In Jharkhand, men like him are crucial to building links to outside academics, journalists, NGOs, and activists that are also rapidly making the Koel Karo a site of international adivasi resistance. These men are the first point of call for the transnational leaders in their grass-roots mobilization. As is clear in Ghosh's description, mediators like Soma are well acquainted with such leaders and can appropriate the discourse of indigeneity when it suits them. In this case, Soma Munda stresses the fact that the patrilineal clan cannot be broken, both because of the protectionary measures of the Chotanagpur Tenancy Act and also because this would violate Munda customs, and anyone who transgresses and sells land risks being hacked to death. But Jharkhand's subaltern populations are divided into classes, and Soma clearly represents a village elite well versed in the discourses of indigeneity, especially when it comes to making claims about adivasi attitudes toward the land.

22. K. Singh (1966, 193).

23. This has been argued in the case of nationalist politics. See Fox (1990).

24. See Baviskar (1997).

25. *Prabhat Khabar*, 28 November 2001, p. 11.

26. As Clifford (2007) notes more generally about indigenous diasporas, geographic mobility is hardly a recent feature of indigeneity.

27. See Roy (1912; 1915), Weiner ([1978] 1988, 154), and the comment by Hardiman (1987, 12) that "the idea that adivasis are autochthonous, or original, inhabitants is belied by the fact that many such groups are known to have migrated in recorded history into the areas in which they are found, often displacing existing inhabitants in the process."

28. See also Skaria's accounts of the importance of mobility (1999, 46) and the temporary nature of villages (54) to adivasi communities in western India.

29. See F. Osella and Gardner (2004) and, specifically for migration from adivasi belts, see Bates (1994b).

30. In 1817, the British had entered Assam to repel a Burmese invasion, and they stayed in the area. In 1834, the British government appointed a committee to report on the possibility of introducing the cultivation of tea into India. The Assam Tea Company, founded in 1839, was the first tea plantation in the northeastern states of India. In 1859, the planters realized that they needed to import labor, as the local people had gone on strikes in 1848 and 1859. At first, the planters attempted to hire Chinese laborers (Weiner [1978] 1988), but there was violence between them and the Assamese. In 1859, a Tea Planters Association was formed to organize a system of labor migration from Lower Bengal (modern Jharkhand was then part of this) to Assam. By 1884 or 1885, nearly 45 percent of the laborers in Assam came from the Chotanagpur Plateau. In 1866, 84,915 laborers were recruited from Chotanagpur (Government of India 1931).

31. Government of India (1861, 2). See also Piya Chatterjee (2001) and K. Ghosh (1999), on how adivasis were transformed from wild savages to

docile laborers through the colonial market for aboriginality, which produced Jharkhand as a coolie nation.

32. See Badgaiyan (1994, 177).

33. Weiner ([1978] 1988, 161).

34. Rogaly et al. (2001) highlight the problems of quantifying the scale of seasonal migrant labor in an interesting attempt to estimate the number of seasonal migrants entering Bardhaman District, West Bengal, in the rice-harvesting season.

35. The classic scholarly study is Meillassoux ([1975] 1981), which shows how the Marxist concept of primitive accumulation results from peasants' entering capitalist labor markets through temporary and rotating labor migration, which preserves and exploits the domestic agricultural economy and brings the two economies (feudal and capitalist) together. See also the excellent work of Breman on western India (1985; 1994; 1996), as well as the studies by S. Mukherji (1985) and Standing (1985).

36. See Gadgil and Guha (1995).

37. This is also the classical scholarly approach, as exemplified by Breman (1985) and G. Shah et al. (1990). In recent years, the migrant has acquired more agency in the literature. Yet, most often he or she is still seen as a rational actor striving for an economic optimum (Lal 1989), or participating in a defensive coping strategy in the context of debt and extreme economic vulnerability. Although some object that the migrant is not just *Homo economicus* and consider social, religious, and ethnic factors, their accounts argue that it is mainly economic choices that drive such migration (De Haan 1994; Rogaly and Coppard 2003). Those who integrate the social and cultural contexts of migration do so more in their analysis of change in the areas receiving immigration (Appadurai 1996), or creating emigration (Gardner 1995; F. Osella and Osella 2000, 2003), rather than in their considerations of why people move.

38. See Breman (1985).

39. *Prabhat Khabar*, 28 November 2001, 11.

40. Willis (1978, 120).

41. See S. Mahmood (2001).

42. In focusing on such migration, marginal but increasingly important to labor studies in India (Breman 1999), I also want to advance important recent contributions to the study of South Asian migration (De Haan 2002; Mosse et al. 2002; F. Osella and Gardner 2004). These show that while economic considerations might shape or constrain seasonal, casual labor migration, it is also a dynamic sociopolitical process.

43. See the postscript of Baviskar (2004).

44. I focus here on brick kiln migration because this was the dominant form of migration in Tapu, and because it was also the central form of migration focused on by the indigenous rights activists. I should note, however, that there were a handful of cases of migrants from Jharkhand traveling to work as agricultural laborers in Punjab. In 2000–2002, three young sadans went to Punjab from Tapu. I should also note that an emerg-

ing concern for the activists is girls who are migrating to Delhi to do domestic labor. There is a slightly different undertone to this campaign against domestic labor migration because some of the migration is facilitated and supported by a Christian organization, and thus the threat to the activists is double: not only are they losing adivasis to Delhi, but the migrants might also be converting to Christianity. There were no cases of domestic labor migration in Tapu. More generally, however, this is clearly a rich research avenue to pursue.

45. See, in particular, the writings of Devi (1997).

46. One kiln owner told me that according to Indian standards, a large brick kiln employs about 500 laborers and produces 3,000,000 bricks a year; a medium-sized one employs about 300 laborers and produces 2,000,000 bricks a year; and a small one produces 1,500,000 bricks a year with about 200 laborers.

47. Parry (2003) notes this in the case of long-distance labor migrants to Bhilai. He also draws attention to this contradiction in Wolf's (1992) data on factory women in Java.

48. This was also the case for the migrants in Tirupur, in Tamil Nadu, described by De Neve (2003).

49. Rogaly and Coppard (2003) report the case of a woman—separated from her second husband—who migrated from Puruliya to the rice fields of Bardhaman in order to have an affair with the labor contractor.

50. See the very interesting analysis of the micropolitics of friendship and flirting in Kerala by C. Osella and Osella (1998).

51. Parry (2001, 808) describes the same thing for casual and contract laborers in Bhilai.

52. This explanation resonates with Parry's (2001, 808) report from Bhilai that husbands and wives generally avoid working at the same construction site because of the sexual banter and flirting that is characteristic of such work sites, and the jealousy that it produces.

53. Chopra (1995, 31 and 59) reports a case in which migration to Punjab allowed an Oraon man from Ranchi District to elope with an unsuitable girl from a lower-status family.

54. In line with their broader argument that migration might amplify gender inequalities in the context of adivasi seasonal labor migrants in eastern India, Mosse et al. (2002, 82) argue that migration puts a strain on the marriage relationship. They cite new liaisons that are formed in the context of migration, and insecurity and suspicion that lead to domestic violence and abandonment, as part of their evidence. However, based on the Jharkhand evidence, I would like to suggest that migration might be a solution to these problems, rather than a cause.

55. See comparative material by Unnithan-Kumar (2003) on the Darana women in Jaipur.

56. Dupont (2000, 109) also notes the importance of familial tensions and quarrels in explaining why homeless people in Old Delhi had migrated to the city. She says that 24 percent of the homeless migrants she surveyed

cited familial tensions as their primary reason for migrating. Of course, people are often reluctant to admit in brief questionnaires that familial tensions resulted in their migration. This is perhaps demonstrated by the fact that of the thirty-six respondents Dupont selected for in-depth interviews, about a third mentioned familial tensions as important in their migration trajectory only when pressed (2000, n. 35).

57. For instance, Bates and Carter note several cases of women in the early twentieth century for whom migration to places such as Assam from the Central Provinces was a way to elope with lovers and escape from husbands back home. The authors say that the problem became so serious that a special clause was entered into the Central Provinces Emigration Rules in 1937 to allow women to be detained for up to three days "if unaccompanied by husbands." They note that "clearly the administration was extremely distressed by such goings-on, though little can be known of the view of the Gonds" (1992, 230). Migration as a means of liberation from social constraints at home was often described in terms of the emotional propensity of adivasis to run away from home. For instance, in his report of the Assam Labour Enquiry Committee, Reverend Van Hecke notes, "The people are of a peculiar temper, they get angry very easily and run away from home"; and Father Hoffman points out, "The Mundas are very impulsive and sensitive; young people often run away from home, after getting a scolding about something" (Government of India 1906, 13). It may be that in those days, economic motives for migrating were more prominent in people's minds than they are for my informants today. However, while motivations may change with the political and economic conditions of the time, it is worth remembering that several movements—such as the spread of Christianity beginning in the late 1800s and the spread of the Tana Bhagats since 1914—probably also produced local tensions of the sort that had prompted Burababa to flee from his puritanical son.

58. Some of the key texts are those by B. Anderson (1983) and Hobsbawm and Ranger (1983).

59. See Douglas (1966).

60. See especially the thought-provoking article by A. Gupta and Ferguson (1992, 17), but also Massey (1994).

61. See Spencer (2003), who draws on the insights of Ranabir Sammadar to make this argument.

62. See also excellent work on the U.S.-Mexico border, where the U.S. government arrests many Mexicans, and hence performatively reinforces the state idea of bounded citizenship, but at the same time negates the effectiveness of these arrests by permitting the labor migration that is fundamental to the U.S. economy (de Genova 2002; Heyman 1995).

63. See the detailed ethnography by Elwin (1946) and the subsequent engagement of this work in S. Gell (1992).

64. There are parallels here with the ways in which Hindu Nationalist discourses evoke notions of femininity in protecting Mother India (van der Veer 1996 is a classic study of such discourses).

65. See Humphries (1988, 118–19). Whether this argument is relevant to Jharkhand is a question for further investigation, but one insightful explanation that Humphries gives for the obsession of ruling-class men with female sexuality is that female infidelity and impurity threaten the integrity of the bloodline (120). Promoting chastity and modesty as ideal female virtues was a way to safeguard property rights, eventually developing into the idea of the control and domination of women themselves as men's property. This ideology was absent among the propertyless colliers, and their alleged sexual promiscuity thus became the focus of the bourgeois investigators.

66. To this extent, I disagree that migration does little to emancipate adivasi women (as is argued of Bhil women by Mosse et al. 2002, 78). The Jharkhand situation suggests that a broader perspective on transforming social relations might reveal that migration enables women, in particular, to be emancipated from village constraints.

67. After her excellent book *Veiled Sentiments*, Abu Lughod wrote an important article warning against the romance of resistance, arguing that resistance should be used as a diagnostic of power (1990). She shows what the forms of Awlad Ali Bedouin women's resistance could reveal about the historically changing relations of power in which they were enmeshed, as they became increasingly incorporated into the Egyptian state and economy.

68. It is extremely encouraging to see efforts from scholars and development consultants—in particular Mosse et al. (2002) and Mosse, Gupta, and Shah (2005), and Rogaly et al. (2001; 2002)—starting with the basis that seasonal labor migration is central to rural livelihoods, and that therefore a key issue is not how to reduce migration, but how to reduce its costs. In western India, Mosse was involved in a project supporting adivasi migrants under the auspices of the U.K. DfID. While most of the planned endeavors are extremely promising, I think that the Jharkhand case gives us reasons to be wary of bureaucratizing migration through registering migrants in migration information centers, and especially via identity cards. As the cases discussed in this chapter suggest, migration also provides a space of escape and liberation, and the registration of migrants might in the long run serve to reduce their freedom. Rogaly et al. (2002) stress that attempts to reverse exclusion should beware of attempting a form of inclusion which goes against the interests of migrants. Moreover, we should not hesitate to think laterally about what we might learn from the debates over identity cards in a cross-country perspective. I am, of course, thinking about the striking parallels with the current debates in England.

6. THE TERROR WITHIN

1. The early Naxalites acknowledged their inspiration by the Chinese Communists, and the first Naxalite party—the Communist Party of India

(Marxist-Leninist), or CPI(ML)—had the approval of the Chinese government. For brief histories, see S. Banerjee (1984) and P. Singh (1995).

2. For summaries of the emergence of different branches of the Naxalite movement, see Bhatia (2000, 46–63) for Bihar, Shanta Sinha (1989) for Andhra Pradesh, and D. Gellner (2003) and Hutt (2004) for Maoists in Nepal. My edited volume with Judith Pettigrew juxtaposes ethnographies of the spread of Maoists in India and Nepal, in order to consider them in one comparative frame (Shah and Pettigrew 2009).

3. The Aurangabad incidents have also been depicted as a sign of the degeneration of the MCC from a fight for social and economic justice to a caste conflict, with only a veneer of a class struggle (Pathak 1993).

4. *Bihar in Flames* is the title of a book by S. K. Ghosh (2000). The imagery of Bihar burning goes back to a 1986 CPI(ML) document which referred to the flaming fields of Bihar.

5. Andhra Pradesh banned its main Naxalite branch, the People's War Group (PWG), in 1992.

6. *Hindustan Times*, Ranchi, 1 November 2001, 2. Indeed, between January 2001 and February 2002, there were several major MCC strikes in Jharkhand against the police. Police reports claim that the lives of seventy-four police officers were lost (see *Hindustan Times*, Ranchi, 1 November 2001, 2).

7. See Bhatia (2000).

8. See Louis (2002).

9. See Corbridge (2002).

10. See *From Our Own Correspondent*, BBC Radio 4, 10 June 2006, and *New York Times*, 13 April 2006. See also the *Guardian*, 9 May 2006.

11. See Buur, Jensen, and Stepputat (2007).

12. Tilly (1985, 170).

13. Ibid.

14. As Gambetta (1993) explains is the case with the Sicilian mafia. Gambetta's important work deconstructs the popular stereotype of the mafia as mere criminals.

15. This is an expansion of Elwert's (1999) term "markets of violence," for arenas of long-term violent interaction in which different organizations employ violence as a strategy to bargain for power and material benefits.

16. This was the case for P. Singh (1995) and R. Gupta (2004).

17. Such studies of the Naxalites in Bihar or Bengal include S. Banerjee (1984), Mukherjee and Yadav (1980), Sankar Ghosh (1974), Louis (2002), and Donner (2005). Stree Shakti Sanghatana (1989) recorded evocative life stories of female survivors of the Telengana People's Struggle.

18. This argument has been made by, for example, Sluka (2000) and C. Mahmood (1996).

19. This is the basis of the research of Bhatia (2000) and Kunnath (2004; 2006) in central Bihar. Note that neither author has much material on the MCC.

20. Bhatia (2000, 79).

21. See, for example, Corbridge (2002, 56 and 69).

22. See Corbridge and Harriss (2000, 206).

23. See *Frontline*, 24 May 2002, 39.

24. There are certainly similarities with so-called revolutionary movements in other parts of the world—some have argued that peasants in the Peruvian Maoist insurgency of the Shining Path were won over to the movement only by force, as most of the members were intellectuals and disillusioned, educated young people (Ivan Degregori cited in Bourque and Warren 1989, 19; Stern 1998). In fact, Starn (1999) beautifully shows how the larger, longer-lasting movement of the Andean poor in the late twentieth century was not the Shining Path, but the formation of village vigilante groups known as *rondas*.

25. Kunnath (2006, 107) also reports antiliquor campaigns in Jehanabad District, Bihar.

26. Dalit critics of the Naxalite movement have accused it of being *Brahminwadi* (higher caste oriented) (Bhatia 2000, 162). A deviation from revolutionary socialist ideologies is not very surprising. Stoll (1993) argues that when people joined the revolutionary movement in Ixil, that did not mean they took the revolution's ideological message to heart. Though undoubtedly polemic, Stoll's argument that rural dwellers in the Ixil region of Guatemala were caught between two armies—that of the guerrillas and that of the state—is an important revisionist account of violence that no doubt raises questions for scholars of other cases.

27. See, for instance, Bhatia (2000; 2005).

28. In his study of Santali involvement in the Midnapore Naxalite uprising, Duyker (1987, 104) argues that the movement was successful in areas where people had already participated in local mass movements.

29. Gambetta (1993) reports that the mafia in southern Italy is also essentially supported by and supports state officials and politicians.

30. The crackdown began in August 2001 when Babula Marandi, the Chief Minister of Jharkhand, claimed he would "crack down on lawlessness which has no place in a civilised society" (www.rediff.com/news/2000/nov/25tara.htm. November 2000) and offered "special benefits" to MCC extremists who were willing to give up the armed struggle and surrender. The "benefits" were a payment of Rs 10,000, an Indira Aawas house, financial assistance of Rs 50,000, free legal aid, free educational facilities for children through primary school, and security. Thirty-seven people surrendered, which made the front page of all the local newspapers and dominated conversations in Ranchi City for many days. Marandi was careful not to investigate whether the surrender was voluntary, under pressure, or orchestrated (*Hindustan Times*, Ranchi, 12 August 2001, p. 2), and was able to repeat his central message about the need to civilize and educate the poor, uneducated masses who joined the MCC. In a sense, the crackdown was political theater. It enabled Marandi to construct a drama whose plot reenacted three related messages. First, it transformed the terrorists into a group of undeveloped savages. Second, the fact that they were still this way

was blamed on the last government's inability to keep its promises of modernization and development. And most important, it enabled the new government to take control of reproducing the civilizing myth of the state.

31. *Prabhat Khabar*, Ranchi, 11 August 2001, p. 4. See also *Hindustan Times*, Ranchi, 15 August 2001, p. 3.

32. The incident had a direct bearing on me, as the next day two jeeps full of armed police, some of whom had come from Ranchi, arrived in Tapu looking for me, to the shock of the villagers. At the time I was in Ranchi, and I was told later that the police asked what I was doing and how I lived, and took a good look at my house through the small window. They also asked if there was anybody living in the forest. Out of politeness, I followed up by going to the office of the Deputy Superintendent of Police in Ranchi, where I was told that it had been just a routine visit to make sure I was well. Later I realized that the visit was a direct result of Chandra Ganjhu's arrest, and I figured that after being tortured, he might have revealed his regional area of responsibility. Concerned about a foreigner living in an MCC zone of expansion, the police must have come to check up on me.

33. See also the story of Spencer's (2000) friend in a Sri Lankan Sinhala village.

34. See, for instance, Scheper-Hughes and Bourgois (2004).

35. See Taussig (1984) and Mitchell (2002).

36. See Kunnath (2004).

37. I am inspired to think in these terms by Parry's (2000) discussion of corruption.

38. The reverse could become the case in MCC-controlled areas where people suspect each other of betraying the MCC. In Bihar, Kunnath (2004) was struck by the degree to which people suspected those around them to be police informers or working for rival Naxal groups, and the degree to which he was constantly living in a state of fear.

39. *Hindustan Times*, Ranchi, 6 December 2001, p. 11.

40. See Spencer (1992, 267–68) for a discussion of the role of rumors and the tenacity with which people hold them to be true in the collective interpretations of collective violence. Das (2007) also has an excellent account of the role of rumor in producing events, and the continuity that they can achieve between events which might seem unconnected. She stresses the role of rumor in how the past may come alive in the act of telling, tracing the continuities between the Partition of India, Sikh militancy in Punjab and the related counterinsurgencies, the assassination of Indira Gandhi, and the subsequent authorization of the horrific violence against the Sikhs. But rumor also plays a role in connecting events that might be spatially quite disparate, so that a particular action of the speaker in Ranchi is suddenly connected to an arrest in Bero, to show the extent of the MCC's reach.

41. There is probably far more to be said about this last incident. What, for instance, were the Maoists doing shooting Muslims? Was it a case, as

has been claimed, of the MCC's simply shooting a gang of criminals who allegedly looted market stalls and raped the mothers and sisters of local men? Or was it playing with communal fire—were the attackers actually members of the militant right-wing Hindu Nationalist Rashtriya Swayam Sevak Sangh (RSS) in disguise, addressing the concerns of a Hinduized political elite in Bero and feeding off the growing Hindu-Muslim tension? Or was it playing out a class battle, as the Narkopi Muslims, landlord descendants, were increasingly buying property and shops in Bero and threatening preexisting Bero elites? Or was it a bit of all of these? I am afraid that despite the massacre's proximity to me in terms of time and location, I was not able to acquire more detailed accounts than those obtained by journalists in Bero and reported in newspapers. This is symptomatic of the larger difficulty of researching a so-called terrorist organization. For example, consider the case of the Ali Sena, reputed in Ranchi circles to be the Narkopi-based Muslim army set up in retaliation for the MCC's atrocities. By the time I left, Ali Sena was said to have disintegrated; in fact, some local people suggested that it might actually have been called Raksha Dal or even Jan Mancha. I cannot be certain whether the organization ever existed, or whether it was part mythical. It is, for instance, easy to imagine a scenario in which local journalists, inspired by the idea of groups such as the Ranvir Sena of central Bihar (created as the landlord descendants' opposition to the MCC), labeled a few Muslim reactionaries the Ali Sena, and in doing so perpetuated a discourse in Ranchi and Bero about the existence of Ali Sena.

42. I know of one case where a man was asked to deliver his gun and rifle to the MCC through his maid's relative, who had allegedly joined the MCC. When the man failed to deliver his weapons, eight men who identified themselves as MCC members came to his house one night when he was absent and blindfolded and kidnapped his wife. They left a note written and signed by his wife saying: "The MCC have kidnapped me. They want our guns. Please send them by 6:00 p.m. or they will kill me." The man sent the gun immediately, but he had left the rifle at the local police station. Fortunately, as he knew the local policemen well, he was able to bribe them to return his rifle, which he then sent off to the MCC. His wife was returned as soon as they received the second weapon and said she had been treated gently and with respect.

43. Taussig (1997) suggests similar activities by the state in Latin America.

44. There are parallels here with the analysis of the sublime and profane qualities that Hansen (2001a, 35) suggests together mark the way the state is imagined. Hansen analyzes this dual aspect of the state in the aftermaths of the very visible brutality of the Hindu-Muslim riots in Bombay in 1992 and 1993, in which the state was implicated, and demonstrates the need for the production of the more sublime and invisible dimensions of the state—the illusion that higher forms of rationality are prevailing, which allows ordinary people to make some sense of the otherwise senseless events, and

through which the state is able to reconfigure its legitimacy, as it tried to do through the public performances of the Sri Krishna Commission inquiry into the riots.

45. Abrams (1988, 82).

46. Taussig (1987).

47. E. Leach was among the first anthropologists to critically consider the continuity between the state and the "terrorist," pointing out that recent history provides striking examples of how the "legitimate" actions of the state become the criminal acts of the "enemy": the deviant characteristics of the hero (the state) and the criminal (the terrorist) are essentially the same (1977, 27). Others have since argued that, as Sluka put it, "the major form of terrorism in the world today is that practised by states and their agents and allies" (2000, 1). In Northern Ireland, the direct input of the British military in the sectarian campaign against the Catholics is exposed (Sluka 2000). And in Latin America, attention is drawn to death squads appearing in states receiving military assistance from the United States (Chomsky and Herman 1979), and to how the Venezuelan state constructs a drama against alleged subversives in order to reenact its own civilizing myths (Coronil and Skurski 1991).

48. See especially Das and Poole (2004) and Hansen and Stepputat (2005).

49. See Kelly and Shah (2006).

50. See Heyman and Smart (1999).

51. In Andhra Pradesh, Shanta Sinha argues, "In many places the first direct contact which the people have had with the state machinery has been through the Maoist movement and the state's reaction to it" (1989, 317).

52. See Taussig's (1984) analysis of the "culture of terror" in the Putamayo rubber-gathering boom in the colonial period. Taussig analyzes the report of Roger Casement to show that the rubber-gathering boom was based on narratives and stories that were used to create and sustain a culture of terror, a high-powered tool for domination and a principal medium of political practice. Part of this culture of terror was that Indians were constructed as so terrifying and savage that the only way to control them was by inspiring terror. Taussig argues that this was a kind of mimetic argument—if those labeled as terrorists are described as less than human, then it becomes permissible to use against them every form of terrorism attributed to them.

53. Das and Poole (2004) explore how events and experiences at the margins of the state shape the state itself.

54. I am thinking of the state in terms of the fascinating and important analysis of sovereignty that has arisen from anthropology after Giorgio Agamben's theories of sovereignty. Diverging from the idea of sovereignty as linked to control over territory, this work has promoted the importance of the constitution of sovereign power within states, through the exercise of violence over bodies and populations. See especially Hansen and Stepputat (2005), as well as Das and Poole (2004) and Buur, Jensen, and

Stepputat (2007). By marking a state of exception, sovereignty here is not bound to the law. Instead, its power arises from its very ability to reconstitute individuals through special laws as populations on whom new forms of regulation can be used. Placing adivasis in refugee camps enables them to be governed through states of exception, which strips them of their special legal rights as adivasis and "civilizes" them into "normal" citizens.

55. Benjamin (1969, 256).

56. Bhatia (2000, 162).

EPILOGUE

1. See Gledhill (1997).

2. Graeber (2004) proposes that our role as radical intellectuals should be to look for possible alternatives, and that since anthropologists are constantly adding to a creative reservoir of the moral imagination, they are very well placed to outline what the world could look like. He suggests that two moments are involved, one ethnographic and the other utopian. I use the phrase "arcadian spaces" to capture the potentialities in these moments as one.

3. See Benjamin (1999, especially 456–89). See also Leslie (2000). I am grateful to Dennis Rodgers for prompting me to seek inspiration from Benjamin here.

4. Latour (1993) has importantly argued that the very idea of the modern world is based on a set of impossible intellectual distinctions, like those between objective nature and subjective culture, science and politics, and the modern and the traditional. My intention in resurrecting arcadian spaces is not to exoticize so-called traditional values and customs, but to move beyond the distinctions of modern and traditional in showing how Munda values and lives today could be the basis of future political visions.

5. See, for example, the classic Scott (1985) and Jean Comaroff (1985).

6. Some of the excellent criticism of the resistance literature has questioned its separation of the body from the mind, and of behavior from consciousness. See Mitchell (1990), but also the critique by Ortner (1995).

7. Hart (2006), in a broader plea against immigration controls, has argued that with the increasing control of the movement of people, we are seeing the globalization of apartheid.

8. Skaria (1999).

9. See Fuller and Harriss (2001) for an extended discussion.

10. An influential line of thought sees the failure of the postcolonial state as India's natural rejection of imposed social change and, furthermore, as evidence of a broader pattern inherent in India's experiments with modernism. The most extreme proponents of this argument are Nandy (1998) and Madan (1997), who believe that a Westernized elite imposed secular Western institutions on ordinary people who considered religion to contain the principles by which social conduct should be governed. Variants of this

argument, albeit less historically and culturally reductionist, are implied in Kaviraj (1984, 1991, 1997) and Partha Chatterjee (1986; 1993), who, following Gramsci, argue that the form of the Western liberal postcolonial state imported for India by its modernizing bourgeoisie was unintelligible for its subaltern populations at the time of independence. Social transformation was not driven from within the society; rather, it was a function of domination attempted through the state and a "passive revolution" that substituted planning for political reform (Kaviraj 1984, 225–27; 1991, 80).

11. See Asad (1973).

Bibliography

Abrams, Philip. 1988. "Notes on the Difficulty of Studying the State (1977)." *Journal of Historical Sociology* 1 (1):58–89.

Abu Lughod, Lila. 1986. *Veiled Sentiments: Honor and Poetry in a Bedouin Society.* Berkeley: University of California Press.

——. 1990. "The Romance of Resistance: Tracing the Transformations of Power through Bedouin Women." *American Ethnologist* 17 (1):41–55.

Agrawal, Arun. 1999. *Greener Pastures: Politics, Markets, and Community among a Migrant Pastoral People*. Durham, N.C.: Duke University Press.

——. 2005. *Environmentality: Technologies of Government and the Making of Subjects*. Durham, N.C.: Duke University Press.

Agrawal, Arun, and K. Sivraramakrishnan, eds. 2000. *Agrarian Environments: Resources, Representations, and Rule in India*. Durham, N.C.: Duke University Press.

Agarwal, Bina. 1992. "The Gender and Environment Debate: Lessons from India." *Feminist Studies* 18 (1):119–58.

Alfred, Taiaiake. 2001. "From Sovereignty to Freedom: Towards an Indigenous Political Discourse." *Indigenous Affairs* 3:22–34.

Anderson, Benedict. 1983. *Imagined Communities*. New York: Verso.

Anderson, David, and Richard Grove. 1987. "The Scramble for Eden: Past, Present and Future in African Conservation." In *Conservation in Africa: People, Policies and Practice*, edited by David Anderson and Richard Grove. Cambridge: Cambridge University Press.

Appadurai, Arjun. 1988. "Putting Hierarchy in Its Place." *Cultural Anthropology* 3 (1):36–49.

——. 1996. *Modernity at Large: Cultural Dimensions of Globalization*. Minneapolis: University of Minnesota Press.

Apter, Andrew. 1987. "Things Fell Apart? Yoruba Responses to the 1983 Elections in Ondo State, Nigeria." *Journal of Modern African Studies* 25 (3):489–503.

Areeparampil, Mathew. 1995. *Tribals of Jharkhand: Victims of Development*. New Delhi: Indian Social Institute.
———. 2003. "Historical Bases of the Name of Jharkhand." In *The Jharkhand Movement: Indigenous Peoples' Struggle for Autonomy in Jharkhand*, edited by Ram Dayal Munda and Sanjay Bosu Mullick. Copenhagen: International Work Group for Indigenous Affairs.
Arnold, David, and Ramachandra Guha. 1995. "Introduction: Themes and Issues in the Environmental History of South Asia." In *Nature, Culture, Imperialism: Essays on the Environmental History of South Asia*, edited by David Arnold and Ramachandra Guha. Delhi: Oxford University Press.
Asad, Talal, ed. 1973. *Anthropology and the Colonial Encounter*. New York: Humanities Press.
Badgaiyan, S. D. 1994. "Tribal Worker in the Industry." In *Tribal Labour and Employment*, edited by D. Thakur and D. Thakur. New Delhi: Deep and Deep.
Bailey, Frederick G. 1957. *Caste and the Economic Frontier: A Village in Highland Orissa*. Manchester, England: Manchester University Press.
———. 1963. *Politics and Social Change: Orissa in 1959*. Berkeley: University of California Press.
———. 1969. *Stratagems and Spoils: A Social Anthropology of Politics*. Oxford: Basil Blackwell.
Banerjee, Mukulika. 2007. "Sacred Elections." *Economic and Political Weekly* 42 (17):1556–67.
Banerjee, Sumanta. 1984. *India's Simmering Revolution: The Naxalite Uprising*. London: Zed.
Banuri, Tariq, and Frederique Apffel Marglin, eds. 1993. *Who Will Save the Forests? Knowledge, Power and Environmental Destruction*. London: Zed.
Barnard, Alan. 2006. "Kalahari Revisionism, Vienna, and the 'Indigenous Peoples' Debate." *Social Anthropology* 14 (1):1–17.
Bates, Crispin. 1994a. "Lost Innocents and the Loss of Innocence: Interpreting Adivasi Movements in South Asia." In *Indigenous Peoples of Asia*, edited by R. Barnes, A. Gray, and B. Kingsbury. Ann Arbor, Mich.: Association for Asian Studies.
———. 1994b. "Regional Dependence and Rural Development in Central India: The Pivotal Role of Migrant Labour." In *Agricultural Production and Indian History*, edited by David Ludden. Delhi: Oxford University Press.
———. 1995. "Race, Caste, and Tribe in Central India: The Early Origins of Indian Anthropometry." In *The Concept of Race in South Asia*, edited by Peter Robb. Delhi: Oxford University Press.
———. 2006. "Human Sacrifice in Colonial Central India: Myth, Agency and Representation." In *Beyond Representation: Colonial and Postcolonial Constructions of Indian Identity*, edited by Crispin Bates. Oxford: Oxford University Press.
Bates, Crispin, and Marina Carter. 1992. "Tribal Migration in India and

Beyond." In *The World of the Rural Labourer in Colonial India*, edited by Gyan Prakash. Delhi: Oxford University Press.

Bauman, Gerd. 1999. *The Multicultural Riddle: Rethinking National, Ethnic, and Religious Identities*. New York: Routledge.

Baviskar, Amita. 1995. *In the Belly of the River: Tribal Conflicts over Development in the Narmada Valley*. Delhi: Oxford University Press.

———. 1997. "Tribal Politics and Discourses of Environmentalism." *Contributions to Indian Sociology*, n.s., 31 (2):195–225.

———. 2004. *In the Belly of the River: Tribal Conflicts over Development in the Narmada Valley*. 2nd ed. Delhi: Oxford University Press.

———. 2005. "Adivasi Encounters with Hindu Nationalism in Madhya Pradesh." *Economic and Political Weekly* 40 (48):5105–13.

Bayart, Jean-François. 1993. *The State in Africa: Politics of the Belly*. London: Longman.

Bayart, Jean-François, Stephen Ellis, and Beatrice Hibou. 1999. *Criminalisation of the State in Africa*. Oxford: James Currey.

Benjamin, Walter. 1969. *Illuminations*. New York: Schocken.

———. 1999. *The Arcades Project*. Translated by Howard Eiland and Kevin McLaughlin. Cambridge: Harvard University Press.

Béteille, André. 1974. "Tribe and Peasantry." In *Six Essays in Comparative Sociology*. Delhi: Oxford University Press.

———. 1983. "The Backward Classes and the New Social Order." In *The Idea of Natural Inequality and Other Essays*. Delhi: Oxford University Press.

———. 1991. "Distributive Justice and Institutional Well-being." *Economic and Political Weekly* 26:591–600.

———. 1998. "The Idea of Indigenous People." *Current Anthropology* 39 (2):187–91.

Bhagwati, Jagdish. 1993. *India in Transition: Freeing the Economy*. Oxford: Clarendon Press of Oxford University Press.

Bhatia, Bela. 2000. "The Naxalite Movement in Central Bihar." Ph.D. diss., University of Cambridge.

———. 2005. "The Naxalite Movement in Central Bihar." *Economic and Political Weekly* 40 (15):1536–50.

Bhatt, Chetan. 2001. *Hindu Nationalism: Origins, Ideologies and Modern Myths*. Oxford: Berg.

Bierschenk, T., J. P. Chaveau, and Olivier de Sardan. 2002. *Local Development Brokers in Africa: The Rise of a New Social Category*. Mainz, Germany: Department of Anthropology and African Studies, Johannes Gutenberg Universität.

Bosu Mullick, Sanjay. 1991. "The Concept of the Supreme Being in the Sarna System of Religion." In *Cultural Chota Nagpur*, edited by Sanjay Bosu Mullick. New Delhi: Central Publishing House.

———. 2003. Introduction. In *The Jharkhand Movement: Indigenous Peoples' Struggle for Autonomy in Jharkhand*, edited by Ram Dayal Munda and

Sanjay Bosu Mullick. Copenhagen: International Work Group for Indigenous Affairs.

Bourque, Susan, and Kay Warren. 1989. "Democracy without Peace: The Cultural Politics of Terror in Peru." *Latin American Research Review* 24 (1):7–34.

Brass, Paul. 1974. *Language, Religion and Politics in North India*. Cambridge: Cambridge University Press.

———. 1997. *Theft of an Idol: Text and Context in Representation and Collective Violence*. Princeton, N.J.: Princeton University Press.

Breman, Jan. 1985. *Of Peasants, Migrants and Paupers: Rural Labour Circulation and Capitalist Production in West India*. Delhi: Oxford University Press.

———. 1994. *Wage Hunters and Gatherers: Search for Work in the Urban and Rural Economy of South Gujarat*. Delhi: Oxford University Press.

———. 1996. *Footloose Labour: Working in India's Internal Economy*. Cambridge: Cambridge University Press.

———. 1999. "The Study of Industrial Labour in Post-colonial India—The Formal Sector: An Introductory Review." *Contributions to Indian Sociology*, n.s., 33 (1 and 2):1–43.

Brody, Hugh. 1987. *Hunters of the Canadian North*. London: Faber and Faber.

Brown, Michael. 1998. "Can Culture Be Copyrighted?" *Current Anthropology* 39 (2):193–222.

———. 2003. *Who Owns Native Culture?* Cambridge: Harvard University Press.

———. 2007. "Sovereignty's Betrayals." In *Indigenous Experience Today*, edited by Marisol de la Cadena and Orin Starn. Oxford: Berg.

Buur, Lars, Steffen Jensen, and Finn Stepputat, eds. 2007. *The Security-Development Nexus: Expressions of Sovereignty and Securitization in Southern Africa*. Uppsala, Sweden: Nordiska Afrikainstitutet.

Campbell, John. 1861. *Narrative by Major John Campbell C.B. of his Operations in the Hill Tracts of Orissa for the Suppression of Human Sacrifices and Female Infanticide*. London: Hurst Blackett.

Cederlof, Gunnel, and K. Sivaramakrishnan, eds. 2005. *Ecological Nationalisms: Nation, Livelihoods and Identities in South Asia*. Delhi: Permanent Black.

Chakrabarty, Dipesh. 2006. "Politics Unlimited: The Global Adivasi and Debates about the Political. In *Indigeneity in India*, edited by B. Karlsson and T. Subba. London: Kegan Paul.

Chambers, Robert. 1983. *Rural Development: Putting the Last First*. Harlow, England: Longman.

———. 1997. *Whose Reality Counts? Putting the First Last*. London: Intermediate Technology.

Chatterjee, Partha. 1986. *Nationalist Thought and the Colonial World: A Derivative Discourse*. 2nd ed. London: Zed.

——. 1993. *The Nation and Its Fragments: Colonial and Postcolonial Histories*. Princeton, N.J.: Princeton University Press.

——. 2004. *The Politics of the Governed: Reflections on Popular Politics in Most of the World*. New York: Columbia University Press.

Chatterjee, Piya. 2001. *A Time for Tea: Women, Labor and Post/colonial Politics*. Durham, N.C.: Duke University Press.

Chaturvedi, Vinayak, ed. 2000. *Mapping Subaltern Studies and the Postcolonial*. London: Verso.

Chomsky, Noam, and Edward Herman. 1979. *The Washington Connection and Third World Fascism*. Nottingham, England: Spokesman.

Chopra, Radhika. 1995. "Maps of Experience: Narratives of Migration in an Indian Village." *Economic and Political Weekly* 30 (49):3156–62.

Clastres, Pierre. 1974. *Society against the State: Essays in Political Anthropology*. New York: Zone.

Clifford, James. 1988. *The Predicament of Culture: Twentieth-century Ethnography, Literature, and Art*. Cambridge: Harvard University Press.

——. 2007. "Varieties of Indigenous Experience: Diasporas, Homelands, Sovereignties." In *Indigenous Experience Today*, edited by Marisol de la Cadena and Orin Starn. Oxford: Berg.

Cohn, Bernard S. 1987. "Structural Change in Indian Rural Society 1596–1885." In *An Anthropologist among the Historians and Other Essays*. Delhi: Oxford University Press.

Collier, Jane. 1976. "Political Leadership and Legal Change in Zinacantan." *Law and Society* 11 (1):131–63.

Comaroff, Jean. 1985. *Body of Power, Spirit of Resistance: The Culture and History of a South African People*. Chicago: University of Chicago Press.

Comaroff, John, and Jean Comaroff. 1997. "Postcolonial Politics and Discourses of Democracy in Southern Africa: An Anthropological Reflection on African Political Modernities." *Journal of Anthropological Research* 53 (2):123–46.

Conklin, Beth, and Laura Graham. 1995. "The Shifting Middle Ground: Amazonian Indians and Eco-politics." *American Anthropologist* 97 (4):695–710.

Cooke, Bill, and Uma Kothari. 2001. *Participation: The New Tyranny?* London: Zed.

Corbridge, Stuart. 1988. "The Ideology of Tribal Economy and Society: Politics in the Jharkhand, 1950–1980." *Modern Asian Studies* 22 (1):1–42.

——. 2002. "The Continuing Struggle for India's Jharkhand: Democracy, Decentralisation and the Politics of Names and Numbers." *Commonwealth and Comparative Politics* 40 (3):55–71.

Corbridge, Stuart, and John Harriss. 2000. *Reinventing India: Liberalisation, Hindu Nationalism and Popular Democracy*. Cambridge: Cambridge University Press.

Corbridge, Stuart, et al. 2005. *Seeing the State: Governance and Governmentality in India*. Cambridge: Cambridge University Press.

Coronil, Fernando, and Julie Skurski. 1991. "Dismembering and Remembering the Nation: The Semantics of Political Violence in Venezuela." *Comparative Studies in Society and History* 33 (2):288–337.

Cowan, Jane, Marie-Benedict Dembour, and Richard Wilson, eds. 2001. *Culture and Rights: Anthropological Perspectives*. Cambridge: Cambridge University Press.

Croll, Elisabeth, and David Parkin, eds. 1992. *Bush Base, Forest Farm: Culture, Environment and Development*. London: Routledge.

Cronon, William. 1995. "The Trouble with Wilderness; or, Getting Back to the Wrong Nature." In *Uncommon Ground: Toward Reinventing Nature*, edited by William Cronon. London: W. W. Norton.

Crook, Richard, and James Manor. 1998. *Democracy and Decentralisation in South Asia and West Africa: Participation, Accountability and Performance*. Cambridge: Cambridge University Press.

Damodaran, Vinita. 2000. "Review of Sumit Guha's *Environment and Ethnicity in India 1200–1991*." *Journal of Political Ecology* 7:12–17.

———. 2006. "Colonial Constructions of Tribe in India: The Case of Chotanagpur." In *Europe and the World in European Historiography*, edited by C. Levai. Pisa, Italy: Pisa University Press.

Das, Veena. 2007. *Life and Words: Violence and the Descent into the Ordinary*. Berkeley: University of California Press.

Das, Veena, and Deborah Poole, eds. 2004. *Anthropology in the Margins of the State*. Santa Fe, N.M.: School of American Research Press.

Das, Victor. 1992. *Jharkhand: Castle over the Graves.* New Delhi: Inter-India Publications.

Dasgupta, Sangeeta 2004. "The Journey of an Anthropologist in Chotanagpur." *Indian Economic and Social History Review* 41 (2):165–98.

de Castro, Eduardo Viveros. 1998. "Cosmological Deixis and Amerindian Perspectivism." *Journal of the Royal Anthropological Institute* 4 (3):469–88.

de Genova, Nicholas P. 2002. "Migrant 'Illegality' and Deportability in Everyday Life." *Annual Review of Anthropology* 31:419–47.

De Haan, Arjan. 1994. *Unsettled Settlers: Migrant Workers and Industrial Capitalism in Calcutta*. Rotterdam, the Netherlands: Verloren.

———. 2002. "Migration and Livelihoods in Historical Perspective: A Case Study of Bihar, India." *Journal of Development Studies* 38 (5):115–42.

De Haan, Arjan, and Ben Rogaly. 2002. "Migrant Workers and Their Role in Rural Change." In "Labour Mobility and Rural Society," edited by Arjan De Haan and Ben Rogaly. Special Issue, *Journal of Development Studies* 38 (5):1–14.

de la Cadena, Marisol, and Orin Starn, eds. 2007. *Indigenous Experience Today*. Oxford: Berg

De Neve, Geert. 2003. "Expectations and Rewards of Modernity: Commitment and Mobility among Rural Migrants in Tirupur, Tamil Nadu." *Contributions to Indian Sociology*, n.s., 37 (1 and 2):251–80.

De Sa, Fidelis. 1975. *Crisis in Chota Nagpur*. Bangalore, India: Redemptorist Publications.

de Sardan, Olivier. 1999. "A Moral Economy of Corruption in Africa?" *Journal of Modern African Studies* 37 (1):25–52.

——. 2005. *Anthropology and Development: Understanding Contemporary Social Change*. London: Zed.

Descola, Philippe, and Gisli Palsson, eds. 1996. *Nature and Society: Anthropological Perspectives*. London: Routledge.

Devalle, Susana. 1992. *Discourses of Ethnicity: Culture and Protest in Jharkhand*. New Delhi: Sage.

Devi, Mahashweta. 1997. *Dust on the Road: The Activist Writings of Mahashweta Devi*. Calcutta: Seagull.

Dirks, Nicholas. 1987. *The Hollow Crown: Ethnohistory of an Indian Kingdom*. Cambridge: Cambridge University Press.

——. 1989. "The Original Caste: Power, History and Hierarchy in South Asia." *Contributions to Indian Sociology*, n.s., 23 (1):59–79.

——. 2001. *Castes of Mind: Colonialism and the Making of Modern India*. Princeton, N.J.: Princeton University Press.

Dombrowski, Kirk. 2001. *Against Culture: Development, Politics and Religion in Indian Alaska*. Lincoln: University of Nebraska Press.

——. 2002. "The Praxis of Indigenism and Alaska Native Timber Politics." *American Anthropologist* 104 (4):1062–73.

Donner, Henrike. 2005. "The Legacy of the Maoists in West Bengal." Paper presented at The Legacy of Maoism in China and India, LSE Asia Research Centre Seminar, London, November.

Douglas, Mary. 1966. *Purity and Danger: An Analysis of Concepts of Pollution and Taboo*. London: Routledge and Kegan Paul.

Dumont, Louis. 1959. "Pure and Impure." *Contributions to Indian Sociology* 3:9–40.

——. 1970a. "The Conception of Kingship in Ancient India." In *Religion/Politics and History in India: Collected Papers in Indian Sociology*, edited by Louis Dumont. The Hague: Mouton.

——. 1970b. *Homo Hierarchicus: The Caste System and Its Implications*. London: Wiedenfeld and Nicolson.

——. 1986. *Essays on Individualism: Modern Ideology in Anthropological Perspectives*. Chicago: University of Chicago Press.

Dumont, Louis, and David Pocock. 1959. "Possession and Priesthood." *Contributions to Indian Sociology* 3:55–74.

Dupont, Veronique. 2000. "Mobility Patterns and Economic Strategies of Houseless People in Old Delhi." In *Delhi: Urban Space and Human Destinies*, edited by E. Tarlo, V. Dupont, and D. Vidal. Delhi: Manohar.

Duyker, Edward. 1987. *Tribal Guerrillas: The Santals of West Bengal and the Naxalite Movement*. Delhi: Oxford University Press.

Einarsson, N. 1993. "All Animals are Equal, but Some Are Cetaceans:

Conservation and Culture Conflict." In *Environmentalism: The View from Anthropology*, edited by K. Milton. New York: Routledge.
Elwert, Georg. 1999. "Markets of Violence." In *Dynamics of Violence: Process of Escalation and De-escalation in Violent Groups*, edited by Georg Elwert, Stephan Feuchtwang, and D. Neubert. Berlin: Duncker and Humblot.
Elwin, Verrier. 1936. *Leaves from the Jungle*. London: John Murray.
——. 1939. *The Baiga*. London: John Murray.
——. 1943. *The Aboriginals*. Bombay: Oxford University Press.
——. 1946. *The Muria and their Ghotul*. Bombay: Oxford University Press.
——. 1955. *The Religion of an Indian Tribe*. Bombay: Oxford University Press.
Escobar, Arturo, and Sonia Alvarez, eds. 1992. *The Making of Social Movements: Identity, Strategy, and Democracy*. Boulder, Colo.: Westview.
Fairhead, James, and Melissa Leach. 1996. *Misreading the African Landscape: Society and Ecology in a Forest-savannah Mosaic*. Cambridge: Cambridge University Press.
Ferguson, James. 1990. *The Anti-Politics Machine: "Development," Depoliticisation, and Bureaucratic Power in Lesotho*. Cambridge: Cambridge University Press.
Feuchtwang, Stephan. 2003. "Peasants, Democracy and Anthropology: Questions of Local Loyalty." *Critique of Anthropology* 23 (1):93–120.
Fine, Ben. 1999. "The Developmental State Is Dead—Long Live Social Capital?" *Development and Change* 30 (1):1–9.
Fox, Richard G., ed. 1990. *Nationalist Ideologies and the Production of National Cultures*. Washington: American Anthropological Association.
Fox, Richard G., and Orin Starn, eds. 1997. *Between Resistance and Revolution: Cultural Politics and Social Protest*. New Brunswick, N.J.: Rutgers University Press.
Frankel, Francine R. 1978. *India's Political Economy, 1947–1977: The Gradual Revolution*. Princeton, N.J.: Princeton University Press.
Freeman, J. 1999. "Gods, Groves and the Culture of Nature in Kerala." *Modern Asian Studies* 32 (2):257–302.
Freid, Morton. 1975. *The Notion of Tribe*. Menlo Park, Calif.: Cummings.
Froerer, Peggy. 2005. "Challenging Traditional Authority: The Role of the State, the Divine and the RSS." *Contributions to Indian Sociology*, n.s., 39 (1):39–73.
——. 2006. "Emphasising 'Others': The Emergence of Hindu Nationalism in a Central Indian Tribal Community." *Journal of the Royal Anthropological Institute* 12 (1):39–59.
——. 2007. *Religious Division and Social Conflict: The Emergence of Hindu Nationalism in Rural India*. Delhi: Social Science Press.
Fuller, C. J. 1992. *The Camphor Flame: Popular Hinduism and Society in India*. Princeton, N.J.: Princeton University Press.
Fuller, C. J., and John Harriss. 2001. "Introduction: For an Anthropology

of the Modern Indian State." In *The Everyday State and Society in Modern India*, edited by C. J. Fuller and V. Benei. London: C. Hurst.

Gadgil, Madhav, and Ramachandra Guha. 1993. *The Fissured Land: An Ecological History of India*. Delhi: Oxford University Press.

———. 1995. *Ecology and Equity: The Use and Abuse of Nature in Contemporary India*. London: Routledge.

Galanter, Marc. 1984. *Competing Equalities: Law and the Backward Classes in India*. Berkeley: University of California Press.

Gambetta, Diego. 1993. *The Sicilian Mafia: The Business of Private Protection*. Cambridge: Harvard University Press.

Gardner, Katy. 1995. *Global Migrants, Local Lives: Travel and Transformation in Rural Bangladesh*. Oxford: Oxford University Press.

Gell, Alfred. 1986. "Newcomers to the World of Goods: Consumption among the Muria Gonds." In *The Social Life of Things: Commodities in Cultural Perspective*, edited by Arjun Appadurai. Cambridge: Cambridge University Press.

———. 1997. "Exalting the King and Obstructing the State: A Political Interpretation of Royal Ritual in Bastar District, Central India." *Journal of the Royal Anthropological Institute* 3:433–50.

Gell, Simeron M. S. 1992. *The Ghotul in Muria Society*. Chur, Switzerland: Harwood Academic Publishers.

Gellner, David, ed. 2003. *Resistance and the State: Nepalese Experiences*. Delhi: Social Science Press.

Gellner, E., and J. Watterbury, eds. 1977. *Patrons and Clients in Mediterranean Societies*. London: Duckworth.

Geschiere, Peter. 1997. *The Modernity of Witchcraft: Politics and the Occult in Postcolonial Africa*. Translated by Peter Geschiere and Janet Roitman. Charlottesville: University Press of Virginia.

Ghosh, Abhik. 2006. *The World of the Oraon: Their Symbols in Time and Space*. Delhi: Manohar.

Ghosh, Kaushik. 1999. "A Market for Aboriginality: Primitivism and Race Classification in the Indentured Labour Market of Colonial India." *Subaltern Studies* 12:8–48.

———. 2006. "Between Global Flows and Local Dams: Indigenousness, Locality and the Transnational Sphere in Jharkhand, India." *Cultural Anthropology* 21 (4):501–34.

Ghosh, Sankar. 1974. *The Naxalite Movement: A Maoist Experience*. Calcutta: Mukhopadyay.

Ghosh, S. K. 2000. *Bihar in Flames*. Delhi: APH Publishing.

Ghurye, G. S. [1943] 1963. *The Scheduled Tribes: The Aborigines So-called and Their Future*. Bombay: Ramdas Bhatkal for Popular Prakashan.

Gill, S. S. 1998. *The Pathology of Corruption*. New Delhi: HarperCollins.

Gilsenan, Michael. 1977. "Against Patron-Client Relations." In *Patrons and Clients in Mediterranean Societies*, edited by E. Gellner and J. Watterbury. London: Duckworth.

Gledhill, John. 1997. "Liberalism, Socio-economic Rights and the Politics of Identity: From Moral Economy to Indigenous Rights." In *Human Rights, Culture and Context: Anthropological Approaches*, edited by R. Wilson. London: Pluto.

Gold, Anne G., and Bhoju Ram Gujar. 2002. *In the Time of Trees and Sorrows: Nature, Power, and Memory in Rajasthan*. Durham, N.C.: Duke University Press.

Goldman, Marcio. 2001. "An Ethnographic Theory of Democracy: Politics from the Viewpoint of Ilheus's Black Movement." *Ethnos* 66 (2):157–80.

Goody, Jack. 1996. "Man and the Natural World: Reflections on History and Anthropology." *Environment and History* 2 (3):255–70.

Government of India. 1861. *Emigration to Assam: Commission of Enquiry*. Calcutta: Office of the Superintendent of Government Printing.

——. 1906. *Proceedings of the Assam Labour Enquiry Committee in the Recruiting and Labour Districts*. Calcutta: Office of the Superintendent of Government Printing.

——. 1931. *Report of the Royal Commission on Labour in India*. London: Her Majesty's Stationery Office.

Graeber, David. 2004. *Fragments of an Anarchist Anthropology*. Chicago: Prickly Paradigm, distributed by the University of Chicago Press.

Greenough, Paul. 2001. "Standard Environmental Narrative." In *Agrarian Studies: Synthetic Work at the Cutting Edge*, edited by James Scott. New Haven, Conn.: Yale University Press.

Grove, Richard. 1995. *Green Imperialism: Colonial Expansion, Tropical Island Edens and the Origins of Environmentalism, 1600–1860*. Cambridge: Cambridge University Press.

Guha, Ramachandra. 1989. *The Unquiet Woods: The Ecological Bases of Peasant Resistance in the Himalayas*. New Delhi: Oxford University Press.

——. 1999. *Savaging the Civilised: Verrier Elwin, His Tribals, and India*. Chicago: University of Chicago Press; New Delhi: Oxford University Press.

Guha, Ranajit. 1982. "On Some Aspects of the Historiography of Colonial India." *Subaltern Studies* 1:1–8.

——. [1983] 1999. *Elementary Aspects of Peasant Insurgency in Colonial India*. Durham, N.C.: Duke University Press.

——. 1998. *Dominance without Hegemony: History and Power in Colonial India*. Delhi: Oxford University Press.

Guha, Sumit. 1999. *Environment and Ethnicity in India 1200–1991*. Cambridge: Cambridge University Press.

Gujit, Irene, and Meera Shah. 1998. *The Myth of the Community: Gender Issues in Participatory Development*. London: Intermediate Technology.

Gupta, Akhil. 1995. "Blurred Boundaries: The Discourse of Corruption, the Culture of Politics and the Imagined State." *American Ethnologist* 22 (2):375–402.

——. 1998. *Postcolonial Developments: Agriculture in the Making of Modern India*. Durham, N.C.: Duke University Press.

——. 2005. "Narratives of Corruption: Anthropological and Fictional Accounts of the Indian State." *Ethnography* 6 (1):5–34.

Gupta, Akhil, and James Ferguson. 1992. "Beyond 'Culture': Space, Identity and the Politics of Difference." *Cultural Anthropology* 7 (1):6–23.

Gupta, Ranjit Kumar. 2004. *The Crimson Agenda: Maoist Protest and Terror*. Delhi: Wordsmiths.

Hale, Charles. 1997. "Consciousness, Violence and the Politics of Memory in Guatemala." *Current Anthropology* 38 (5):817–38.

——. 2006. "Activist Research v. Cultural Critique: Indigenous Land Rights and the Contradictions of Politically Engaged Anthropology." *Cultural Anthropology* 21 (1):96–120.

Haller, Dieter, and Chris Shore, eds. 2005. *Corruption: Anthropological Perspectives*. London: Pluto.

Hallett, M. G. 1917. *Ranchi: Bihar and Orissa District Gazetteers*. Patna, India: Government of India.

Hansen, Thomas Blom. 1999. *The Saffron Wave: Democracy and Hindu Nationalism in Modern India*. Princeton, N.J.: Princeton University Press.

——. 2000. "Predicaments of Secularism: Muslim Identities and Politics in Mumbai." *Journal of the Royal Anthropological Institute* 6 (2):255–72.

——. 2001a. "Governance and Myths of the State in Mumbai." In *The Everyday State and Society in Modern India*, edited by C. J. Fuller and V. Benei. London: Hurst.

——. 2001b. *Wages of Violence: Naming and Identity in Postcolonial Bombay*. Princeton, N.J.: Princeton University Press.

Hansen, Thomas Blom, and Finn Stepputat, eds. 2001. *States of Imagination: Ethnographic Explorations of the Postcolonial State*. Durham, N.C.: Duke University Press.

——, eds. 2005. *Sovereign Bodies: Citizens, Migrants and States in the Postcolonial World*. Princeton, N.J.: Princeton University Press.

Hardiman, David. 1987. *The Coming of the Devi: Adivasi Assertion in Western India*. Delhi: Oxford University Press.

——. 1994. "The Power in the Forests: The Dangs, 1820–1940." In "Essays in Honour of Ranajit Guha," edited by David Arnold and David Hardiman. Special issue, *Subaltern Studies* 8:89–147.

Harris, Olivia, ed. 1996. *Inside and Outside the Law: Anthropological Studies of Authority and Ambiguity*. London: Routledge.

Harriss, John. 2002. *Depoliticizing Development: The World Bank and Social Capital*. London: Anthem.

Harriss-White, Barbara. 1996. *A Political Economy of Agricultural Markets in South Asia: Masters of the Countryside*. New Delhi: Sage.

Hart, Keith. 1973. "Informal Income Opportunities and Urban Employment in Ghana." *Journal of Modern African Studies* 11 (1):61–89.

———. 2005. *Formal Bureaucracy and the Emergent Forms of the Informal Economy*. http://www.thememorybank.co.uk/papers/emergent-forms.
———. 2006. "The Globalisation of Apartheid." Presentation for the first Rethinking Economies workshop, "Unequal Development: The Globalization of Apartheid," Goldsmiths College, London, March 24. http://www.thememorybank.co.uk2008/09/04/the-globalisation-of-apartheid.
Heesterman, J. C. 1971. "Priesthood and the Brahmin." *Contributions to Indian Sociology*, n.s., 5 (1):43–47.
Heuze, Gerard. 1996. *Workers of Another World: Miners, the Countryside and the Coalfields in Dhanbad*. New Delhi: Oxford University Press.
Heyman, Josiah. 1995. "Putting Power in the Anthropology of Bureaucracy: The Immigration and Naturalization Service at the Mexico–United States Border." *Current Anthropology* 36 (2):261–87.
Heyman, Josiah, and Alan Smart, eds. 1999. *States and Illegal Practices*. Oxford: Berg.
Hobsbawm, Eric, and Terence Ranger. 1983. *The Invention of Tradition*. Cambridge: Cambridge University Press.
Hocking, Russel. 1994. "The Potential for BJP Expansion: Ideology, Politics and Regional Appeal—The Lessons of Jharkhand." *South Asia* 17:157–68.
Hoffman, J. 1909. *Social Works in Chota Nagpur*. Calcutta: Catholic Orphans Press.
———. [1915] 1961. "Principles of Succession and Inheritance among the Mundas." *Man in India* 41 (4):324–38.
Humphrey, Caroline. 2002. *The Unmaking of Soviet Life: Everyday Economies after Socialism*. Ithaca, N.Y.: Cornell University Press.
Humphries, Jane. 1988. "Protective Legislation, the Capitalist State and Working-Class Men: The Case of the 1842 Mines Regulation Act." In *On Work*, edited by R. Pahl. Oxford: Basil Blackwell.
Hutt, Michael, ed. 2004. *Himalayan "People's War": Nepal's Maoist Rebellion*. London: Hurst.
Ingold, Tim. 1992. "Culture and the Perception of the Environment." In *Bush Base, Forest Farm: Culture, Environment and Development*, edited by Elisabeth Croll and David Parkin. London: Routledge.
———. 2000. *The Perception of the Environment: Essays on Livelihood, Dwelling and Skill*. London: Routledge.
Jackson, Cecile, and Molly Chattopadhyay. 2000. "Identities and Livelihoods: Gender, Ethnicity, and Nature in a South Bihar Village." In *Agrarian Environments: Resources, Representations, and Rule in India*, edited by Arun Agrawal and K. Sivaramakrishnan. Durham, N.C.: Duke University Press.
Jalais, Annu. 2005. "Dwelling on Morichjhanpi: When Tigers Become 'Citizens,' Refugees 'Tiger Food.'" *Economic and Political Weekly* 40 (17):1757–62.

James, Deborah. 2007. *Gaining Ground? "Rights" and "Property" in Southern African Land Reform*. Abingdon, England: Routledge-Cavendish.
Jean-Klein, Iris, and Annelise Riles. 2005. "Anthropology and Human Rights Administrations: Expert Observation and Representation after the Fact." POLAR: *Political and Legal Anthropology Review* 28 (2):173–202.
Jeffery, Roger, and Nandini Sundar. 1999. *A New Moral Economy for India's Forests? Discourses of Community and Participation*. New Delhi: Sage.
Jeffrey, Craig, Patricia Jeffery, and Roger Jeffery. 2008. *Degrees Without Freedom? Education, Masculinities, and Unemployment in North India*. Stanford, Calif.: Stanford University Press.
Jensen, Steffen. 2004. "Claiming Community: Local Politics on the Cape Flats, South Africa." *Critique of Anthropology* 24 (2):179–207.
Jewitt, Sarah. 2000. "Mothering Earth? Gender and Environmental Protection in Jharkhand, India." *Journal of Peasant Studies* 27 (2):94–131.
Jha, J. C. 1990. *History of the Freedom Movement in Chotanagpur (1885–1947)*. Patna, India: Kashi Prasad Jayaswal Research Institute.
Karlsson, Bengt. 2003. "Anthropology and the 'Indigenous Slot': Claims to and Debates about Indigenous People's Status in India." *Critique of Anthropology* 23 (4):402–23.
———. 2005. "Sovereignty through Indigenous Governance: Reviving 'Traditional Political Institutions' in Northeast India." NEHU *Journal of Social Sciences* 3 (2).
Kaviraj, Sudipta. 1984. "On the Crisis of Political Institutions in India." *Contributions to Indian Sociology*, n.s., 18 (2):223–43.
———. 1991. "On State, Society and Discourse in India." In *Rethinking Third World Politics*, edited by J. Manor. Harlow, England: Longman.
———. 1993. "The Imaginary Institution of India." *Subaltern Studies* 7:1–39.
———. 1997. The Modern State in India. In *Dynamics of State Formation: India and Europe Compared*, edited by M. Doornbos and S. Kaviraj. Delhi: Sage.
Kelkar, Govind, and Dev Nathan. 1992. *Gender and Tribe: Women, Land and Forests in Jharkhand*. London: Zed.
Kelly, Tobias, and Alpa Shah. 2006. "A Double-edged Sword: Protection and State Violence." *Critique of Anthropology* 26 (3):251–59.
Kenrick, Justin, and Jerome Lewis. 2004. "Indigenous Peoples' Rights and the Politics of the Term 'Indigenous.'" *Anthropology Today* 20 (2):4–10.
Keshri, B. P. 2003. *Cultural Jharkhand (Problems and Prospects)*. Ranchi, India: Nagpuri Sansthan.
Knight, James. 2000. *Natural Enemies: People-wildlife Conflicts in Anthropological Perspective*. London: Routledge.
Kreuger, Anne. 1974. "The Political Economy of the Rent-Seeking Society." *American Economic Review* 64:291–303.
Kumar, Sanjay. 2004. "Social Capital, Local Politics and Sustainable Rural

Livelihoods: A Case Study of the Eastern India Rainfed Farming Project." Ph.D. diss., University of Cambridge.

Kunnath, George. 2004. "Under the Shadow of Guns: Negotiating the Flaming Fields of Caste/Class War in Bihar, India." *Anthropology Matters* 6 (2). http://www.anthropologymatters.com/journal/2004-2/kunnath_2004_under.htm.

——. 2006. "Becoming a Naxalite in Rural Bihar: Class Struggle and Its Contradictions." *Journal of Peasant Studies* 33 (1):89–123.

Kuper, Adam. 1988. *The Invention of Primitive Society: Transformations of an Illusion*. London: Routledge.

——. 2003. "The Return of the Native." *Current Anthropology* 44 (3):389–402.

Lal, D. 1989. *The Hindu Equilibrium*. Vol. 2: *Aspects of Indian Labour*. Oxford: Clarendon Press of Oxford University Press.

Latour, Bruno. 1993. *We Have Never Been Modern*. Translated by Catherine Porter. Cambridge, Mass.: Harvard University Press.

Leach, Edmund 1977. *Custom, Law, and Terrorist Violence*. Edinburgh: Edinburgh University Press.

Leach, Melissa, and Robin Mearns. 1996. "Environmental Change and Policy: Challenging Received Wisdom in Africa." In *The Lie of the Land: Challenging Received Wisdom on the African Environment*, edited by Melissa Leach and Robin Mearns. London: International African Institute.

Leslie, Esther. 2000. *Walter Benjamin: Overpowering Conformism*. London: Pluto.

Lévi-Strauss, Claude. 1966. *The Savage Mind*. Translated by Doreen Weightman. London: Weidenfeld and Nicolson.

Lewis, David, and David Mosse. 2006. *Development Brokers and Translators: The Ethnography of Aid and Agencies*. Bloomfield, Conn.: Kumarian.

Lewis, David, Dennis Rodgers, and Michael Woolcock. 2008. "The Fiction of Development: Literary Representation as a Source of Authoritative Knowledge." *Journal of Development Studies* 44 (2):198–216.

Li, Tania Murray. 2000. "Articulating Indigenous Identity in Indonesia: Resource Politics and the Tribal Slot." *Comparative Studies in Society and History* 42 (1):149–79.

Linz, Juan J., Alfred Stepan, and Yogendra Yadav. 2007. "'Nation State' or 'State Nation': India in Comparative Perspective." In *Democracy and Diversity: India and the American Experience*, edited by K. S. Bajpai. Delhi: Oxford University Press.

Lofving, Staffan. 2005. "Silence and the Politics of Representing Rebellion: On the Emergence of the Neutral Maya in Guatemala." In *No Peace No War: An Anthropology of Contemporary Armed Conflicts*, edited by P. Richards. Oxford: James Currey.

Louis, Prakash. 2002. *People's Power: The Naxalite Movement in Central Bihar*. Delhi: Wordsmiths.

Lund, Christian. 2006. "Twilight Institutions: An Introduction." In "Twilight

Institutions: Public Authority and Local Politics in Africa," edited by Christian Lund. Special Issue, *Development and Change* 37 (4):673–84.

Mackenzie, John. 1987. "Chivalry, Social Darwinism and Ritualised Killing: The Hunting Ethos in Central Africa up to 1914." In *Conservation in Africa: People, Policies and Practice*, edited by David Anderson and Richard Grove. Cambridge: Cambridge University Press.

MacPherson, Samuel. 1865. *Memorials of Service in India*. London: John Murray.

Madan, T. N. 1987. "Secularism in its Place." *Journal of Asian Studies* 46 (4):747–59.

——. 1997. *Modern Myths, Locked Minds: Secularism and Fundamentalism in India*. Delhi: Oxford University Press.

Mahmood, Cynthia Keppley. 1996. *Fighting for Faith and Nation: Dialogues with Sikh Militants*. Philadelphia: University of Pennsylvania Press.

Mahmood, Saba. 2001. "Feminist Theory, Embodiment, and the Docile Agent: Some Reflections on the Egyptian Islamic Revival." *Cultural Anthropology* 16 (2):202–36.

Malkki, Liisa. 1992. "National Geographic: The Rooting of Peoples and the Territorialization of National Identity among Scholars and Refugees." *Cultural Anthropology* 7 (1):24–44.

——. 1995. *Purity and Exile: Violence, Memory and National Cosmology among Hutu Refugees in Tanzania*. Chicago: University of Chicago Press.

Mamdani, Mahmood. 1976. *Politics and Class Formation in Uganda*. New York: Monthly Review.

Marriott, McKim. 1968. "Caste Ranking and Food Transactions: A Matrix Analysis." In *Structure and Change in Indian Society*, edited by Milton Singer and Bernard S. Cohn. Chicago: Aldine.

Massey, Doreen. 1994. *Space, Place and Gender*. London: Polity.

Mauss, Marcel. [1925] 1990. *The Gift: The Form and Reason for Exchange in Archaic Societies*. Translated by W. D. Halls. London: Routledge.

Mawdsley, Emma. 2002. "Redrawing the Body Politic: Federalism, Regionalism and the Creation of New States in India." *Commonwealth and Comparative Politics* 40 (3):34–54.

——. 2004. "India's Middle Classes and the Environment." *Development and Change* 35 (1):79–103.

——. 2005. "The Abuse of Religion and Ecology: The Vishva Hindu Parishad and Tehri Dam." *Worldviews* 9 (1):1–24.

——. 2006. "Hindu Nationalism, Neo-traditionalism and Environmental Discourses in India." *Geoforum* 37 (3):380–90.

Mayer, Adrian. 1981. "Public Service and Individual Merit in a Town of Central India." In *Culture and Morality: Essays in Honor of Christoph von Fürer-Haimendorf*, edited by Adrian Mayer. Oxford: Oxford University Press.

Meillassoux, Claude. [1975] 1981. *Maidens, Meal and Money: Capitalism and the Domestic Community*. Cambridge: Cambridge University Press.

Menchú, Rigoberta. 1984. *I, Rigoberta Menchú*. Edited by Elisabeth Burgos-Debray; translated by Ann Wright. London: Verso.
Merlan, Francesca. 2007. "Indigeneity as Relational Identity: The Construction of Australian Aboriginal Land Rights." In *Indigenous Experience Today*, edited by Marisol de la Cadena and Orin Starn. Oxford: Berg.
Mitchell, Timothy. 1990. "Everyday Metaphors of Power." *Theory and Society* 19 (5):545–77.
———. 1991. "The Limits of the State: Beyond Statist Approaches and Their Critics." *American Political Science Review* 85:77–96.
———. 2002. *Rule of Experts: Egypt, Techno-politics, Modernity*. Berkeley: University of California Press.
Mitra, Subrata Kumar. 1991. "Room to Maneuver in the Middle: Local Elites, Political Action and the State in India." *World Politics* 43 (3):390–413.
Mooij, Jos. 1992. "Private Pockets and Public Policies: Rethinking the Concept of Corruption." In *Law as a Resource in Agrarian Struggles*, edited by F. von Benda-Beckmann and M. van der Velde. Wageningse, the Netherlands: Wageningse Sociological Studies.
Morris, Brian 1997. "In Defence of Realism and Truth: Critical Reflections on the Anthropological Followers of Heidegger." *Critique of Anthropology* 17 (3):313–40.
Mosse, David. 1994. "Authority, Gender and Knowledge: Theoretical Reflections on the Practice of Participatory Rural Appraisal." *Development and Change* 25:497–526.
———. 2001. "Irrigation and Statecraft in Zamindari South India." In *The Everyday State and Society in Modern India*, edited by C. J. Fuller and V. Benei. London: C. Hurst.
———. 2005. *Cultivating Development: An Ethnography of Aid Policy and Practice*. London: Pluto.
———. 2007. "Power and the Durability of Poverty: A Critical Exploration of the Links between Culture, Marginality and Chronic Poverty. Working paper 107. Manchester: Chronic Poverty Research Centre.
Mosse, David, Sanjeev Gupta, and Vidya Shah. 2005. "On the Margins in the City: Adivasi Seasonal Labour Migration in Western India." *Economic and Political Weekly* 40 (28):3025–38.
Mosse, David, et al. 2002. "Brokered Livelihoods: Debt, Labour Migration and Development in Tribal Western India." *Journal of Development Studies* 38 (5):59–88.
Mukherjee, Kalyan, and Rogendra Singh Yadav. 1980. *Bhojpur: Naxalism in the Plains of Bihar*. Delhi: Radhakrishnan.
Mukherji, S. 1985. "The Process of Wage Labour Circulation in Northern India." In *Labour Circulation and the Labour Process*, edited by G. Standing. London: Croom Helm.
Munda, Ram Dayal. 2000a. "Adi-Dharam: Religious Beliefs of the Adivasis of India." *Sarini* 3:3–48.

——. 2000b. "Autonomy Movements in Tribal India: With Particular Reference to the Jharkhand Movement; A View from Inside." Paper presented at the workshop, "Indigenous Peoples: The Trajectory of a Contemporary Concept in India," at Uppsala, Sweden, Seminar for Development Studies, Kursgarden.

Nandy, Ashish. 1998. "The Politics of Secularism and the Recovery of Religious Tolerance." *Alternatives* 8:177–94.

Nathan, Dev. 1988. "Factors in the Jharkhand Movement." *Economic and Political Weekly*, January 30, 185–87.

——. 2003. "Jharkhand: Factors and Future." In *The Jharkhand Movement: Indigenous Peoples' Struggle for Autonomy in Jharkhand*, edited by Ram Dayal Munda and Sanjay Bosu Mullick. Copenhagen: International Work Group for Indigenous Affairs.

Neocleous, Mark. 1996. *Administering Civil Society: Towards a Theory of State Power*. London: Macmillan.

Nicholas, Colin. 1996. "A Common Struggle: Regaining Control." In *Indigenous Peoples of Asia: Many Peoples, One Struggle*, edited by Colin Nicholas and Raajen Singh. Bangkok, Thailand: Asia Indigenous Peoples Pact.

Norman, Will. 2004. "Living on the Frontline: Politics, Migration and Transfrontier Conservation in the Mozambican Villages of the South Africa–Mozambique Borderland." Ph.D. diss, Department of Anthropology, London School of Economics and Political Sciences, University of London.

Nugent, David. 2001. "Before History and Prior to Politics: Time, Space and Territory in the Modern Peruvian Nation-state." In *States of Imagination: Ethnographic Explorations of the Postcolonial State*, edited by Thomas Blom Hansen and Finn Stepputat. Durham, N.C.: Duke University Press.

Nuijten, Monique. 2003. *Power, Community and the State: The Political Anthropology of Organisation in Mexico*. London: Pluto.

Nyerges, A. Endre, and Glen Martin Green. 2000. "The Ethnography of Landscape: GIS and Remote Sensing in the Study of Forest Change in West African Guinea Savanna." *American Anthropologist* 102 (2):271–89.

Ortner, Sherry. 1995. "Resistance and the Problem of Ethnographic Refusal." *Comparative Studies in Society and History* 37 (1):171–93.

Osella, Caroline, and Filippo Osella. 1998. "Friendship and Flirting: Micro-politics in Kerala, South India." *Journal of the Royal Anthropological Institute* 4 (2):189–206.

Osella, Filippo, and Katy Gardner, eds. 2004. *Migration, Modernity and Social Transformation in South Asia*. New Delhi: Sage.

Osella, Filippo, and Caroline Osella. 2000. "Migration, Money and Masculinity in Kerala." *Journal of the Royal Anthropological Institute* 6 (1):117–33.

——. 2003. "Migration and Commoditisation of Ritual: Sacrifice, Spectacle and Contestations in Kerala, India." *Contributions to Indian Sociology*, n.s., 37 (1 and 2):109–39.

Padel, Felix. 1995. *The Sacrifice of Human Being: British Rule and the Konds of Orissa*. Delhi: Oxford University Press.

Parry, Jonathan. 1979. *Caste and Kinship in Kangra*. London: Routledge.

———. 1998. "Mauss, Dumont, and the Distinction between Status and Power." In *Marcel Mauss: A Centenary Tribute*, edited by W. James and N. J. Allen. New York: Berghahn.

———. 1999. "Two Cheers for Reservation: the Satnamis and the Steel Plant." In *Institutions and Inequalities: Essays in Honour of André Béteille*, edited by Ramachandra Guha and Jonathan Parry. New Delhi: Oxford University Press.

———. 2000. "The 'Crisis of Corruption' and 'The Idea of India': A Worm's Eye View." In *Morals of Legitimacy: Between Agency and System*, edited by I. Pardo. New York: Berghahn.

———. 2001. "Ankalu's Errant Wife: Sex, Marriage and Industry in Contemporary Chhattisgarh." *Modern Asian Studies* 35 (4):783–820.

———. 2003. "Nehru's Dream and the Village 'Waiting Room': Long Distance Labour Migrants to a Central Indian Steel Town." *Contributions to Indian Sociology*, n.s., 37 (1 and 2):217–49.

———. 2008. "The Sacrifices of Modernity in a Central Indian Steel Town." In *On the Margins of Religion*, edited by Frances Pine and Joao de Pina-Cabral. New York: Berghahn.

Parry, Jonathan, and Maurice Bloch. 1989. *Money and the Morality of Exchange*. Cambridge: Cambridge University Press.

Patel, G. D. 1954. *The Indian Land Problem and Legislation*. Bombay: N. M. Tripathi.

Pathak, B. 1993. *Rural Violence in Bihar*. Delhi: Concept.

Peabody, Norbert. 1991. "Kota Mahajagat, or the Great Universe of Kota: Territory and Sovereignty in Eighteenth Century Rajasthan." *Contributions to Indian Sociology*, n.s., 25:29–56.

———. 2003. *Hindu Kingship and Polity in Precolonial India*. Cambridge: Cambridge University Press.

Peluso, Nancy. 1993. "Coercive Conservation: The Politics of State Resource Control." In *The State and Social Power in Environmental Politics*, edited by R. Lipschutz and K. Conca. New York: Columbia University Press.

Pigg, Stacey Leigh. 1992. "Inventing Social Categories through Place: Social Representations and Development in Nepal." *Comparative Studies in Society and History* 34 (3):491–513.

Pinney, Christopher. 1990. "Colonial Anthropology in the 'Laboratory of Mankind.'" In *The Raj: India and the British, 1600–1947*, edited by C. Bayly. London: National Portrait Gallery.

Platteau, Jean Philippe. 1994. "Behind the Market Stage Where Real Societies Exist." Pts. 1 and 2. *Journal of Development Studies* 30:533–77 and 753–817.

Posey, Darrell. 1982. "Keepers of the Forest." *Garden* 6:18–24.
Prakash, Amit. 2001. *Jharkhand: Politics of Development and Identity*. Hyderabad, India: Orient Longman.
Prasad, Archana. 2003. *Against Ecological Romanticism: Verrier Elwin and the Making of an Anti-modern Tribal Identity*. New Delhi: Three Essays Collective.
Rangan, Haripriya. 1996. "From Chipko to Uttaranchal: Development, Environment and Social Protest in Garhwal Himalayas, India." In *Liberation Ecologies: Environment, Development, Social Movements*, edited by R. Peet and M. Watts. London: Routledge.
Rangarajan, Mahesh. 2006. "Ideology, the Environment and Policy: Indira Gandhi." *IIC Quarterly* 33 (1):50–64.
——. Forthcoming. "Environment, Ecology and Colonial India: Departures and Beginnings." In *India and the British Empire*, edited by N. Gooptu and D. Peers. Oxford History of the British Empire Companion Series. Oxford: Oxford University Press.
Rao, Nitya. 2003. "Jharkhand Vision 2010: Chasing Mirages." *Economic and Political Weekly*, 38 (18):1755–58.
Redford, K. H. 1990. "The Ecologically Noble Savage." *Orion* 9 (3):22–37.
Reid, J. 1912. *Final Report on the Survey and Settlement Operations in the District of Ranchi 1902–1910*. Calcutta: Government of India.
Richards, Paul. 1985. *Indigenous Agricultural Revolution: Ecology and Food Production in West Africa*. London: Hutchinson.
Robertson, A. F. 2006. "Misunderstanding Corruption." *Anthropology Today* 22 (2):8–12.
Rogaly, Ben, and Daniel Coppard. 2003. "'They Used to Go to Eat, Now They Go to Earn': The Changing Meanings of Seasonal Migration from Puruliya District in West Bengal, India." *Journal of Agrarian Change* 3 (3):395–439.
Rogaly, Ben, et al. 2001. "Seasonal Migration, Social Change and Migrants' Rights: Lessons from West Bengal." *Economic and Political Weekly* 36 (49):4547–59.
——. 2002. "Seasonal Migration and Welfare/Illfare in Eastern India: A Social Analysis." *Journal of Development Studies* 38 (5):89–114.
Rowlands, Michael, and Jean-Pierre Warnier. 1988. "Sorcery, Power and the Modern State in Cameroon." *Man*, n.s., 23 (1):118–32.
Roy, Sarat Chandra. 1912. *The Mundas and Their Country*. Ranchi, India: Catholic Press.
——. 1915. *The Oraons of the Chota Nagpur: Their History, Economic Life and Social Organisation*. Ranchi, India: Catholic Press.
Rudolph, L., and S. H. Rudolph. 1987. *In Pursuit of Lakshmi: The Political Economy of the Indian State*. Chicago: University of Chicago Press.
Russell, R. V., and Hira Lal. 1916. *The Tribes and Castes of the Central Provinces of India*. London: Macmillan.
Ruud, Aril Engelsen. 2001. "Talking Dirty about Politics: A View from a

Bengali Village." In *The Everyday State and Society in Modern India*, edited by C. J. Fuller and V. Benei. London: C. Hurst.

Saberwal, Vasant, and Mahesh Rangarajan. 2003. *Battles over Nature: Science and the Politics of Conservation*. Delhi: Oxford University Press.

Saberwal, Vasant, Mahesh Rangarajan, and Ashish Kothari. 2001. *People, Parks and Wildlife: Towards Coexistence*. Delhi: Orient Longman.

Saberwal, Vasant, et al. 1994. "Lion-human Conflicts in the Gir Forest, India." *Conservation Biology* 8 (2):501–7.

Sachidananda. 1976. *The Tribal Voter in Bihar*. Delhi: National Publishing House.

Sahlins, Marshall. 1976. *Culture and Practical Reason*. Chicago: University of Chicago Press.

Salafsky, N., et al. 2001. "A Systematic Test of an Enterprise Strategy for Community-based Biodiversity Conservation." *Conservation Biology* 15:1585–95.

Scheper-Hughes, Nancy. 1995. "The Primacy of the Ethical: Propositions for a Militant Anthropology." *Current Anthropology* 36 (3):409–20.

Scheper-Hughes, Nancy, and Philippe Bourgois, eds. 2004. *Violence in War and Peace: An Anthology*. Malden, Mass.: Blackwell.

Schnepel, B. 1995. "Durga and the King: Ethnohistorical Aspects of Politico-ritual Life in a South Orissan Jungle Kingdom." *Journal of the Royal Anthropological Institute* 1:145–66.

Scott, James. 1979. *The Moral Economy of the Peasant: Subsistence and Rebellion in Southeast Asia*. New Haven, Conn.: Yale University Press.

———. 1985. *Weapons of the Weak: Everyday Forms of Peasant Resistance*. New Haven, Conn.: Yale University Press.

Shah, Alpa. 2006a. "The Labour of Love: Seasonal Migration from Jharkhand to the Brick Kilns of Other States in India." *Contributions to Indian Sociology*, n.s., 40 (1):91–118.

———. 2006b. "Markets of Protection: The 'Terrorist' Maoist Movement and the State in Jharkhand, India." *Critique of Anthropology* 26 (3):297–314.

———. 2007a. "The Dark Side of Indigeneity: Indigenous People, Indigenous Rights and Indigenous Development in India." *History Compass* 5:1806–32.

———. 2007b. "'Keeping the State Away': Democracy, Politics and Imaginations of the State in India's Jharkhand." *Journal of the Royal Anthropological Institute* 13 (1):129–45.

Shah, Alpa, and Judith Pettigrew. 2009. "Windows on a Revolution: Ethnographies of Maoism in South Asia." Special issue. *Dialectical Anthropology* 33 (3–4):225–51.

Shah, G., et al. 1990. *Migrant Labour in India*. Surat City: Gujarat: Centre for Social Studies.

Sharan, Ramesh, Prabhat K. Singh, and Suresh P. Sahu. 1999. "Present Status of Traditional System of Governance among the Tribals of Bihar." *Social Change* 29 (3–4):287–301.

Sharma, B. D. 2001. *Tribal Affairs in India: A Crucial Transition*. New Delhi: Sahyog Pustak Kuteer Trust.
Shiva, Vandana. 1988. *Staying Alive: Women, Ecology and Survival in India*. New Delhi: Kali for Women.
Sieder, Rachel, and Jessica Witchell. 2001. "Advancing Indigenous Claims through the Law: Reflections on the Guatemalan Peace Process." In *Culture and Rights: Anthropological Perspectives*, edited by Jane Cowan, Marie-Benedict Dembour, and Richard Wilson. Cambridge: Cambridge University Press.
Singh, Kumar Suresh. 1966. *The Dust Storm and the Hanging Mist*. Calcutta: Firma K. L. Mukhopadhyay.
———. 1982. "Tribal Autonomy Movements in Chotanagpur." In *Tribal Movements in India*, edited by Kumar Suresh Singh, vol. 2. Delhi: Manohar.
Singh, Prakash. 1995. *The Naxalite Movement in India*. New Delhi: Rupa.
Singh, Raajen. 1996. "The Adivasis in Jharkhand and Northeast India." In *Indigenous Peoples of Asia: Many Peoples, One Struggle*, edited by Colin Nicholas and Raajen Singh. Bangkok, Thailand: Asia Indigenous Peoples Pact.
Singh, V. B., and S. Bose. 1988. *State Elections in India: Data Handbook on Vidhan Sabha Elections 1952–1985*. Vol. 4, pt. 2: *The North: Bihar and Uttar Pradesh*. New Delhi: Sage.
Sinha, Shanta. 1989. *Maoists in Andra Pradesh*. Delhi: Gyan.
Sinha, Subir, Shubhra Gururani, and Brian Greenberg. 1997. "The 'New Traditionalist' Discourse of Indian Environmentalism." *Journal of Peasant Studies* 24 (3):65–99.
Sinha-Kerkhoff, Kathinka. 2004. "Voices of Difference: Partition Memory and Memories of Muslims in Jharkhand, India." *Critical Asian Studies* 36 (1):113–42.
Sivaramakrishnan, K. 1998. "Modern Forestry: Trees and Development Spaces in South-west Bengal, India." In *The Social Life of Trees: Anthropological Perspectives on Tree Symbolism*, edited by L. Rival. Oxford: Berg.
———. 1999. *Modern Forests: Statemaking and Environmental Change in Colonial Eastern India*. Stanford, Calif.: Stanford University Press.
———. 2003. "Nationalisms and the Writing of Environmental Histories." *Seminar*, http://www.india-seminar.com (accessed 12 September 2009).
Skaria, Ajay. 1997. "Shades of Wildness Tribe, Caste, and Gender in Western India." *Journal of Asian Studies* 56 (3):726–45.
———. 1999. *Hybrid Histories: Forests, Frontiers, and Wildness in Western India*. Delhi: Oxford University Press.
Sluka, Jeffrey. 2000. *Death Squad: The Anthropology of State Terror*. Philadelphia: University of Pennsylvania Press.
Smith, Carol. 1999. "Why Write an Exposé of Rigoberta Menchú?" *Latin American Perspectives* 26 (6):15–28.
Solway, Jacqueline, and Richard Lee. 1990. "Foragers, Genuine or Spu-

rious? Situating the Kalahari San in History." *Current Anthropology* 31 (1):109–46.

Spencer, Jonathan. 1992. "Problems in the Analysis of Communal Violence." *Contributions to Indian Sociology*, n.s., 26 (2):261–79.

———. 1997. "Post-colonialism and the Political Imagination." *Journal of the Royal Anthropological Institute* 3 (1):1–19.

———. 2000. "On Not Becoming a 'Terrorist': Problems of Memory, Agency, and Community in the Sri Lankan Conflict." In *Violence and Subjectivity*, edited by V. Das, M. Ramphele, and P. Reynolds. Berkeley: University of California Press.

———. 2003. "A Nation 'Living in Different Places': Notes on the Impossible Work of Purification in Postcolonial Sri Lanka." *Contributions to Indian Sociology*, n.s., 37 (1–2):1–23.

Spivak, Gayatri. 1988a. "Subaltern Studies: Deconstructing Historiography." In *Selected Subaltern Studies,* edited by R. Guha and G. Spivak. Oxford: Oxford University Press.

———. 1988b. "Can the Subaltern Speak?" In *Marxism and the Interpretation of Culture*, edited by C. Nelson and L. Grossberg. Chicago: University of Illinois Press.

Srinivas, M. N. 1956. "A Note on Sanskritisation and Westernisation." *Far Eastern Quarterly* 15 (4):481–96.

Standing, G., ed. 1985. *Labour Circulation and the Labour Process*. London: Croom Helm.

Starn, Orin. 1999. *Nightwatch: Politics and Protest in the Andes*. Durham, N.C.: Duke University Press.

Stavenhagen, Rodolfo. 1996. "Indigenous Rights: Some Conceptual Problems." In *Constructing Democracy: Human Rights, Citizenship and Society in Latin America*, edited by E. Jelin and E. Hersberg. Boulder, Colo.: Westview.

Stern, Steve. 1998. *Shining and Other Paths: War and Society in Peru, 1980–1995*. Durham, N.C.: Duke University Press.

Stirrat, R. L. 1996. "The New Orthodoxy and Old Truths: Participation, Empowerment and Other Buzz Words." In *Assessing Participation: The Debate from South Asia*, edited by S. Bastian and N. Bastian. New Delhi: Konark.

Stoll, David. 1993. *Between Two Armies in the Ixil Towns of Guatemala*. New York: Columbia University Press.

———. 1999. *Rigoberta Menchú and the Story of All Poor Guatemalans*. Boulder, Colo.: Westview.

Stree Shakti Sanghatana. 1989. *We Were Making History: Life Stories of Women in the Telengana People's Struggle (Lalita Vasantha Kannabiran, Rama Melkote, Uma Maheshwari, Susie Tharu and Veena Shatrugna)*. London: Zed.

Sukumar, R. 1989. *The Asian Elephant: Ecology and Management*. Cambridge: Cambridge University Press.

Sundar, Nandini. 1997. *Subalterns and Sovereigns: An Anthropological History of Bastar, 1854–1996*. Delhi: Oxford University Press.

———. 2005a. "'Custom' and 'Democracy' in Jharkhand." *Economic and Political Weekly* 40 (41):4430–34.

———. 2005b. "Teaching to Hate: The RSS's Pedagogical Programme." *Economic and Political Weekly* 38 (16):1605–12.

Sylvain, Renee. 2002. "Land, Water and Truth: San Identity and Global Indigenism." *American Anthropologist* 104 (4):1074–85.

Taussig, Michael. 1984. "Culture of Terror, Space of Death: Roger Casement's Putumanyo Report and the Explanation of Torture." *Comparative Studies in Society and History* 26 (3):467–97.

———. 1987. *Colonialism, Shamanism, and the Wild Man: A Study of Terror and Healing*. Chicago: University of Chicago Press.

———. 1997. *The Magic of the State*. New York: Routledge.

Taylor, Charles. [1931] 1992. *Multiculturalism and "the Politics of Recognition."* Princeton, N.J.: Princeton University Press.

Taylor, F. E. A. 1940. *Final Report on the Revisional Survey and Settlement Operations in the District of Ranchi (1927–1935)*. Patna, India: Government of India.

Tete, Peter. 1990. *The Kharias and the History of the Catholic Church in Biru*. Ranchi, India: St. Albert's College, Faculty of Theology.

Thompson, E. P. 1971. "The Moral Economy of the English Crowd in the Eighteenth Century." *Past and Present* 50:76–136.

Thornton, Allan, and Dave Currey. 1991. *To Save an Elephant: The Undercover Investigation into the Illegal Ivory Trade*. London: Doubleday.

Tilly, Charles. 1985. "War Making and State Making as Organised Crime." In *Bringing the State Back In*, edited by P. Evans, D. Rueschemeyer, and T. Skocpol. Cambridge: University of Cambridge Press.

Toye, John. 1987. *Dilemmas of Development: Reflections on the Counterrevolution in Development Theory and Practice*. Oxford: Basil Blackwell.

Transparency International. 2005. *India Corruption Study*. London: Transparency International.

Tsing, Anna. 2005. *Friction: An Ethnography of Global Connection*. Princeton, N.J.: Princeton University Press.

Turner, Terence, and Vanessa Fajans-Turner. 2006. "Political Innovation and Inter-ethnic Alliance: Kayapo Resistance to the Developmentalist State." *Anthropology Today* 22 (5):3–10.

Unnithan-Kumar, Maya. 2003. "Spirits of the Womb: Migration, Reproductive Choice and Healing in Rajasthan." *Contributions to Indian Sociology*, n.s., 37 (1 and 2):163–88.

van der Veer, Peter. 1996. *Religious Nationalism: Hindus and Muslims in India*. Delhi: Oxford University Press.

van Schendel, Willem. 1992. "The Invention of the 'Jummas': State Formation and Ethnicity in Southeastern Bangladesh." *Modern Asian Studies* 26 (1):95–128.

Vartak, V. D., and Madhav Gadgil. 1981. "Studies in Sacred Groves along the Western Ghats from Maharashtra and Goa: Role of Beliefs and Folklores." In *Glimpses of Ethnobotany*, edited by S. K. Jain. New Delhi: Oxford and IBH.

Vidyarthi, L. P., and K. N. Sahay. 1976. *The Dynamics of Tribal Leadership in Bihar: Research Project on Changing Leadership in a Tribal Society, 1967–1971*. Allahabad, India: Kitab Mahal.

Vishvanathan, Shiv, and Harsh Sethi. 1998. *Foul Play: Chronicles of Corruption, 1947–1997*. New Delhi: Banyan.

Vitebsky, Piers. 1993. *Dialogues with the Dead: Moments of Inarticulacy in Tribal India*. Cambridge: Cambridge University Press.

von Furer Haimendorf, Christoph. 1948. *Raj Gonds of Adilabad: A Peasant Culture of the Decan*. Vol. 3, book 1: *Myth and Ritual*. London: Macmillan.

Wade, Robert. 1982. "The System of Administrative and Political Corruption: Canal Irrigation in South India." *Journal of Development Studies* 18:287–328.

———. 1985. "The Market for Public Office: Why the Indian State Is Not Better at Development." *World Development* 13:467–97.

Warren, Kay. 1998. *Indigenous Movements and Their Critics: Pan-Mayan Activism in Guatemala*. Princeton, N.J.: Princeton University Press.

Webster, G. K. 1875. *Land Tenure of Ranchi: Government of India—Indian Civil Service*. Delhi: Indian Civil Service.

Weiner, Myron. [1978] 1988. *Sons of the Soil: Migration and Ethnic Conflict in India*. Princeton, N.J.: Princeton University Press.

West, Harry. 1999. "Betwixt and Between: 'Traditional Authority' and Democratic Decentralisation in Post-war Mozambique." *African Affairs* 98:455–84.

———. 2005. *Kupulika: Governance and the Invisible Realm in Mozambique*. Chicago: University of Chicago Press.

Williams, Glyn. 2004. "Evaluating Participatory Development: Tyranny, Power and (Re)politicisation." *Third World Quarterly* 25 (3):557–78.

Williams, Raymond. 1980. "Ideas of Nature." In *Problems of Materialism and Culture*, edited by Raymond Williams. London: Verso.

Willis, Paul. 1978. *Learning to Labour: How Working Class Kids Get Working Class Jobs*. Westmead, England: Saxon House.

Willmsen, Edwin. 1989. *Land Filled with Flies: A Political Economy of the Kalahari*. Chicago: University of Chicago Press.

Wilshusen, Peter, et al. 2002. "Reinventing a Square Wheel: Critique of a Resurgent 'Protection Paradigm' in International Biodiversity Conservation." *Society and Natural Resources* 15 (1):17–40.

Wolf, Diane. 1992. *Factory Daughters: Gender, Household Dynamics, and Rural Industrialization in Java*. Berkeley: University of California Press.

Wood, Geoff. 2003. "Staying Secure, Staying Poor: The 'Faustian Bargain.'" *World Development* 31 (3):455–71.

World Bank. 1992. *Governance and Development*. Washington: World Bank.

——. 2007. *Strengthening World Bank Group Engagement on Governance and Anticorruption*. Washington: World Bank.

Xaxa, Virginius. 1999. "Tribes as Indigenous People of India." *Economic and Political Weekly* 34 (51):3589–96.

Yan, Yunxiang. 1996. *The Flow of Gifts: Reciprocity and Social Networks in a Chinese Village*. Stanford, Calif.: Stanford University Press.

Yorke, Michael. 1976. "Decisions and Analogy: Political Structure and Discourse among the Ho Tribals of India." Ph.D. diss., School of Oriental and African Studies.

Passages in this book have previously appeared in various published forms. I would like to acknowledge permission from the following:

Journal of Royal Anthropological Institute for "Keeping the State Away: Democracy, Politics and Imaginations of the State in India's Jharkhand," 13 (1) (2007): 129–45. Copyright © Wiley-Blackwell Publishers.

History Compass for "The Dark Side of Indigeneity: Indigenous People, Indigenous Rights and Indigenous Development in India," 5 (2007): 1806–32. Copyright © Wiley-Blackwell Publishers.

Palgrave Macmillan (New York) for "Corruption: Insights into Combating Corruption in Rural Development," in *Ethnographies of Moral Reasoning: Living Paradoxes of a Global Age*, edited by Karen Sykes (2009), 117–35.

Contributions to Indian Sociology (n.s.) for "The Labour of Love: Seasonal Migration from Jharkhand to the Brick Kilns of Other States in India," 40 (1) (2006): 91–118. Copyright © Institute of Economic Growth, Delhi 2006. All rights reserved. Reproduced with the permission of the copyright holders and the publishers, Sage Publications India Pvt. Ltd., New Delhi.

Critique of Anthropology for "Markets of Protection: The 'Terrorist' Maoist Movement and the State in Jharkhand, India," 26 (3) (2006): 297–314. Copyright © Sage Publications United Kingdom, London. All rights reserved.

Journal of Development Studies for "Morality, Corruption and the State: Insights from Jharkhand, Eastern India," 45 (3) (2009): 295–313. http://www.informaworld.com. Copyright © Routledge.

Index

ALPA SHAH IS A LECTURER
IN THE DEPARTMENT OF
ANTHROPOLOGY AT GOLDSMITHS,
UNIVERSITY OF LONDON.

Library of Congress Cataloging-in-Publication Data
Shah, Alpa
In the shadows of the state: indigenous politics, environmentalism, and insurgency in Jharkhand, India / Alpa Shah.
p. cm.
Includes bibliographical references and index.
ISBN 978-0-8223-4744-6 (cloth : alk. paper)
ISBN 978-0-8223-4765-1 (pbk. : alk. paper)
1. Adivasis — India — Jharkhand — Social conditions.
2. Adivasis — India — Jharkhand — Economic conditions.
3. Adivasis — India — Jharkhand — Politics and government.
4. Jharkhand (India) — History — Autonomy and independence movements. I. Title.
DS485.J4842S53 2010
305.5'6880954127 — dc22 2010000607